CW00496410

I Chose the Storm

J'AI CHOISI LA TEMPÊTE

Marie Chamming's
1923-2022

A Resistance heroine of the Second World War
whose book is dedicated to the men and women who gave
their lives to save France. It also embodies a revolt
against every form of oppression.

I Chose
the Storm

MARIE CHAMMING'S

Translated by Clare Vining

V

VICTORY BOOKS

I Chose the Storm
(originally published in French as *J'ai Choisi la Tempête*)

First published in French by Éditions France Empire 1965, 1984, 1998
This edition published in English by Victory Books 2022
Copyright © Marie Chamming's 2022
English translation copyright © Clare Vining 2022
Book design copyright © Tom & Rieko Vining 2022

All rights reserved. No part of this publication may be reproduced,
stored in a retrieval system, or transmitted in any form
or by any means, electronic, mechanical, photocopying, recording,
or otherwise, without the prior permission of the copyright owner of this book.

Author: Marie Chamming's
Translator: Clare Vining
Editor: Barbara Mellor
Editor: Catherine Cary-Elwes
Researcher: Nichola Lewis
Designer: More Air

• • •

This translation has remained faithful to the text of
the 1984 edition of *J'ai Choisi la Tempête*.

However, some names and place names have been edited for
accuracy; and some footnotes that are not in the French edition
have been added for clarity and reader interest.

First published in print format 2022

Hardcover: ISBN 979-8-8408-1736-0
Paperback: ISBN 979-8-8408-1709-4

To Clare Vining née Cary-Elwes

*In memory of your father, "our" Major Cary-Elwes:
an exceptional man, whom we will never forget!
How I would like these pages to reach out to the
young people of today, who so often seem confused.*

*With my warmest sympathy,
Marie Chamming's*

Clare Vining née Cary-Elwes
11 June 1949 – 13 March 2020

Also in memory of Clare Vining née Cary-Elwes,
who translated this book as a tribute to her father
Lt. Col. O.A.J. Cary-Elwes.

This is a true story.
Which is why I wanted to write it.

Marie Chamming's

CONTENTS

PART III

The End and the Beginning

Appendices

ABOUT THE AUTHOR

Marie Chamming's (née Krebs) was born in Paris in 1923. She was barely nineteen years old when war broke out, and when the Germans overran the capital, she made the courageous decision to join the Resistance group *Organisation Civile et Militaire des Jeunes* (OCMJ). She took the code name Marie-Claire. Among other clandestine activities, Marie helped to organise relief for the families of captured or murdered Maquisards as well those in need following the repressive activities of the occupying forces. In May 1944, she returned to the family home in Concarneau on the coast of Brittany, where her father Louis Krebs was an engineer and shipbuilder, and Mayor of the district of Lanriec. Louis was also secretly engaged in the Resistance, organising escape routes to England by sea. Marie soon joined the local Maquis, and when divisions of the French SAS were parachuted into Brittany ahead of the D-Day landings she became an *agente de liaison*, running messages between the various fighting groups commanded by Pierre-Louis Bourgoin, Henri Deplante and Pierre Marienne. Marie shared their precarious existence, constantly on the move and sleeping under the stars. She cycled across Brittany with messages hidden in her tyre pump or turban and confronted numerous German and Milice patrols en route, each time escaping detection with a combination of luck and quick thinking. Marie was witness to the brutality of the occupying forces, including the aftermath of the massacre of Lieutenant Marienne and his fellow combatants and the bloody battle of Saint-Marcel. She also attended parachute drops from England and assisted Georges Chamming's (known as Geo), a young radio operator, with coding and decoding messages from London. The two young patriots grew close and made plans to marry. In August 1944, the liberation of Brittany was marred by the tragic death of Marie's father Louis. Still in mourning, Geo and Marie married, so hurriedly that the bride was unable to wear her wedding dress made from a parachute.

With the war still raging, Geo rejoined his unit and Marie, already pregnant with her son Louis, formed part of a delegation of Resistance fighters who visited London and Liverpool in 1944. They witnessed the war effort in Britain as well as the devastation in the East End of London during the Blitz. Marie's compelling account of this journey, "Voyage to England", is included in the present volume (pp. 385).

In peacetime, Marie and Georges lived in Paris for seven years, where they had their three children, Louis, Claire and Martine. In 1952, they went to Madagascar, where Geo had been born, and stayed a further seven years. In 1959, at the time of Madagascar's independence, they moved back to France and lived in several cities: Grenoble, Paris, Lorient and finally Montpellier, where Geo died in 2013.

In 1964, Marie published to wide acclaim her wartime memoir *J'ai choisi la tempête*, for which she received the *Grand Prix Vérité*. For her extraordinary bravery during the war she was awarded the *Ordre National du Mérite* in 1972, the *Légion d'honneur* in 2006 (promoted to *Officier de la Légion d'honneur* in 2021), together with the *King's Medal for Courage in the Cause of Freedom*, the *Médaille de la Résistance* in 1949, and the *Croix de Saint Marcel*.

Marie Chamming's died on February 15th, 2022.

A NOTE ON THE TRANSLATION

In 2012, my mother Clare Vining (née Cary-Elwes) completed the English translation of Marie-Claire's wartime memoir *J'ai Choisi la Tempête*. Marie-Claire entrusted the translation of her memoir to my mother, which she undertook in memory of her late father, Lt. Col. Oswald Cary-Elwes. He commanded a team of British SAS soldiers who parachuted into occupied France in June 1944, tasked with gaining intelligence, establishing links and training the underground French resistance effort. During this time, Marie-Claire and Oswald forged a close working alliance, and post-war a lasting friendship.

Ten years passed before my mother's translation was published with its English title, *I Chose the Storm*. Sadly, she passed away in 2020 before it went to print. However, shortly before her death, she expressed her deepest wish for this finally to be released. My mother was determined to honour Marie-Claire's original objective for *"these pages to reach out to the youth of today"*, and to stay true to the original book she would regularly liaise with the author. As a family, especially my brother's Richard, Gerald and I, have been deeply moved to read the words translated so diligently by our mother. The effort required for her to produce such a beautiful translation whilst living with bipolar disorder only adds to the pride that we all feel. Our grandfather, like many others of his generation, said very little about his experience, so learning about this has meant a great deal to us.

During this project, we have been immensely grateful for the help of my mother's sister, Catherine Cary-Elwes, and Saint-Marcel resident Nichola Lewis, who both helped with historical research and editing, as well as editorial consultant Barbara Mellor who provided the final edit to bring out more of the nuances in Marie-Claire's style, its rhythms and cadences, and with this a greater sense of the book's urgency and poignancy. And I would like to thank my wife Rieko, and Joe Harrison, for both helping with the book design. My father Jeremy also supported my mother with the translation of *I Chose the Storm* and played a big part in realising the project.

We recently discovered that in 1944 Marie-Claire had written 'Voyage to England', a lively account of a trip she made to London together with a company of Resistance fighters who had been invited to visit their British allies. Marie-Claire's account offers a unique glimpse into the lives of ordinary Britons in the Blitz as well as the warmth and gratitude that flowed between our two nations in those desperate times. My aunt Catherine translated Marie-Claire's report of her trip, which is included in the appendices.

On his return to England, my grandfather wrote an account of Operation 'LOST' entitled, 'Looking back to the French S.A.S in Brittany, 1944', a copy of which was published in Christopher Westhorp's *The SAS Pocket Manual: 1941-1945*. Christopher kindly shared the transcribed text for us to include in the appendices.

The publication of the English edition has been a labour of love and undertaken in honour of the extraordinary courage and determination of Marie-Claire Chamming's, a woman who risked her life for the freedoms we enjoy today. Through it, we also pay tribute to those who fought alongside her and the many who did not live to see the final victory and the rebuilding of their countries. Our debt to them is immeasurable.

Thomas Vining

INTRODUCTION

After the end of the Second World War, many French people tried to forget the horrors of the Occupation, of Vichy and of collaboration, and to get on with the job of rebuilding the country. But the reality of the war years was continually recalled, as Resistance fighters who had returned to civilian life began to write their memoirs. Very different from the flood of war memoirs penned by ex-soldiers, these books were written by civilians and dealt with the shadowy world of Resistance, with its mixture of complex politics, the terrible tension of clandestine activity and the ever-present threat of betrayal. And there was also a handful of more personal memoirs by rank-and-file resisters, explaining their small role in events and often written with the aim of bringing home to a younger generation what exactly their parents and grandparents had lived through. This book by Marie Chamming's, first published in 1965, is an example of this more personal genre, and it is a gem.

It is not simply an account of how a shy, studious teenager became involved in two very different kinds of Resistance activity, before and after D-Day. It is also a love story, telling how she fell in love with Free French parachutist Geo Chamming's, and also of her deep love for her father, Resistance member Louis Krebs, who was killed shortly before his town in Brittany was liberated.

The book is divided into three parts, each corresponding to a different aspect of Marie's life and Resistance activity in 1943-4. The first deals with her role in Paris as a courier for the Organisation Civile et Militaire, an intelligence-gathering network that was decimated by betrayals and Gestapo raids during this period, as grimly outlined in Marie's vivid telling. Running through this section is the parallel narrative of Geo's preparations for parachuting into Brittany on D-Day, foreshadowing how her life was soon to turn on a hinge of fate as she met her future husband in the heat of battle. In the second part, Marie criss-crosses the countryside as an indefatigable bicycle courier for Free French and British troops working behind enemy lines to sabotage the German war effort and support the Allied offensive in Normandy, in a narrative that fuses dramatic military memoir with the romance of her growing affection for Geo. The final section encapsulates the bittersweet emotions of so many after Liberation. Freedom had come, but at a terrible price. For Marie, the joy of falling in love with Geo – and in making urgent wedding plans featuring a bridal gown made from parachute silk – was now mixed with her immense distress at the death of her father.

Therein lies the power of this memoir. It shows how a young woman who 'chose the storm' found love and lost it in the horror of war. Her small but vital contribution to the defeat of the Nazis, and the powerful emotions she lays bare, can be seen as typical of so many people caught up in war, then and now. Chance events shaped Marie's life, taking her to the heights and depths of human experience within a matter of weeks, at an age when she was barely an adult. Her extraordinary story deserves to be read by all who want to understand what it was like back then, and what it is still like, for so many, today.

Matthew Cobb, June 2022
(author of *Eleven Days in August*)

FOREWORD

to the first edition, 1965

The girl known to her companions in the movement as "Marie-Claire" was nineteen years old when she threw herself into the great adventure of the Resistance. So much of her freshness of spirit remains unchanged that, when reading her story, one would think it had been written yesterday.

The young men and women who are now reaching their twentieth year were yet to be born. Marie-Claire fought in order that they should be born free. Day by day, she learned the hard clandestine work of the French Resistance; hers was an existence that was permanently imbued with fear, for the absence of fear could only come from a moment of forgetfulness and it was better by far that the senses be on constant alert. Marie-Claire knew what it meant when a friend suddenly went missing, or when someone was slightly late for a meeting, or when she heard the crunch of a footstep, or the screech of tyres on sudden braking. She was afraid, as we all were, but she carried on because she had to, until the end, until the Liberation that was our goal. She carried on at barely twenty years old, when every day that dawned, every night that fell could have been the day or night of her arrest.

Marie-Claire was suddenly torn from the exhausting army of the shadows and thrust into open warfare and the heat of action in her beloved Brittany where, on the nights of 5 and 6 June 1944, SAS parachutists were dropped under the command of Colonel Bourgoin – one of the finest heroes of Free France.

The chief radio officer of one of the companies of the Bataillon du Ciel [the 4th SAS], commanded by Captain Botella, was a tall young man by the name of Georges Chamming's, who was French despite the sound of his name. Marie-Claire fell in love with him, and they became husband and wife. The story of this Resistance girl of nineteen would have had a fairytale ending, had she not learned, as she neared Concarneau the day before its liberation, that her father, Louis Krebs, had been killed by the enemy at seven o'clock that very morning. He had been a member of the Brittany group of the Confrérie Notre-Dame network that I had founded four years earlier. It was his daughter who informed me of his death, as we all hardly knew one another, and it was better that way if we were captured.

Earlier I mentioned the young men and women who this year, 1965, will be twenty years old. They should read *I Chose the Storm:* in its pages they will find a worthy example. I am moreover convinced that were circumstances to be repeated – which heaven forfend – they would display the same patriotic spirit that so inspired the heroine in this book.

RÉMY
(*Nom de guerre* of Gilbert Renault, 1904-1984)

PROLOGUE

Yesterday, today, tomorrow.

Everything is held in time and space, and who can remain indifferent to human history?

Memorable events – good or evil – mark successive periods of history. Thus the invasion of Europe by the Nazis and the terrible war in the Pacific, from 1940 to 1945, deeply affected us, whoever we were.

We can now see more clearly the dangers that threaten us, the inhabitants of the planet Earth; dangers that must constantly be challenged.

That is why I believe this story has lost none of its relevance so many years after this devastating upheaval, which, in different countries and in different ways, continues to this day.

Marie Chamming's
"Marie-Claire"

Part I

Preparation

CHAPTER 1

Concarneau

The sand flows through my fingers, soft, warm and white, very white, like all the sand in the Bay of Concarneau. The sun is slightly veiled but to the south the sky is clearing. Not a breath of wind comes to ripple the water. I am alone on the beach at Portzou. As I dig my heels into the sand, I can feel the dampness of the sea.

The fresh seawrack brought in by the last storm smells good. I might go for a swim, but the tide is coming in slowly and is still a long way out. The sea will be cold and clear, and to reach it I will have to walk out a long way on the firm, glistening grey sand of low tide.

How long will it be before the Germans take over our beach? Over there, in Le Cabellou, they are busily sawing off the low branches of trees and razing the heathland to the ground to prevent any spies from concealing themselves there. They are building blockhouses everywhere, buried in the depths of the sand dunes.

I'm on my own. My friends have all gone. Georges was the last one I was able to see before he left France for Spain. Isn't it extraordinary that his group managed to take that boy who was left stranded after Madame Jullien was arrested? Thanks to me. I am a young girl of no importance, yet what I do will change the course of events for centuries to come, in however minor a way. To take action or not to take action. To do nothing at all. To shut my eyes against the sun's now dazzling rays. Feel the warm sand against my bare skin. Forget the time. I don't have a notebook, or anything to type up, or any plans to hide. I'd like to have the plans of the fortifications at Le Cabellou, however. But reconnaissance agents must already have made those.

Is it important? Concarneau is just a little port: not a naval port like Lorient, with its U-boat base, so terribly bombed. About nine o'clock every evening, when we're all sitting around together at home, I say to the others: "Here come the planes." You can't hear them yet, but I can sense them coming, and a few seconds later we can just make out a gentle humming that very quickly crescendos into a deafening roar, just over the Iles des Glénans. Off Le Cabellou and Concarneau the anti-aircraft guns boom. In my head I say over and over: "Please don't let them be hit!" Once already I've watched as a light suddenly sank into the sea, like a setting sun, and I thought of the horrific deaths of the airmen, burning alive or drowning in the black waters. And I thought too of those who were waiting for them back in England. But perhaps it's better to be swallowed up by the sea than to die in a concentration camp?

This was how I whiled the time away, daydreaming on the beach day after day as I waited for Charles, who never came. And yet he had told me he would see me again during the summer, as he wanted to set up the Organisation Civile et Militaire des Jeunes (OCMJ) in Brittany, and had asked me to make some contacts in my local area. My father had helped me, and one evening when I came back from Portzou I found Jacques Gloaguen in the sitting room. He was the representative of a group of young men from the region, who were well organised but wanted directives from Paris and weapons. I told him about Charles, and gave him and his friend Herlédan, who came with him for other meetings, the instructions that I had passed on so often in Paris in the spring: to form small groups, about thirty being a good number, and above all to get training if possible from officers or NCOs. To teach the boys to handle weapons, taken from the enemy if necessary. Not to go into action too soon. To make preparations to be fully ready for D-Day. Only to carry out acts of sabotage that were of certain use to the Allies in order to keep up the boys' morale.

"All done already," they told me. What more could I do? Not a word from Charles. He must have been caught. So I set about looking for another contact. General de Penfentenyo, whom I already knew, put them in touch with the "Vengeance" group in Quimper.

Summer would soon be over. Every Saturday evening from the beginning of the holidays, my father would say: "Marie, make lunch for tomorrow, we'll be leaving early." The Germans still allowed us to go sailing, and we would have a heady feeling of escaping as we watched the coastline disappearing behind us. As night fell it would have been so easy not to return to harbour, to steer a course for England! Many had done it in 1940 and since, but now there was no good reason for us to do so: it was better to stay in France and prepare for action.

That Sunday, 19 September 1943, was close to the autumn equinox: a strong wind was whipping from the south, the sky was leaden and the sea green. "The barometer's falling," said my father, consulting it as he did every morning, "the weather's bad." The lunch bags were waiting in the hall; I had prepared the line and bait at the boatyard, and in the waterproof box I had checked the logbook and our *Ausweis* (German ID cards), which we would have to show to the *Gast* (German customs) at the pier. I loved the swell and the wind, I loved the storm. What would the skipper decide? He could see my impatience: "Let's go. If the wind gets up too much we'll come back. This will be our last outing. Next week we'll lay up the *Marsouin*. The Germans are getting too jumpy and the good weather will be over." I sighed with joy. Then my father went on: "Be careful, Marie, don't love the storm too much. You have already chosen a different one,

one that is far more terrible: I give you my approval, but you mustn't love it." He said no more, and we set off.

Never had the *Marsouin* been so sprightly, never had she traced her course more elegantly, hard on the wind with the storm jib up, and rising over the rollers. My father held the helm, still so handsome, with his white canvas jacket that he'd had since he was young, his polo-neck jumper bought long ago in England, and a sou'wester on his head. We were soaked by great sprays of water. My youngest brother Arthur's fair hair hung down over his face or was suddenly swept back by the wind. I felt on amazing form, following every movement of the *Marsouin*, at one with her, in perfect communion with the elements. Could it be that somewhere there were grey towns where you couldn't see the sky, or dark prisons to be filled?

"Go about," said my father, who had given me the helm. And we raced towards the coast with the wind at our backs, on the majestic surge of a huge swell.

The landing that we had been expecting daily was nowhere in sight, and the little suitcase that I took out every night was always put away again the next morning, whatever the moon and the tides. Since my secretarial course was starting up again in Paris, my sister and I decided to return to the capital. The Russians had yet to reach the Pripet Marshes, the Allies had only taken Naples, and the only fighting was in Corsica. We never missed a single news bulletin! A few minutes before they started my father would come to the foot of the stairs, his voice ringing up to the top of the house: "Madeleine, it's the bulletin!" or "Madeleine, it's de Gaulle!" Then Maman would hurry to fetch her big blue exercise book and go down to the sitting room, where she would sit down at a little table and write up a summary or full transcription of the BBC broadcasts such *Les Trois Amis* and *Les Français parlent aux Français*, with a bit of Radio-Paris thrown in for variety. She hid her precious exercise books, blue for the radio and green for her personal reminiscences, in a little gap between the attic ceiling and the roof. While she was writing we wouldn't say a word. The only sounds in that carefully shuttered room were the voice of London, the scratching of her pen on the paper, the clicking of our knitting needles and the hiss of the kettle on the stove where we burned offcuts of wood from the boats being built in our boatyard.

Every time I left Brittany it was a wrench, but this time was worse than ever. Even if Charles had been caught, even if the OCMJ was no more, as soon as I reached Paris I knew I would be starting my Resistance work again, which would be far more all-consuming and dangerous than anything I'd managed to do in Concarneau during the holidays. I couldn't stand on the sidelines of this most intense and demanding of wars any longer. I had known it from that day in March when I'd first met Charles.

CHAPTER 2

Rue d'Assas

In Paris, the Rue d'Assas was its usual reasonable, quiet, settled self. Nothing had changed. The people I passed looked at me, but they didn't stop to stare. Yet my life was no longer to flow like a tranquil river, but more like a tumultuous torrent: not just for a few months, or a few years, but forever.

"You know, don't you, that we're far more likely to be killed than other people. Think carefully about it." The room was dark, with bars at the windows. He looked me straight in the eyes. "Yes, I know," I said, and my voice sounded confident.

But now, outside the student hostel at 12 Rue d'Assas as night fell, I was frightened, frightened that I had signed my own death warrant. As I followed the stream of people towards the Sèvres-Babylone métro station, I gazed at every shop window, every house, every road, as if I were seeing them for the last time. The gate to the peaceful, sheltered garden of my childhood had closed forever. And I had shut it myself.

It was hard to imagine that two hours earlier I'd been waiting my turn for the piano audition at the Parent Conservatoire on Rue de Tournon. How childish my fears had been! But I was scared that under the strict and anxious gaze of my elderly teacher I would inevitably get stuck on the same passage, in front of those splendid mothers and all those happy, beaming teenagers, most of them so confident of getting to the end of their piece without any mistakes. I envied them. It felt as though everyone was following their chosen path with confidence and would be successful at whatever they did. Was I ever confident about anything? I was consumed with nerves before even the most minor exam, and whenever I had to make a decision I was always terrified of getting it wrong.

I headed back via the Rue des Saints-Pères to my sister Elisabeth's apartment, where I had been living for the previous few months. Her husband was a prisoner-of-war in Austria.

The apartment gave on to the paved courtyard of an old townhouse on Rue de Lille. Once you were inside the carriage entrance, it felt as peaceful as being in the country. A horse chestnut tree marked the changing seasons for us. A deep silence greeted me: Elisabeth was not back yet from the Tuileries Gardens where she had taken her four-year-old daughter Claude for a walk.

Plunged into a state of anguish over what I'd let myself in for, I didn't hear my sister opening the front door and shutting it behind them. She was already busy preparing dinner when Claude came to give me a kiss, clambering onto my lap and wrapping her cool, chubby little arms around my neck. I pressed my cheek to hers, so soft and pink, and her fine blonde hair brushed against my forehead. What a happy and loving little girl she was, and how I loved her! Could I put her at even the tiniest risk of being caught, taken away, put in a camp to die of cold and hunger, separated from her mother? Would anything I could do for France be important and valuable enough to put such a precious young life in the balance? Could there be anything more precious than Claude's life? I'd lost the strength to think, and I was doubting everything. I told myself: "You will be extremely careful. You will take every precaution. Nobody will ever know about this address on Rue de Lille."

Dinner was over before I'd managed to find the right moment to say something.

The cleaning lady only came in the mornings, and in the evening Elisabeth and I did the washing up together. It was a chore that lent itself to conversation and reflection, for my sister had taught me to be as methodical as she was. Our precise, efficient movements gave us the freedom to think. "Now is the moment," I told myself. "Don't delay any longer."

I was washing the plates and my sister was putting them away in the kitchen cupboard. Don't wait. Quickly, say it. "Elisabeth, I've joined the Resistance."

She swung round. "Mie, don't you ever!" There was a heavy silence as we stared at each other. Then Elisabeth relaxed. She put down the dish she was still holding. "I suppose you must do as you wish." Picking up a plate from the draining board, she started to dry it.

It was to Jean-Marie that I owed the moment I had been waiting for since the beginning of the war. It was he who introduced me to Francis and Michel from Pontivy, with whom I would get to work with the French parachutists of the Special Air Service.

How could I have known that Geo was boarding the SS Orduna at Tamatave in Madagascar, setting course for England via the Cape? Just off the coast of Africa, a torpedo missed his ship by a whisker, but eventually, after an arduous two-month journey, he disembarked in Liverpool with a large group of comrades from Madagascar, all of them determined to undergo the most rigorous training and face the greatest dangers for their country, a country they had never seen. Before leaving Madagascar, they had signed up with the Free French Paratroopers, and now they were sent straight to the camp at Camberley, where they joined the veterans.

My only regret was not joining the Resistance in Brittany, the region to which I was most attached, as I'd spent most of my childhood and youth there. I couldn't have known, on that day in 1943 when I met Charles, that circumstances and the choices I made would inexorably take me back there.

Jean-Marie lived a few houses away from us on Rue de Lille, with his uncle and aunt Faussemagne. As soon as we'd arrived in Paris we'd become regular guests at their Sunday gatherings. With her charming smile, Madame Faussemagne would usher us into her high-ceilinged drawing room, where a pale light fell through tall, narrow windows framed by heavy curtains. She would invite us to sit in the bergère armchairs or on the sofa. We would talk about literature, art and music, and of course the war. Old Colonel Faussemagne, who was blind, never missed a news bulletin from England, Vichy or Switzerland, always sitting in the same armchair, in the shadow of one of the tall curtains. While his wife was convinced of our eventual victory however disastrous the news, the Colonel was a prophet of doom who Sunday after Sunday would have us quaking with fear over the potential progress of the war.

Jean-Marie and I both loved music and the sea – he was at the Merchant Navy College – which was enough for us to get on well together. I was often the beneficiary of the concert tickets that he used to get hold of by standing in interminable queues.

One night we were coming home from one of these concerts in the pitch dark, as there was no street lighting in Paris. After crossing the Boulevard St Germain, we were walking the length of the white barriers around the Hotel Montalembert, which had been completely taken over by the Germans, when we were overcome with a profound anger that in our own city, our own country, there were places that were out of bounds to us. No, it was intolerable. That was how we'd felt from day one of the invasion. On 18 June 1940, de Gaulle had rallied our hopes. Ever since then, I'd been looking for a way to contribute to the liberation that had to happen. But I still looked like a child, despite being seventeen, and I had never managed to make contact with the intelligence agents who were operating in Brittany. In a low voice I told Jean-Marie about all my fruitless efforts and hopes. He said nothing.

"Promise me that if you see a way I can do something you'll tell me."

"You can count on it."

I wasn't convinced, but I was wrong. Jean-Marie didn't say much, but he always kept his word.

A few days later, he telephoned me: "Hello, it's Jean-Marie, I have something for you." I didn't understand at first. He insisted: "Remember? The other night…"

For a moment, everything inside me went quiet. "When can I see you?"

The rendezvous was fixed. My life was decided.

• • •

Charles was to contact me, and the waiting began. And waiting is bad, because your darkest thoughts grow, and all your aims begin to seem ultimately pointless, devoid of sense. You want to go back to the age when grown-ups would say: "She's not responsible, she's too young." But that time was long gone, and what each one of us did from now on would have incalculable consequences. I pounded the piano relentlessly so as not to think, and Jean-Marie would come round to urge patience, settling himself in the armchair beside the fireplace.

The room doubled as our dining room and my bedroom. The Directoire bed fitted perfectly in the alcove and the same flowery pattern brightened up the bedspread and the bergère armchair. Everything in the room felt welcoming: the pink carpet, the piano, the old prints, the rustic armoire, the square table covered with an Indian shawl in warm tones. We had taken to living in this room, Elisabeth and I, because it was so sunny. Spring was coming but the sitting room and study, which faced north over the entrance courtyard, had kept their winter chill, and our coal ration was so tiny that we only lit a small stove in the one room.

Before he spoke, Jean-Marie would tap his pipe against the ashtray on the standard lamp, fill it with care, and light it with his tinder lighter. He would cross his legs, take a few puffs, and then start to tell me about his boys, the ones it was his job to train and arm. Already he spoke with the authority of a ship's captain, and I could easily imagine him on the bridge, binoculars in hand, unflinchingly navigating his vessel to her destination. My sister and I liked listening to the news bulletins from London with him and hearing his commentaries.

• • •

At another meeting on Rue d'Assas the part I was to play became clearer at last. Charles took me to the Library. We sat down at a long table, opposite each other. All I knew from Jean-Marie was that he was the leader of the youth wing of the Organisation Civile et Militaire,[1] then one of the most important Resistance movements. He moved in a mysterious world, dangerous and fascinating, that I was only allowed to discover bit by bit, and never in its entirety. There was no choice but to put blind trust in men whom you knew only outside their normal lives. I'd noticed that he walked with long, confident strides, like my father, and when he shook my hand it hurt.

I took in his square chin, stubborn forehead and the strange expression in his eyes, which were an almost transparent blue, deep-set and particularly striking against his very dark hair and eyebrows. Could he read my thoughts? You felt he was possessed by the goal

---

1. See appendix: Organisation Civile et Militaire des Jeunes (OCMJ), (Organisation of Civilian and Military Youth).

he had set himself: to organise young people in the struggle against the occupiers. Anyone who came to join him had to leave all other concerns behind. He was only twenty.

"The Allies are going to land soon," he said. "We don't have much time to prepare. Can you drive?"

"No, but I can soon take my test."

"Good, we'll need girls to drive the ambulances on D-Day. Learn how to set up a first-aid post and how to navigate with a map. Buy the little book with all the German army badges and ranks that they sell opposite the Ministry of War. You have to be able to collect intelligence of all kinds. What are you doing at the moment?"

"A secretarial course."

"Perfect. I have work for you to do straight away."

And he gave me a date for our next meeting.

We were about to go our separate ways when he added: "Can you be free on D-Day?"

I thought for a moment before replying: "I think that will be possible."

CHAPTER 3

Action

"Type this for me for tomorrow. It's urgent. Instructions for parachute drops: ten copies and to be sent to the regional heads." Charles would put the papers on the table, one after another: circulars, diverse instructions and, on narrow strips, in code or unscrambled, intercepted conversations and messages between Vichy France and Germany, from Laval in particular. I would put it all in a satchel, documents and rolled-up strips in among innocent-looking exercise books, and every time I would say: "It will be done for tomorrow." I would work after supper, until midnight or one in the morning.

But I still went regularly to my Femme Sécrétaire course, I took singing lessons and I joined an art class at a studio in the Rue de Seine, something I had dreamed of doing for years.

Elisabeth made no comment on the meetings I had with Charles or Jean-Marie, and never asked me any questions.

The evening when I first received an incriminating document at the Rue de Lille is forever imprinted on my memory. It was a plan of a parachute drop. Where should I put it? I hadn't thought about the matter of hiding places and merely slid it under my mattress, but I knew that would be no good. Did I sleep at all that night? I was convinced I could hear footsteps on the stairs. The Gestapo. They had come for the three of us. The doorbell rang. No, it was the clock at the Institut chiming, or at the Louvre. I tossed and turned in the big bed, as a cold sweat trickled down my spine. My throat was constricted as if in a vice: I wouldn't have been able to speak. Possibly by the morning my hair would have turned white.

"When you scare so easily, my child," I told myself, "you don't fling yourself into something like this; you take up embroidery or knit layettes for your little nephews." My teeth were chattering. Did I really want to fight on D-Day, and drive ambulances under fire? I only had to look in the mirror now: did I look as if I had what it took? I'd probably get used to it, but I couldn't be certain – not one little bit. I was chewing the sheets. No, I wanted to live, I wanted to love and to experience all the riches of the earth, and to give life, and to finish what had only just begun.

Daylight dispelled my fears and I started looking for solutions. I needed to keep luck on my side. The first thing was to find some good hiding places. I looked around the pink bedroom, the cupboard, the alcove, the wardrobe, the beautiful unblemished parquet floor, the prints, the mantelpiece with a mirror above. I went over to the black marble mantelpiece. Slowly an idea came to me. I could do something with the fireplace. I moved the heavy wireless and the candlesticks and with one heave lifted up the marble, revealing a very uneven plaster surface. It was quite soft, and I started hollowing it out with a spoon. A big hole on the right, a big hole on the left, and there was enough space to hide quite a lot of documents: an excellent hiding place. That night I slept more soundly.

Except that before long there were too many papers and the marble top stayed permanently pushed up a little. The piano became my overflow hiding place. The top part to start with, except that when you played it the notes were muffled by the papers. The lower part worked much better. Behind the wooden panel, which I could easily lift off, I had all the room I needed. Correspondence from London, in buff post office envelopes, stayed there between two legs on its journey. I gazed on those envelopes with awe: they were the tangible evidence of the fearsome mystery of clandestine action, and the outcome of the war might depend upon it.

Of course I had no idea that, as early as 1940, Rémy had set up the first Resistance intelligence network, the Confrérie Notre-Dame, better known by its initials, CND. In April 1943, it had been decided that Colonel Touny, then head of the Organisation Civile et Militaire (OCM), should start up a special network called "Centurie" to gather intelligence and send it to London via the CND.[2] Thus we had an intelligence channel through which to send information. There were others, and often the same information collected by different agents reached London via different routes. The Allies received thousands of these pieces of information, without which they would not have been able to plan the liberation of Europe with such precision and such a good chance of success.

Those post office envelopes contained military intelligence (the largest category), political information, directions on where to find supplies and the like, all written on the thinnest paper possible. They came to us from the east, the north, the west, from all over. In 1942, at the Allies' request, we sent detailed plans of "Brittany's coastal defences on the Quiberon Peninsula" and at Saint Nazaire. In February 1943, more information arrived from Brittany on the "possibilities of making a landing on the Quiberon Peninsula".

A plan of the Atlantic Wall in the Calvados region was audaciously plotted by the artist Duchez, who worked for Organisation Todt (the German organisation that was building the wall) which, coupled with aerial reconnaissance, made it possible to plot the exact spot for the landings; a report on the work at the Renault factory at Billancourt;

---

2. The OCM later formed a special network, NAVARRE, founded by the lawyer Jacques-Henri Simon, code name Sermoy.

a plan of the German airfield at Creil, and I don't know what else besides! The information went on its way, spending as short a time as possible at one house or another – in Elisabeth's piano, for example – and was then handed over to the post office (hence the envelopes), put into mail bags, and transported to an Atlantic port. Which one, in 1943? There were several. Among them Pont-Aven and the fishing boat *Les Deux Anges*, and Concarneau, my own port. There it was Dr Nicolas, the engineer Henri Cevaer, my father and the manager of our boatyard who would watch over the trawler's departure. A British vessel, the N.51, based in the Scilly Isles, would be waiting out at sea to pick up the bags and sometimes passengers.

Neither my father nor I had any idea how closely connected we were by our "work".

Secretarial and liaison work. Forged documents. I did a lot of both. Departures for Spain too – until the day when I found myself at the bottom of the stairs at Madame Jullien's house, where I was to give her photographs of the two "candidates". I would then give them the details of their final rendezvous. I hesitated for a long moment on the bottom step, uneasy, with a strange feeling that I shouldn't go up. There was nothing suspicious about the house. Rue Allasseur is a quiet street: I was the only person there. The house itself was completely silent. Should I go up or not? The boys had to go. I left though. The Germans had laid a trap in Madame Jullien's apartment, and she had been arrested. I found out the following day.

• • •

Whit Sunday, 1943: the youth pilgrimage to Chartres. The long procession meandered along the white road, between fields of green wheat. We prayed, we sang and we were very footsore, for it was ages since we'd had any proper leather shoes: most of us ended up walking barefoot along the earth paths. All suffering on the way to the Virgin of Chartres was good. If it rained, so much the better.

It cut straight through to our bones. Would we then be sufficiently humbled and mortified for Our Lady to bless us with her light? We all hoped so: Charles, talking about freedom with the chaplain of our chapter, the young men around him who in the months to come would choose between the STO[3] or joining the Maquis, the young women who would perhaps have to leave their families for active war duties, like me.

We knew we had to pray on doggedly, on the rain-lashed road, in the cathedral minus its stained-glass windows, and in the crypt of the Black Virgin, where Father Bernart said again in his warm vibrant voice, reading our thoughts: "Pray, my children, pray without respite to follow the right path."

"Where's Charles?" I said suddenly.

"He has to catch the train to Lyon tonight," someone answered.

Lyon today, a different city tomorrow. Lyon: I would have liked to meet the people who were preparing for the liberation there. People said there were a lot of them. But I was far too small a cog for that ever to happen.

Yet the following Thursday, Charles telephoned: "Can you leave for Lyon tomorrow?" So there I was, queuing at the railway station for a ticket and boarding pass, since I couldn't reserve a seat. To get a seat I would have had to spend all night there. There were so few that people would get up at dawn, sleeping in the hotels around the station, or even on the ground wrapped up in blankets, to be sure of being at the front of the ticket queue. I was to take a large suitcase with me, to be filled with underground newspapers and leaflets in Lyon, and on my person I had stamps to be copied and letters to pass on. Somebody would be waiting for me at the station. It was my first mission outside Paris, a very important one, Charles told me, to set up links between the southern and northern zones.

---

3. Service du Travail Obligatoire: during the occupation there was forced enlistment and deportation of French workers to Germany.

Although it was still early when I left on the Sunday morning, it was scorching hot and every carriage was packed with three times the normal number of passengers. At stations people even clambered in through the windows. Just before we reached Châlons, my fellow passengers started to get restless. One of them warned me in a friendly way that German border guards were about to check the train, compartment by compartment, since we were crossing the demarcation line between the occupied zone and what used to be called the free zone. "They almost always catch someone," he said. I had put the stamps between two photographs in my wallet. The broad grey-green figures were coming ever closer, creating a general commotion, although all you could hear were their guttural exclamations: nobody said a word. Everyone looked at each other, and you could see the anxiety in their eyes when the two Germans bent over the proffered papers. They looked me up and down with scorn: "Ach, you, mademoiselle, no need to bother with you." Too young, too small. It was a bit of luck that I would exploit right up to the end. I had suffered enough from being a "cut-down version": at least now I could make use of it!

When I arrived there was no one waiting for me: it wasn't easy to find Jean-Louis, about whom Charles had told me so much. So this slim young man with his dashing blonde moustache had been in London only a few weeks earlier! I eyed him with curiosity. He could tell me what life was like on the other side of the Channel. Not straight away though, as the Longchambons (punningly known as the Courtjarrets), with whom I had eventually arrived, were convinced that the Gestapo were about to make an appearance: they were making their final preparations to leave, but even so they kindly gave me a cool drink and some biscuits and asked if I would like a bath, as I had been traipsing all over the city trying to find one or other of my contacts. Jean-Louis[4] took me to the Parc de la Tête d'Or, where we could talk undisturbed. A light mist was rising from the river and the trees provided a welcome shade. We sat down on a bench beside a pond. When we had gone over what we had to say about young people and the Resistance and the growing part we would play in the war, he told me about life in England after the great battle in the skies over London. I didn't dare ask him how he came to be in this region of France and what he was going to do next. He went on:

"Are you from Paris, or do you have ties in the provinces?"

"Yes, I do. In Brittany."

He turned to look at me.

"Whereabouts?"

"Concarneau, in Finistère."

"That's near me. I'm from Le Faouët."

We almost felt we were family. He started drawing planes in the sand with a stick.

"Do you think the Allied landings will come soon?" I asked. "It really is about time. Every morning, people on the coast get up and scan the sea, hoping to see boats, masses of boats, but moon after moon goes by and still there's nothing."

The poplar trees around us trembled in the breeze. "Before the autumn leaves fall..." and he left the sentence unfinished. We were already in July.

My suitcase was so heavy that the handle had broken. I had done so much walking that my canvas sandals, which I'd made myself, had come apart, and then before I left I heard that the man I had waited for so long after dinner in a café had been arrested and taken to Fort Montluc. It was as hot as ever, and of course the train was packed. But I was glad to have seen Jean-Louis and to have done what I had to do. Exhausted, I stretched out in the corridor. People jostled me and

---

4. Jean-Louis Fraval, sent to France by the BOA (Office of Aerial Operations) sent to contact General de la Porte du Theil, High Commissioner for the youth movement.

trod on me, but I was asleep, dreaming of Brittany and the coolness of the sea. Would Jean-Louis board a ship bound for England from some deserted beach? There wasn't a single deserted beach now: the Germans were building a wall, a great thick, impenetrable, concrete wall that would stand for generations. As soon as I was back in Brittany, where I was going to spend the summer holidays with my sister and her daughter, I went to gaze upon it.

What had become of Geo during all this time?

After training at the camp in Camberley, he and his friends went through the Polish training camp at Largo in Scotland. They weren't jumping yet, but they were learning how to fall, and it was no joke.

The real work started at Ringway: after jumping from balloons, they jumped from aeroplanes. Geo, like the others, sported the parachutists' badge, or more precisely the three badges: the French one on his chest, the British one on his sleeve, and on one of his pockets the Polish eagle, talons to the fore, as the Poles, like the British, were pleased with their students. The Free French even made an impression. "Now," thought Geo, "we're sure to be among the first to leave for France." It was 30 August 1943.

The Allied landing in Sicily on 10 July had made them all hope that they would soon be leaving for the "second front". Many of them reckoned that they shouldn't risk missing this departure by going to training schools with passing out dates that seemed too far off. The best thing was to make yourself indispensable, now.

CHAPTER 4

Mists

Paris seemed numbed and calm after the fiery inferno of Nantes. Our train had rumbled along the length of the Quai de la Fosse through a nightmarish landscape. The shells of venerable old houses with exquisite balconies were silhouetted against the sky, windows gaping and roofs caved in, and heaps of indescribable debris sprawled right up to the railway track. Some of the staircases were still in flames, burning beams creaked as they fell, and a sinister glow lit up our blacked-out train.[5] The passengers pressed up against the windows in silence, their faces flushed red in the reflections of the flames. They whispered with horror that over a hundred people had screamed in their death throes in the cellars of the Citroën plant, and no one had been able to save them. The Allies were pounding the coast of Brittany relentlessly, but not a single air raid warning had disturbed the capital since our return. Perhaps because of the mists that stifled it, shrouding its streets empty of cars in an even eerier silence.

Then winter really set in. A mist still rose from the Seine every morning and evening, but a biting north wind dispersed it during the day. By that time, I was taking care of internal liaison for the OCMJ

---

5. The Civil Defence (Défense Passive) banned lights on trains and buses.

at the same time as doing the secretarial work for Richard, who was Charles's deputy, and every day I had to pass his documents and orders on to Irène, who would then see the heads of the different departments: Maxime, in charge of police surveillance; Pierre and Joseph, in charge of the press; Doranges, in charge of the regions; Jean-Marie, in charge of industrial sabotage; Raymond, in charge of forged papers; and Deleuze, in charge of students.

The racing around Paris started up again, as did the countless hours at the typewriter and the endless secret meetings at my sister's apartment and elsewhere. I spent much of my time waiting, at crossroads, outside métro stations, even in cafés, watching our occupiers go by. I loathed their presence and what many of them had become. But who were we to judge them? My reading and upbringing had taught me to "put myself in other people's shoes", and it was an attitude that had its uses when it came to the Germans as well. After all, they had been taught from an early age to worship war. If I had been brought up like all these women in grey uniforms who strolled back and forth in front of me with such a cheerful air, mightn't I have been just like them? They had been moulded. With their companions, they had been put in a cage that they could no longer see. We wanted nothing to do with that cage.

Elisabeth's apartment was right beside the embankment. I often used it for my own rendezvous. Night after night, Irène would be waiting for me under a streetlamp on the corner of the Pont du Carrousel. The last rays of the setting sun would be playing on the water, and the dried leaves would swirl away in the wind. Sometimes it would be snowing. I no longer noticed the Japanese prints and the exquisite Chinese goddesses in the window of the antique shop on the other side of the street: I could barely make out Irène's silhouette, tall, dark and motionless. She was weary of always running, weary of waiting, weary of being cold and frightened. She would say: "Why do we go to so much trouble? We think we're doing something useful, but we're not doing anything. If we disappeared, the war would carry on just the same."

I would get home, chilled to the depths of my soul, sit down beside the stove and, while I got the feeling back in my fingers, I would try to think calmly and rationally, saying to myself over and over again, "Keep a cool head, my little Mic, keep a very cool head."

But the next day Irène had been reading the newspaper: "Marie-Claire, have you read the terrible article about that railway accident? They say it was caused by sabotage. German carriages were mixed in with French carriages, and a lot of innocent people have died. Who knows whether some of our young people might not have carried out that sabotage? It doesn't bear thinking about."

I couldn't sleep that night for thinking about it. War always leads to acts that you can only deplore. Was it better not to fight, to shift all the responsibility on to other people? But we couldn't possibly allow the deportation of the unfortunate Jews, we couldn't accept the sight of our young people being taken off to Germany, and we had to throw off this enslavement. We had to get organised in France to help the Allies and ensure that France took her place again in the world as a "great nation", thanks to the recognition of our part in the war.

Meanwhile, life carried on around us with apparent tranquillity. My girlfriends would tell me about their brothers who had gone to the Chantiers de Jeunesse, youth camps set up by Marshal Pétain. They thought it was the right thing to do, guided by a fine vision of France's recovery, like Pétain. You could understand it, and our shared hopes of renewal were not dissimilar. Further attempts were made to tighten links with Vichy, but I had transcribed Ribbentrop's letter to Pétain, which we had intercepted, and we could see that Pétain was nothing more than a prisoner now, a total prisoner. The gap was growing gradually wider every day, and there was nothing we could do. Why were we so sure we were right? Why must we always go after the truth? I would sit over lunch and dinner not saying a word, which was out of character for me; Elisabeth would often gaze at me, puzzled. I don't know what stopped me from telling her that I was giving it all up.

I would have liked to help Irène, so that we could quash our doubts together, but as yet I couldn't.

Paul wanted to escape and was asking for false papers. I was going to get them for him. Everything of this kind that I could do helped to justify my actions in my own eyes.

One night I waited for Irène in vain. I never saw her again. She had vanished like a dream into the frozen mists of winter.

• • •

"Marie-Claire, you will take Irène's place." Charles finished counting the banknotes that had just been given to him to distribute between the different departments of the OCMJ. They covered the table.

"Very good," I replied, "where shall I meet the boys?"

"At the Étoile de la Bourse," and he showed me where the café was on the map of Paris. So now I would have to combine this long daily trip with visits to the "dead letterboxes" for which I had recently become responsible: the Escargot d'Or near Les Halles, and Odette Vidon, a secretary at the BNCI (Banque nationale pour le commerce et l'Industrie). Every evening I would telephone Odette and the restaurant at Les Halles and ask for news of Marguerite's aunt. If she was unwell, I had to race to the métro to fetch the mail that had been dropped. Then I would melt into the seven o'clock rush hour, among the exhausted, thin, sombre crowds, including a lot of German men and women. We would be squashed up against each other. Clutching the clandestine papers in my fur muff, I would feel the same frisson of exhilaration mixed with fear that I might have felt if I'd had a bomb in my bag. Brushing with danger and getting away with it. Slipping through German round-ups. Fooling them every time. Exactly the same thrill of pleasure as I felt aboard the *Marsouin*: tacking near the rocks and then veering away at the last moment, calculating precisely the speed with which the boat would respond. Making the right calculations and winning.

It was in the Étoile de la Bourse that I met him, Bernard, the Judas. I had some leaflets to give to Doranges, but he wasn't there. The owner advised me to wait.

"You'll be sure to see one of your lot here soon," he told me.

And before long, a man I didn't know was coming towards me, a grey felt trilby pulled down low over his eyes.

"Are you waiting for Doranges?" he asked me point blank.

My blood ran cold. What if he was Gestapo?

"No, I don't know him," I answered.

"It's OK, you can talk," he said, "I'm Bernard, his second-in-command." I hesitated. I shot a quick glance at the owner: he seemed quite relaxed and Bernard had just been talking to him. So he knew him. He nodded his head, clearly to say "Go ahead." Eventually I handed the leaflets to the stranger. He took the package and disappeared down the stairs to the basement.

"You've got to get them to Doranges as quickly as possible: it's urgent," I called after him.

"Don't worry about a thing, him or me, it's all the same."

As soon as I got outside, I was seized by doubt. Frozen with fear. I didn't trust that boy one bit.

A rendezvous at the Rue du Bac métro station brought us face to face again. "He's in charge of helping prisoners of war to escape," Doranges had told me. This interested me for Paul: Raymond hadn't managed to obtain the papers he had asked for from Louis our printer, documents on special squared paper that was hard to reproduce with our homemade equipment. Bernard came right up close to me so that no one would overhear. I was to give him the information about Paul. His cold inquisitorial stare, his sallow complexion, his dark, straggly hair, his swaggering air and his breath on my face all repulsed me. I said nothing. All we did was to agree to meet again.

Towards the end of the year, the boys stopped meeting at the Étoile de la Bourse. The owner said he was being watched by the Gestapo. And it is probably true that the Gestapo had found out a lot about us. But the fruit was not yet ripe for picking. I had had enough of my doubts: I pushed them right down deep inside me and refused to allow them back up to the surface. What we were doing was necessary. To convince myself even more I had to re-read the extraordinary memorandum signed by Darnand, Déat, and Luchaire in September 1943 and addressed to the German authorities. What an admission of impotence in the face of the will and the increasing actions of the French people! No more soul searching: better to leave your little self where it belongs and to think about other people. About those whom the war was hurting most cruelly: the ever-growing numbers of political prisoners we knew about; their families who could receive no official help; the Jews with the yellow star on their chests, of whom we saw fewer and fewer on the streets as they went into hiding or were arrested; the young men in the Maquis who had nothing, no warm clothes, no food, no shoes, nothing. What our group needed was its own welfare department. I needed three things: the approval and support of Charles, money and premises.

Early one morning, before anyone had gone to work, I met Charles on the Pont d'Alma. We walked part of the way along Avenue Bosquet. I listened to him but couldn't pluck up the courage to talk to him about my idea, feeling horribly inexperienced. But I was determined, really determined. There was that at least. And it was to be a joint venture, with Jean-Marie and his sister Honour, now in Paris; my brother-in-law's sister Marie-Louise; my friend Françoise; and of course Sylvie. Richard had introduced her to me one day: a very tall young woman with brown hair, light eyes, severe eyebrows but a gentle mouth, and above all a regal carriage. She made an instant impression, giving you the feeling that she knew everything, though she didn't say very much. She often came to our apartment and Elisabeth would ask her advice on all manner of different topics.

Everything she did would be well thought-out, considered, essential. But I found her intimidating, even though to start with she did exactly the same work as me, and with me. I put her in the picture concerning the organisation and I gave her documents to type up. Sometimes she would stay up all night doing them. Her abilities and very soon her complete autonomy would lead her to ever more involving and varied work. I knew almost nothing about her family, and it was only because we were brought together by events and also a growing friendship that she gradually opened up to me about them, giving me her address and sharing her personal problems with Elisabeth and me. We were the same age.

Charles and I were about to part when I said: "Charles, don't you think that a welfare department would be useful? Could you help me?" He liked the idea. "Agreed, Marie-Claire," he said. "I could let you have biscuits and condensed milk. You will be on the OCMJ budget alongside the other departments." I couldn't have asked for more. Now I just had to find premises. Marie-Louise put a little room off her bedroom at our disposal.

The first meeting took place one Monday evening after dinner, and we decided that it would be at the same time every week. I would collect Honour, Jean-Marie's sister, and we would meet at Marie-Louise's apartment with Françoise, Sylvie and two new recruits, Marie-Odile and Annie. Marie-Louise would make coffee for us and we would huddle around the fireplace, where lumps of coal glowed red in the grate. In this cosy room with its thick carpet, ensconced in comfortable armchairs, watching the blue flames dancing, sipping our scalding hot coffee, we felt good. The war hadn't reached us yet. The restrictions and the constraints had come little by little and we'd had time to get used to them. We imagined its horrors through accounts that we read and heard. I had seen a town in flames, but from a train. "It's so quiet," said Françoise, "you'd think we were in the country." The apartment gave onto a little courtyard with a garden, like at the Rue de Lille. "Let's get down to work," said someone else. "Let's pick a code name, just for the welfare department, and find a code for making a note of the names of the people we'll be helping." We wrote it all down on a tiny scrap of onion-skin paper.

"Marie-Louise, do you have a hiding place?"

She thought for a couple of seconds. "Here," she said, removing one of the ball finials from the bed end. She slid the precious code into the hole and, pressing down on it a little, replaced the finial.

Our programme was finalised that first night and we stuck to it rigorously:

— Make a list of all the deportees we knew of, the Jews, the young men in hiding, the families of the deportees, the members of the organisation who, unable to work as they used to, found it hard to make ends meet, the Maquisards in need.

— Build up stocks of provisions: flour, biscuits, canned food, *pain d'épices*, dried milk, sugar, potted meat, etc. I had to get on the right side of the regional groups so that they would provide me with ration coupons, which they did. We also received some via Sylvie from the Comité Anti-Déportation (CAD).

— Give vouchers to the press department to print and then resell to increase our resources.

Everyone set about helping us. From my numerous meetings I no longer came back with just papers, but was also laden with tins of condensed milk, boxes of sugar and tins of food. Jean-Marie salvaged sweaters from the Navy, Doranges shoes, Raymond cigarettes. Sylvie gave us ration coupons for bread and other things –fifteen on the fourteenth of the month and another fifteen on the thirtieth. So many that we all had to get rid of twenty or thirty sheets within the day or else they would have gone out of date.

Madame Faussemagne and her sister, Elisabeth, friends, and all of us would set out on the hunt with big bags, going to lots of different shops so as not to startle people with our unusually large supply of coupons.

Every fortnight, Elisabeth's and Madame Faussemagne's apartments were transformed into huge grocery depots. On the evenings when we met, Jean-Marie would come and help me transport this assortment of goods in bags and suitcases, piling them up on the luggage rack of my bicycle. When there were heavy snowfalls, progress was difficult in the Rue de Lille, which was never swept and fortunately quite deserted. We avoided going past the Hôtel Montalembert, which had been taken over by the Germans.

Faithfully, month after month, we met every Monday evening until Easter. From half-past ten, there would always be the same chorus: "I must go," Marie-Odile would say, "I'm going to miss the last métro."

"You've got at least another five minutes," we would chorus in reply. Curfew was at midnight. This was when – once all the work had been allocated, visits, parcels, food supplies and even trips to the country to find potted meat and butter and set up other centres – we would talk about the Gestapo. "What shall we do if they come knocking?" "What shall we say?" We would work out our responses and consider all the possible tortures they could inflict: drowning us in freezing baths, tearing us limb from limb, pulling out our nails, branding us with hot irons.

I would stare into the fire and instinctively curl up my toes up inside my shoes. I was afraid that if I was in too much pain I would talk. How would you be able to think of anything but making the pain stop? But Marie-Odile was reassuring: "There must be a state of grace." This wasn't convincing enough to quell the fear. Arrests were happening at such a pace that it seemed obvious to us that our group would be affected, that one day we would be arrested. Unless the Allies landed.

The comfort, security and warmth of these evenings enveloped us as far as the carriage entrance on Rue du Bac, but after that we would find ourselves back in a dismal Paris where huddled, shadowy figures, worried about the curfew, scurried home to their darkened houses. I thought about Irène. Had she really given it all up? The poor thing! After my doubts, my convictions seemed strangely to have grown stronger.

Sometimes midnight would strike on Saint-Germain-des-Prés before Honour and I reached Rue de Lille. We didn't want to run, though, for fear of alerting the German police patrols.

CHAPTER 5

Enter the Gestapo

There was a Christmas truce at Concarneau, with midnight Mass at seven in the morning, because of the regulations imposed by the occupiers. From the gallery, we looked down over a sea of traditional white coifs pressed using homemade alternatives to the starch that was no longer to be found. The glossy black of the shawls highlighted the elegance and lightness of the headdresses. The brig and schooner ex votos swayed at our level. My brother Arthur sang the psalm *Consolamini* in his tenor voice: the light and pure soprano of the year before had gone. Time was passing.

> *The parachutists who were finishing their training at Cupar in Scotland were thinking about their next Christmas, in 1944, and praying to God that they would be alive still and in France on that day. They were now integrated into a British brigade that was part of the Special Air Service (SAS), famous for fighting Rommel's Afrika Korps in Africa under Colonel Stirling. The new commander of the French parachutists, Pierre Bourgoin, known as "le Manchot" because he had lost an arm, had just come from there.*

On my return I found our welfare department had expanded. Sylvie had been delegated to the Comité féminin anti-deportation

(CFAD),[6] a branch of the CAD, run by Hamon. The department grew yet further when we made contact with Marie-Hélène Lefaucheux who, using the Red Cross as her cover, ran a clandestine and remarkably well-organised welfare service that had spread its tentacles throughout the whole of the northern zone.[7] She received her funds directly from Algiers and supported the welfare services of the Resistance movements. Her husband was head of the FFI[8] subdivision of the Paris region.

One day, Charles finally spoke to me seriously, calling me "*petite fille*", as he invariably did when he had something important to ask me:

"There's an organisation in Nancy that's sheltering men from Alsace who've deserted from the German army and now they're going to send them to us. It will be your job to receive, house and clothe them, to supply them with the correct papers and steer them towards the Maquis."

Soon everything was ready. We had chosen a suburban villa standing in its own grounds for transit purposes. All that remained was to make contact. "It's for tonight," Charles told me. "We'll eat together at the Écu de France. I'll be waiting for you there downstairs at half-past seven."

"Could you tell me where the Écu de France is?" I asked. He laughed. My ignorance amused him and he didn't fully grasp the provincial quietness and simplicity of our lives in the seventh arrondissement. I was forever learning new things.

"Near the Gare de l'Est, little goose, since that's where the trains from Nancy come in, but you probably didn't know that either!" I

---

6. Comité féminin d'action contre la déportation (Women's anti-deportation committee).

7. After the war, Marie-Hélène Lefaucheux (1904-1964) was highly decorated for her Resistance work and became a prominent women's and human rights activist. In 1946, she was the only woman to represent France at the United Nations.

8. Forces Françaises de l'Intérieur (French Forces of the Interior).

blushed, and vowed to myself that next time I would seem more "in the know".

By eight o'clock the Nancy agent had not arrived and we started to eat. "His train must have been delayed," said Charles. "You know when you're leaving, but never when you're going to arrive."

I ate my ice cream tiny spoonfuls at a time, and took tiny sips of my cherry cordial. Long silences stretched between us. In the end we were the only ones there, under the impatient gaze of the waiters. At eleven o'clock we had to go. Some men had left the restaurant a few minutes before us, disappointed, Gestapo men. The man we were waiting for had been caught, along with forty others: he had written down our rendezvous in his notebook. The men from Alsace never came.

Failures here, successes there. Faces that disappeared and new faces to get to know. Constant comings and goings, and above all an air of mystery shrouding all these faces, all these comings and goings. A name overheard or an unambiguous phrase caught in passing gave clues as to the formidable tasks that were underway. There were many movements, many networks, but had they managed to create unity at the top? A wide range of networks was an absolute necessity for survival. One network would go up in flames, another would carry on and could pick up elements of the first one. Viewed from below, this diffuse structure was worrying when it came to results. It had been drummed into us for too long that strength lay in unity. I would often discuss these problems in the Resistance (so clear to see in the records of the OCM) with Claude Desjardins in the Luxembourg Gardens, where we used to meet. Passionate in his beliefs, he published our newspaper *l'Avenir*, as well as *l'Essor* for students and *l'Effort* for workers. He was never short of ideas for articles, never tired of building the France of the future. Charles was working to bring together all the different youth movements – Jeunes Chrétiens,

OCMJ, MUR[9] and so forth — and finally managed it. He appeared at Rue de Lille in triumph with the masthead of the first newspaper of the FUJP (Forces Unies des Jeunes Patriotes), to be called *Jeune Combattant*, while the youth groups would come together as La Jeune Résistance.

One evening in January, Charles's secretary Nicole appeared at the usual time. "Marie-Claire, I've just been to the doctor," she said. There's nothing for it: he wants me to go to the country. For a month. A fortnight will be enough." She stopped, convulsed by a bout of coughing.

"You should have gone ages ago," I told her. At around six o'clock she would arrive exhausted and breathless, yet always in a rush. She would curse her wooden-soled shoes. With a sharp kick she would send them flying across the carpet and examine the daily disaster: no heels to her stockings! She did it again that evening, as usual. It was warm in the room, but she had wrapped herself up in the shaggy beige fur coat her parents had given her. Her dark hair was dishevelled, and by the light of the candle (we were in the middle of a power cut) her eyes seemed greener than usual.

"Marie-Claire," she went on, "you must take my place. Here are all my meetings." She took a notebook out of her pocket and explained who I would be seeing. People from the *Extérieur*, from other movements. There followed a stream of names and positions. I was penetrating right to the heart of the great machine.

Then Daniel, our regional head in the West, was arrested. I had already met him at Mondoubleau, with Michel, his Breton second-in-command, and at the Hôtel de Saumur in Rue de Bellechasse, where he stayed when he came to Paris. Madame Gilles, the manageress, looked after him like a son. It was a quiet, unremarkable place, a proper family hotel. Until then, Madame Gilles thought her

---

9. Mouvements Unis de Résistance (United Resistance Movement) was a Resistance movement in the southern zone that combined three movements: Combat, Libération-Sud, and Franc-Tireurs.

resident guest, Philippe Henriot of Radio-Paris,[10] was just an affable bourgeois gentleman, and our head of Region M (West) was just her little Daniel.

I went round there a little later than usual; it was well after nightfall and a light rain made the darkness even denser. The gas lamps shed only little islands of light. After parking my bicycle with the pedal against the pavement right in front of the hotel, I went in.

Madame Gilles spotted me from her desk and rushed towards me, her face crumpled, her beautiful doe eyes distraught. "Daniel has just been arrested by the Gestapo," she said. "It's dreadful, poor boy! He was just coming in, quiet as you please! He spotted the prison van. He understood immediately and turned on his heels. Too late: the plain clothes men spotted what he was about to do and jumped on him. He tried to defend himself, but they bundled him into the van. Since then they've kept watch outside the hotel, to arrest the 'accomplices' I heard them say. They've searched his room."

"What did they find? What did he have with him?"

She told me all this very rapidly, in a low voice that was trembling with emotion. I was in a fine mess! Clearly the man in the raincoat who I had almost brushed against as I passed him was a Gestapo agent. He would read my name and address on the number plate – mandatory, alas! – on my bike. As luck would have it, I had replaced my number with "Finistère" on the rear mudguard, as my father had got me papers from Lanriec. So they wouldn't be able to trace me through the Paris police stations. I had taken this precaution as soon as I'd started to pick up mail from the Escargot d'Or. But now I had to get out of the hotel, and my bag was stuffed with compromising documents. Madame Gilles looked at me, shaking.

---

10. Philippe Henriot was an extreme right-wing, antisemitic journalist, appointed Vichy Minister for Information in 1943, who was dubbed "the French Goebbels" for his propaganda broadcasts for Radio Vichy and Radio Paris. He was killed by the Resistance on 28 June 1944.

Slowly I walked out of the door; calmly I took my bicycle. The man was there: I could see him without turning to look, I could follow every movement he made. He made no move to cross the two metres separating us: what was he waiting for? I sat on the saddle, one foot on the ground. I waited a few seconds, then settled into the saddle. My heart was beating so wildly that I had the crazy thought: "If he listens, he'll hear it." I rode off. Suddenly, he lifted his torch and shone it straight at my "Finistère" plate. Would I stop when he ordered me to or would I race right up to the crossroads and vanish into the impenetrable blackness of Rue de l'Université? Yes, that was what I would do, because of the papers. I felt the torchlight on my back, but still he said nothing. I turned the corner. The silence went on, and I was safe.

Then I went like the wind. I had to warn the others, straight away. They would be caught in the trap. Making a detour via Rue des Saints Pères and checking to make sure no one was following me, I arrived at Elisabeth's apartment. I took the stairs four at a time: it was nearly half-past seven and our dear friend Claire was coming to dinner.

What should I say to my sister? I had to leave again immediately. I always tried to protect the smooth running of our family and our social life, but that night it was impossible. She came running to meet me and grabbed me by the arm: "Richard has just been here. Daniel has been arrested. Whatever you do, don't go to the Hôtel de Saumur, you'll be arrested on the spot."

"I've just come from there. What about Sylvie and the others? Did Richard say anything about them?"

"Yes, he said you must go to Sylvie's house."

I was expecting this. Sylvie knew Daniel very well and it was even thanks to him that she had entered the movement. There were lots of records and documents at her house, and the Gestapo at Rue des Saussaies had all the means at their disposal to make anyone talk, no matter who.

Elisabeth had barely finished her sentence before I was outside, racing furiously through the deserted streets, along Boulevard Saint-Germain and Boulevard Saint-Michel in the rain, now torrential, and with every bump in the road repeating the same words: "Daniel has been arrested, Daniel has been arrested ..." Since October other people had been disappearing, but not us. It was one thing to be afraid of disasters, but quite another to have to believe in them. The bastion of my little precautions wouldn't be strong enough, and I thought intensely of Paul in Austria, who was happy for me to live in his house, with his wife and daughter. Dear Lord, what should I do? What should I do now? Just try to save those who could be saved.

At last I reached Sylvie's street, near the Val-de-Grâce. My arrival at this late hour and in this state would astonish her family. Too bad. I had to take the documents away.

"No," said Sylvie. "It's vital not to forget any: it will take me a while; I'll come round to you later."

I don't know what our friend Claire thought when I appeared at the end of dinner, scarlet-faced, soaked through and with my hair all over the place. "I'm sorry, I've had problems with my bicycle," I said, and I didn't need to say any more. I was worried most of all about the military records that Richard had recently entrusted to me, which were now in the bag of the vacuum cleaner. I thought it was a good hiding place, but what were we to do with the papers Sylvie was bringing? Why is it that men can't do without pieces of paper? Why do we have to bolster their feeble memories! There was nothing to say on that score about the records we already had. Richard and I regularly weeded out those that could safely be destroyed, and I burned them in the little stove in my bedroom: we only kept what was essential for the present and the future.

We were devouring the last crumbs of the ersatz chestnut cake (made from beans) when Sylvie rang the doorbell. "It's good to be here at last," she murmured, heaving a deep sigh and propping a large satchel, stuffed to bursting, against the wall.

"We must find somewhere to put these papers," I told her. "I don't want to keep them here in this apartment." We were sitting on either side of the chest, utterly exhausted, as we wondered who else had been arrested, and who was about to be. We had to fear the worst: we didn't know who was denouncing the victims.

Sylvie went on: "I'm going to stay with Charles's parents. They're wonderful. I'll ring you tomorrow morning at half-past seven."

"Sylvie, come and have your meals here; I'm sure Elisabeth will agree."

"That's kind of you, Marie-Claire. It would be nice."

With Sylvie coming every day, we would be able to talk undisturbed, as we were always rushed at our meetings. I still found her intimidating, but perhaps I would discover the secret of her assurance and authority. As I waved to her before she disappeared round a bend in the stairs, I thought, "I don't really know her."

I kept the door open: Jean-Marie was arriving to warn me, him as well, in case I didn't know already.

CHAPTER 6

Turbulence

"I've found a new head for Region M." Jean-Marie was gazing at the smoke rising from his pipe as he spoke. "A friend of mine, Francis, a very good chap who works for us already; I'll talk to Charles about it tomorrow. If he agrees, we'll give Francis his 'letters of command' and I'll ask you to come and meet him at my house so that you can tell him all you know about Brittany." The BBC news bulletin was just beginning: we listened to it in silence. Churchill said a few words in his colourful and robust French. But the background interference made the most appalling din; you would have thought an army of witches was swirling around us casting evil spells, and Churchill faded away. I tried to imagine England preparing for the landing and I wondered what the men who were working on them thought about us. The meeting of the two armies, the one here and the other one over there, would be a strange encounter – and one not to be missed. You couldn't live through the most extraordinary times of the century without throwing yourself into them heart and soul. I looked at Jean-Marie with gratitude: without him, I might have stayed on the sidelines to the end. Jean-Marie was in charge of industrial sabotage (SI), under orders from the department. Since there was no hope of listening to the news bulletin, he agreed to explain something of his activities to me. First of all, he had to make contact with workers in the major armaments factories in Paris and in the provinces in order to organise sabotage: this he had already done in part. Then he had to bring himself up to date with all the different ways of destroying things. He collected bottles of poison and special products for jamming machines or damaging their delicate parts. Dynamite and plastic explosives held no secrets for him. "I think we are well on the way to doing some interesting work at the Renault factory," he said as he got up to leave. "Tomorrow I'll bring something over that will astonish you. And I'll tell you when you can meet Francis."

The next day he unfolded on the table a remarkably detailed plan of the Renault factory at Billancourt. All the plants and machinery were plotted.

"Everything is ready, Marie-Claire. When the time is right, the order to go into action will be given. Some of the workers will blow up the power plant, here on the plan," and his index finger pointed to a red dot, "and these other main centres."

I could already hear the tremendous explosion, I could see the windows shattering into tiny splinters, the Germans arriving to arrest the fleeing workers, who would be only too happy about the disaster. Jean-Marie went on: "The factory will be out of action for months. And the Allied bombings and their unavoidable loss of life will become unnecessary." I looked at him with respect. I would never have guessed that he could organise an action on such a scale.

"While we wait for this major coup," he added, "my team of Renault workers and I have developed a method of sabotage that has proved to be amazingly effective. We pour a corrosive liquid into the engines of the vehicles made for the German Army: tanks, small tracked vehicles, lorries and the like, which puts them out of action after 100 kilometres. Impossible to detect the slightest thing at the final inspections before they leave the factory. It's wonderful.

The Germans are in a constant state of fury. There are already large numbers of vehicles that are completely useless except for their outer shells. My men are ace: they do it surreptitiously and there's no way they'll get caught. We've started up a newspaper specially for them, and for all the other workers we've been to establish contacts with in other factories." Then he dropped the subject of workers and factories to tell me about our press organisation, our printer and his escapes to the country with Louis from the post office.

"I'm going there tomorrow. You'll never guess why. To send messages to London, our own messages and those of the OCM and the CNR.[11] Louis's boss at the post office sometimes lets him have a radio transmitter. It's terribly heavy. We lug it around in a suitcase, with the generator, and while Louis transmits, I crank the generator."

I met Francis two days later. Madame Faussemagne had gone ahead of me to show me the way to Jean-Marie's room. At the back of the apartment, in her own bedroom, she opened the door of a cupboard that was one of a pair, but instead of finding shelves of linen inside, I stubbed my toes against the steps of a tiny spiral staircase. At the top was the "den", the free zone of the industrial saboteur.

Francis was sitting on a low chair, his legs crossed, his beige raincoat half open and trailing on the floor, holding a glass of Banyuls. He put it down, got up and shook me by the hand. I looked at him intently. The Brittany regional network that he hailed from meant far more to me than the other regions, not only because it was my favourite place, but also because I felt deep inside that something really important was going to happen there, for the war and for me: not necessarily the landing, but something.

A pale young man. Slight. Too slight, perhaps. And he looked so very young. Can you go to war when you look so young? I wondered

---

11. Conseil National de la Résistance (National Council for the Resistance)

about this for him, for me and for the others. But the answer was already clear: it had to be yes.

The desk and table were piled with papers of all sorts: identity cards, demobilisation forms, census certificates, work permits, a residence permit from the town hall, forms that Jean-Marie would give to his boys, forms that by now I knew so well how to fill in. I had a complete set for myself, which took five years off my age and gave my birthplace as Ergué-Armel, a little hamlet near Quimper. I had lived there since 17 April 1934, under the name of Marie-Claire Kerauden. I had re-read the aide-memoire we gave out with each set of papers many times over:

"And don't forget that:

Your name is: Kerauden

You were born on 3 May 1928

Therefore you are: 16 years of age

You are: without a profession

You live in: Ergué-Armel

You were registered on:

Your work permit was given to you on the:

You were demobilised on:"

And of course on the bed and on the floor were copies of *l'Avenir* and *l'Effort*, and the first edition of *Jeune Combattant*, from which Jean-Marie had read an article out loud to me with the headline '*L'Union est faite. En avant!*':

"The young people of our country feel their very existence is threatened. Hemmed in on all sides, by the enemy from without and by the enemy within, they are moreover called upon daily to betray France in favour of the Germans. To these dangers and to these threats they have given the only possible answer: unity and, thanks to this unity, action. This is the clearest result obtained by the enemy: the young people of France, too often divided in the past by either politics or religion, have found unity."

I told Francis all I knew about South Finistère, and particularly about the departures for England via Concarneau, which were now very difficult according to my father's letters, and about a forest in Anjou "put at the disposition of young men avoiding STO" by a woman friend from Brittany. Just as I was about to go, Jean-Marie took a bottle containing a yellow liquid from among the others on his table: "Here, give this to Elisabeth from me. It's a lot better than onion juice!"

I found myself back at the top of the dark narrow passageway again. "Not exactly spacious, Jean-Marie: better not put on weight!"

"Not much danger of that with what they leave us to eat. I've worked out that the armchair is the right width to jam the opening perfectly. If the Germans come, I'll have time to escape or put up a fight: I've got a good revolver."

It was a few days later when they came.

They rang the doorbell at eight o'clock in the morning, three Gestapo men in plain clothes. Madame Faussemagne had already left to go to buy food, because of the queues. Jean-Marie's mother opened the door. "We want to see Colonel Faussemagne, known as Felix de Schomberg, alias Camille," grunted the men.

"You are mistaken, gentlemen, Colonel Faussemagne is eighty years old and housebound."

They insisted: "We want to see him."

Jean-Marie was still asleep in his room, amid all the stuff that we know about. One of the three men left for the police station to do some checks and Madame West showed the other two into the large drawing room. She was consumed by terrible fear: to mask it she began to knit, struggling to keep her hands from shaking. The Colonel's breakfast was laid out on a tray. Steam was rising from the teapot: two thin slices of bread sat on a plate waiting to be buttered. Madame Faussemagne came back, grasped the situation and didn't waste a second. She grabbed the tray. The men thought she was going to offer them some tea. There was a slight wavering in their viciousness and fury as they refused almost politely.

Then she raced along the passages, plonked the tray down in front of the Colonel, who was in bed, and climbed up the steep, narrow stairs, calling: "Jean-Marie, quickly, get dressed, the Gestapo are here!"

This was enough to rouse him instantly from the deep sleep of the just. He leapt to the foot of the bed and cast a glance over the many dangers that littered his room. "Quick, give it all to me," said his aunt, "we'll take it up to the attic."

Jean-Marie stuffed his revolver awkwardly into his pyjama pocket and followed Madame Faussemagne, his arms, like hers, laden with papers and bottles.

"Quickly, quickly," she kept saying, pushing heavy curtains aside, shoving doors open with her shoulder, going hell for leather. From the drawing room there rose the murmur of voices. To gain time, Madame West was attempting to make polite conversation with the unwelcome guests. No one on the landing: the third accomplice had not yet returned. So they climbed nonchalantly up to the attic room, where Jean-Marie heaped the papers and other material into the empty suitcases. Then he settled down, lit his pipe and waited for someone to come and tell him the danger was over.

Madame Faussemagne went back to the drawing room as if nothing had happened. A few minutes later, the men roughly insisted on searching the apartment, finally suspecting that there might be someone other than the Colonel to look for.

"Certainly! Go ahead," said the two women.

They got as far as the back bedroom, where they came to a halt in the doorway, feeling slightly awkward at the sight of the blind Colonel in bed, very dignified and poised.

"Do you know Camille, alias Felix?" they asked.

"No," replied the Colonel.

"You are requested not to leave the flat."

"I scarcely could if I wanted to."

They flung open all the doors and arrived in front of the pair of cupboards. The sisters watched anxiously. Up above them, the bed was unmade, still warm. There were bound to be some papers still lying around and the room looked like a battlefield. The men hesitated for a moment, opened the genuine cupboard, and left.

The net was closing in on us. Who had betrayed Jean-Marie? We were just about getting over the arrest of Daniel, but the Faussemagne alert made us question everything again.

Elisabeth said nothing.

I gave up my art class.

I gave up secretarial college.

Then a dramatic dragnet operation in the northern zone dealt a terrible blow to the adult section of the OCM, especially with the capture of our leader, Colonel Touny. One by one the "veterans" were disappearing. Who would be left to welcome the Allies? Would nothing be left of this edifice that had been built with such painstaking care? It was crumbling around our ears. Were there enough of us left to fill the gaps? The weight of waiting for an arrest that began to feel inevitable was sometimes so crushing that you fell prey to thinking that if the Gestapo would only come for you then that would be the end of the matter.

As I listened to my brother Arthur playing a Liszt rhapsody, I thought to myself: "Let's hope that at least a few of us will be left to say, 'Look! This is what they did.'"

I organised things to keep some time free on the days when my brother, who was at boarding school at Versailles, came to spend a few hours with us. I immersed myself in his music. He had shot up and I wasn't used to him being so much taller than me. He didn't talk much: we both kept our private thoughts secret, thinking it would somehow reflect badly on us if we expressed them. We never kissed each other and we hardly ever even shook hands.

There was relaxation in Arthur's concerts, and in long conversations with Elisabeth. In the evenings, we would share our thoughts on the books we were reading (the métro allowed me the luxury of reading still), or remind ourselves of what we needed to do the next day: tracking down some cooking oil, or the weekly hundred grams of meat, or trying out some new recipe. I would tell her about my latest driving lesson, as I was going to take my driving test, Rennes Auto-Ecole having started up again with cars converted to run on gas.

Elisabeth would make plans for parties, just small bridge parties, as there was no dancing now,[12] made up of young men and women who boasted both a surname and first name, and whose families and addresses we knew. Within our Resistance group, the reduction of our identities to a constantly changing first name had something unreal about it, turning us into mere shadows, without substance, weight or future. Jacques, Rémy, Georges .... From one day to the next they had disappeared or were going to disappear, and I would have lost touch with my natural peer group; but Elisabeth watched over me and showed me how to role-play being a young girl, and the idea was coming back to me. The irreplaceable years of my youth were passing me by, and sometimes I had a wild desire to go out and forget it all, to go to parties or grand balls, to fall in love and get married. But then I thought that nothing solid or lasting could come of it. War work had to take priority over feelings.

The coldest days of winter fell suddenly in February. We had virtually nothing left to burn in the stove. The ice on the window in the bedroom was so thick it blocked the light. I made myself some mittens from canvas lined with the fur of the rabbits we had eaten at Kerancalvez, but even so the bicycle had to stay in the garage. You could gradually thaw out in the métro, and I arranged more and

---

12. Dancing, whether in public or private, was banned.

more meetings there, but I still often had to trudge through the snow to wait for Raymond, Jean, Jean-Louis and the others.

The mornings-only job as a secretary that I had taken in October had become so annoying! Most of the others had given up everything: I had to as well. One evening, I said to myself: "I'll write to my father about it; I can't go on wasting so much time every day!"

My father wrote back: "I understand why you're not keen on staying with your architect." There were no reproaches from him either. I put his letter down on the table, suddenly wanting so much to see him again. A strange light enveloped me: it was starting to snow again.

In England too it was snowing. Geo had left behind the moors and forests of the north, where a few days earlier he had been sleeping in the open in his sleeping bag, under the hanging branches of fir trees, where the snow couldn't reach. But it surrounded him and covered the trees with a thick mantle. With his stick of paratroopers, he had been carrying out dummy missions in a frozen wilderness.

Along with other young men who had been taught that radio operators would be the key factor in the success of their operations, he had thus left romantic Scotland. Their training course was at Henley-on-Thames. But it was not without a certain regret that he left his friends to learn how to drive a train or blow up a factory.

The Americans had invaded England, which was now nothing but one big army: when Geo wiped the condensation from the train windows he saw a snowy landscape full of camps, and more camps.

I left my job.

CHAPTER 7

Ripe Fruit

When did Charles, Richard and Nicole start coming regularly to Elisabeth's apartment? I can't remember. Though she didn't say anything, my sister was worried about all these meetings that I was going to all over the place, and it seemed safer to her to have us, or some of us at least, under her wing. They all won her over. The flowers they brought filled the apartment with their scent all day long. Nicole amused her with stories of her giddy life, Charles fascinated her with his masterly expositions on the war, and Richard charmed her with his affection and kindness. Little Claude would go from one to another for kisses and cuddles. Their changing names amazed her, but she wasn't fooled. One evening she whispered in Charles's ear: "You, you're not Philippe," (this was the name we had given him at the time), "you're Charles. That's what your name is."

I made the lucky six who met up at Rue de Lille promise on all they held most dear that they would be tortured, chopped up in little pieces or killed rather than reveal my sister's name and address. None of them did.

Richard stayed behind. I could see how those last few months had left their mark on him. Would it be exhaustion that would force us into submission in the end? Elisabeth had brought him a cup of mint tea: it sat steaming on the corner of the table, and we let the time go by.

Even though he was terribly concerned about anything that didn't work or that ought to have worked better, Richard created an atmosphere of confidence and stability around him. When he began to talk about the Resistance, I was fascinated. For generations and to this day, my family had always been passionate about history, and now we were living through one of its greatest periods, we were making history. Working with Richard made me feel I was doing something effective: our comings and goings, our meetings, our scraps of paper were not a futile waste of effort. When liberation came, this work would produce results that were worthwhile: factories and bridges would be blown up, roads would be cut off – as long as we weren't caught.

"Richard," I said eventually, "is this D-Day that we've been trying to plan for actually going to happen? Have we planned well enough, both us and the Allies? Our future and that of our children depend on it!"

"Yes," said Richard, "but what more can we do? We have to spend our time on repairing links that have been broken. Daniel arrested, Deleuze, in charge of students, and his deputy both arrested. Frédéric has taken over from him, but all these changes weaken the strength of the whole …"

He sighed. I carried on:

"It's true that we're gradually developing into useful tools, worn in in all the right ways. Take me, for instance – I can memorise any telephone number I want to, or addresses, or anything else, and I can forget them too. I feel I'm turning into an effective agent in the war that I have to wage, and it would be more inconvenient to lose me now than it would have been a year ago. The same goes for all of us."

Then I added:

"Richard, if you and Charles are arrested, who will take over from you?"

"Jacques Nord."

"And if he's arrested too?"

"The welfare department," he said with a laugh.

The all-clear sounded: the warning had given us time for a good long talk. I put on my coat, as I had just enough time to get to the rendezvous I'd arranged with Raymond at the Odéon métro station: he was at last to give me my brother-in-law's papers to help him escape. Richard watched as I slung my big leather bag across my body. Michel, from the western region, had had one made for each of us, Nicole, Sylvie and me, by the Ferrière Maquis in the Loiret. Proper army haversacks, into which we could stuff newspapers, plans, identity cards, demobilisation papers, work certificates, parachute drop instructions, photographs and I don't know what else! I used often to run the palm of my hand over the soft leather, still pale and new. Now we only had faux materials, we only ate ersatz food. Imitation leather, imitation wool, imitation soap, imitation oil, imitation coffee, and possibly even imitation fish in that disgusting grey paté that you could buy off-ration. Richard and Charles didn't like those bags, telling us they could give us away; but we couldn't bring ourselves to part with them. I still have mine and it will still be good for my grandchildren!

• • •

"Don't worry," said Raymond, "Louis couldn't get the papers done for me for tonight, but I promise you'll have them tomorrow." Not tomorrow, Raymond! The Gestapo arrested you and Louis that day, with all the material you had put in a box in a cellar because you could "feel the heat".

Cartier took over from Raymond. The papers had gone: we had to find another template. My brother-in-law's sister managed to persuade a Beaux-Arts student who had just come back from Germany to lend her his papers for two or three days, the time it would take to copy them: in the meantime, he would stay holed up in his room! I was terrified that the new forged papers department would mislay them. Twice they had to start again as the prints were no good. Then at last we were able to put the unfortunate boy back into circulation.

"You'll have them in a week, Marie-Claire, I promise," said Cartier.

• • •

The latest arrests, plus giving up my secretarial job, meant that I was doing much more travelling around Paris and in the provinces. I followed spring's triumphant progress on the horse chestnut tree in the courtyard. My energies had been depleted by the cold, and with the sun's return I found new reserves of determination and endurance.

But on some days the sudden arrival of spring could prove enervating, and for no reason you felt convinced you had a death sentence hanging over you. I used to walk along the edge of the pavement. My weary spirit made this calculation: "I mustn't step on the cracks. If I do I'll be arrested. Death is watching my every move, waiting to spot the first sign of weakness." As I lengthened my stride so my foot landed plumb in the middle of the paving stone, I would say to myself: "This is just childish: pure superstition. The last thing we need is more reasons to be agitated and anxious." But such calculations of risk were hard to resist.

I often went into the church at Saint-Germain-des-Prés to pray. I prayed that we would win the war. And what about the German girls, were they praying for their country's victory? Of course they were. It didn't matter: prayer has its own intrinsic worth. God is the champion of just causes. He put Joan of Arc at the head of an army.

The distant hum of the city, the shadowy light and shafts of colour in this church, with its medieval decoration, and the regular clatter of the door to the confessional enveloped my thoughts. They were mired in contradictions. First I would build a future for myself, then I would think: "It would probably be better if I died now, for the perfection of my life. I have reached a state of detachment that I will find hard to keep up in peacetime."

· · ·

The end of March already. Heady days under the flowering horse chestnut trees in the Luxembourg and Tuileries gardens, buzzing with thousands of insects. The buds on the plane trees were bursting, young shoots were spreading: I would daydream, leaning my elbows on the embankment wall. Daydream beside the Seine, green and tranquil, with its passing barges. I was waiting. Waiting for Cartier and my brother-in-law's papers. I didn't dare make any more promises to Elisabeth: I would give them to her when I got them, and that was that. She already had the identity card, and the form Paul would need to obtain a food ration card when he got to Paris after his escape. But I still didn't have the crucial travel pass.

I waited for Doranges outside the Académie des Belles Lettres.

And Doranges didn't come.

Then I waited for the two Jeans whom I saw every day: Jean, liaison agent for Doranges and Bernard, and Jean-Louis, liaison agent for Hache,[13] in charge of the Paris region, tall and lanky, dressed in black with a soft trilby and big glasses, towering above the crowds and older than the rest of us.

---

13. Doctor Claude Mairesse ("Hache") was head of the Bureau Central de Renseignements et d'Action (BCRA) in the Aisne. After being forced to take refuge in Paris, he became head of the OCMJ, and with our team pulled off some remarkable coups, including setting a fire that consumed 50,000 Service de Travail Obligatoire records at the Ministry of Labour. On 2 July 1944 he died in a cattle truck during deportation.

The two skinny teenagers told me that nobody knew what had happened to Doranges, that he hadn't turned up for any of his meetings.

It was a glorious morning and I was waiting for the two Jeans again. I was dreaming of the sea and the countryside, as I was leaving. I told them: "On Tuesday I won't be here. Nicole will come instead of me to our half-past two rendezvous at Rue Guénégaud. I'm leaving on a mission to Brittany."

On Tuesday 4 April, the two Jeans were at Rue Guénégaud on time. Not Nicole. Bernard was also there, which was odd: he shouldn't have known about the rendezvous. Perhaps he'd heard Jean-Louis reminding Jean about it. He said: "I was being followed but I've just managed to shake them off." Then suddenly: "Run! They're here! Even though I took a roundabout route to lose them!"

But the Gestapo had arrived, at the time appointed by Bernard. They shoved the two Jeans into a Citroën Traction Avant.

"Who is Dominique?" (my new name) they demanded.

"A tall lad with very fair hair." They made a careful note of the description.

Nicole never did arrive, and the small dark-haired girl who was Dominique was in Brittany, travelling from one town to another on behalf of the welfare departments of the OCMJ and Marie-Hélène Lefaucheux.

Bernard went on his way, a free man. A zealous member of the Resistance, above suspicion …

CHAPTER 8

The Break

My father was home early. From the hall I could see him in the sitting room, bending over a plan.

"Marie, come and see," he said. He never called me "Mie" like the others. He always used the proper names for everything, and he never swore. He would say "Germans" and not "Boche", "the Fritz", "*fridolins*" or "*doryphores*" (Colorado beetles), as we used to. I sometimes heard him talk about "*la verdure*" (a reference to the grey-green of the German uniforms). I went up beside him and was stunned to see the plan of a 30-foot boat, elegant and spacious. "I'm going to build it as soon as the war is over. We shall be able to go on cruises. I shall put winches for the halyards, as I am getting old now, and we shall need a sturdy engine." We discussed it for ages, down to the tiniest detail. "If we go on a long trip, we'll take a sailor with us …"

In my mind I was already on the jetty on launch day.

The next day, Easter Sunday, he took me to the boatyard to show me the boats that were up on jack stands. It was a marvellous day: the air smelt of tar and freshly cut wood. He and I were growing closer.

The following Tuesday morning the time crawled by as I waited for the postman. I was writing my diary up in my bedroom. Through the open window I could see the sea, very blue in the westerly breeze, and I watched the scudding shadows of the cumulus clouds that had broken away from the distant mist. Blackthorn in full bloom fringed the path leading to the beach and the scent came drifting up to me. In the past two days the youngest beech tree had come into leaf, the earliest of all the trees in the wood where my father wanted to build a house. I put down my pen and looked, thinking: "What is it about this view that casts a spell over me every time? Is it the curve of the field, sheltered by the hill with its windmill? Is it the tall poplars in the little valley that carries on the dip in the land, almost opposite us? Or is it the constantly changing surface of the sea, framed by Le Cabellou and Beg-Meil? Perhaps all these lines, intersecting and extending each other, add up to make a perfect equation, a golden number. For me it all adds up to complete inner peace." My thoughts roamed on, undisturbed. My grandmother with her well-powdered hair looked down on me from the oval-shaped gilt frame that added a gentle air to my room; the figure on the impressively large wooden crucifix brought back from the Black Forest by a forebear also kept an eye on me. Framing the window, the airy pale green net curtains that my mother had managed to buy off-ration rippled in the breeze. I felt good.

Above me I could hear my sister Françoise shifting her chair from time to time to "get some distance" as she painted. Downstairs in the kitchen, I could hear Anna clattering pots and pans and busying herself around the hay box, a proper piece of furniture into which she would put the stewpot of dried haricot beans to cook for hours and hours. In the dining room, Arthur was playing "Forest Murmurs" from Wagner's *Siegfried*.

"The postman is so late this morning!" I kept saying to myself. At last a firm hand banged the garden gate open: it was him! I charged downstairs and recognised Sylvie's writing on the envelope. We had agreed she would send me news, but can you ever know what you'll find in a letter? The news was worse even than I could have feared. Jean-Marie, Richard and others had fallen ill: it wasn't difficult to work out what it meant. "Don't come back!" she wrote. I wanted to go that very evening. My parents wisely dissuaded me: "Wait for another letter, otherwise you'll be throwing yourself into the jaws of the beast." Two days later, another one came: the evil was spreading, Charles and Cartier had been caught, and many others with them. This time I decided I had to go.

"Where will you go?" asked Mother. "The house in Rue de Lille is shut up."

"To Albert on Rue Madame," I replied.

Mother couldn't deny that I would be fine with my brother and his wife, but she wanted me to wait longer. Nothing was going to hold me back any longer now, however: I was too scared that I might not have put the papers away carefully enough. Would they still be safely in the vacuum cleaner bag and inside the piano? Had I burned the carbon copies? The typewriter too could be proof positive for the

La Vue

Gestapo and get us all arrested, even at Concarneau! My parents, Elisabeth and all rest of the family. I would have to find somewhere else to put it. In the end, my father brought forward a business trip and took the train with me, resolved to bring me back a week later.

In Paris, a letter from Sylvie was waiting for me:

> Dear Friend,
>
> I wanted you to find this little note from your fellow worker when you arrive. Gosh, how lucky you are to get out of Paris and breathe some Breton air! Meanwhile I've carried on breathing this disease-infested air, and how infested it is! A thousand thanks for your long letter. I'm so touched that you've kept your promise like this. Give me a ring as soon as you can, so I can tell you all about our last bridge party at your relative's house. I feel for you really, as now you're going to have to get back in the swing of it all again.
>
> Affectionately,
>
> Sylvie

I saw her again at Marie-Louise's in Rue du Bac. We felt like two survivors of a terrible storm. I leafed through the now outdated worksheets: we would need new ones, lots of them.

In code I wrote: *Richard...*

Richard had been glad that he'd gone to the cinema with Sylvie the night before. "We need to relax," he had said, "or we'll lose our nerve." He had a rendezvous with Claude Desjardins, Mabille and Bernard in Rue Velpeau, near Le Bon Marché, at five o'clock. Mabille and Bernard were already there waiting. Richard and Bernard started to talk as they walked. Claude had just arrived and was about to join them. But suddenly Bernard took a step forward and turned round to face Richard, who tried to push past him. As he did so, he turned around and saw three men behind him. Now he understood everything, right from the start. Possessed by a furious rage, he head-butted Bernard in the stomach, catching him off-balance, then shoved him aside and ran towards Rue de Babylone, while Mabille ran towards the Velpeau métro entrance. There he was caught by a German policeman. Richard was trying to get into Square Boucicaut by the side gate and slip through the gardens and into the métro at the Sèvres road junction, which is always crowded at that time of day. The three Germans fired, shattering a café window, but Richard got away. Not realising why he was running, the park keeper grabbed hold of him. Gasping for breath, Richard yelled: "Let me go! The Gestapo are after me."

The keeper released his grip, but it was too late. The Germans caught up and arrested him. As he climbed into the car, Richard spotted Claude in the crowd, watching, stock still.

In his briefcase Richard had military documents and others signed with his alias, de Lionne, inside a geography book. At his first interrogation, the Germans hadn't found them. So far so good. Richard could breathe again. From Rue des Saussaies they took him back to Fresnes prison.

By his second interrogation they had found them. "You are de Lionne. Admit it..."

"No, no, he's a tall fair chap with glasses." They probably didn't believe him, but still matters could be worse.

Third interrogation: "You are the second-in-command to Charles Verny." Richard knew his number was up.

The Gestapo men knew that there was a Nicole and a Marie-Claire.

"Descriptions," they demanded.

"Marie-Claire is very tall, nearly six foot, and lives near Place Clichy." They wrote it all down in a notebook.

I wrote down another name: *Jean-Marie...*

Several of the boys used to meet up at the restaurant on the corner of Rue de Babylone and Rue du Bac. As soon as Claude saw Richard and Mabille being arrested, he knew it was compromised. How to warn them? He discussed it with Charles Verny's mother. In the end he suggested she should send her granddaughter to be the look-out in front of the restaurant, as she knew them all and no one would suspect her, especially if she was racing up and down the pavement on her roller-skates. This she duly did, relentlessly, bumping into each of the boys on purpose and whispering in their ear: "Claude says not to go in, it's dangerous." Then she would pick herself up and streak away again.

But Jean-Marie did go there that night. As soon as he sat down, he felt uneasy about the shady-looking individuals at the next table.

Before long the café owner called out: "Monsieur Jean-Marie, telephone call for Monsieur Jean-Marie."

Jean-Marie recognized Bernard's voice. "What do you want?" "Nothing in particular. Just to check you've arrived."

Unsettled, Jean-Marie hastily finished his dinner. As he was about to leave, the men at the next table got up and arrested him. At that very moment, his mother and sister came running to tell him to get out as quickly as he could, as one of Charles's brothers had come to warn them that his cover was blown.

They too fell into the clutches of the Gestapo, who took the whole family off towards the Sèvres junction.

"I was walking down the side of the square," Sylvie told me, "with my bag stuffed with papers. I saw Jean-Marie, but didn't spot his escort or his mother and sister a little way behind. I headed towards him. He held up his hands, which were handcuffed. I carried on walking and passed him without saying anything. Had one of the policemen spotted the prisoner's gesture? He followed me and soon accosted me, asking to see what was in my bag. I took my time, picked out a few uncompromising papers and showed them to him with a smile. He let me go."

Sylvie couldn't tell me anything about how the two Jeans were arrested: they had simply not turned up, like Charles, at a rendezvous at Auteuil, like Hache, like others I didn't know so well. "We've managed to re-establish contact with the departments," Sylvie said. "Jacques Nord is running the OCMJ with Frédéric. It's lucky you gave him Marie-Louise's address for sending parcels from Normandy. That was the only way left to find us." She went on: "Annie has disappeared too, Nicole is still going strong. I'd like you to meet Marie: she's your replacement."

So I had been replaced. What was there left to do? The bitter feeling of no longer being indispensable was some consolation for having to go back with my father. Would Charles's plans for me never come to fruition? Would I live through the landings with my family in Brittany?

• • •

With my father, I set about helping the Resistance in Concarneau, fighting like him against any splitting into factions and rivalries. He told me about his activities in more detail, but without going into any depth. Prudence dictated that both of us should know as little as possible about what the other did. It was only years later that I found out how it had all begun for him.

In 1941, my best friends' mother had invited him to the Manoir du Bois, near where we lived. She was going to Morocco.

"I believe you are the person," she said, "to whom I can entrust the password for the escape network for British and Canadian airmen brought down in France. It is 'The buffaloes are on the prairie.' If anyone says this to you, you can believe them and help them. Here is the network." And she gave him all the information in her possession. So it was that my father was caught up in the system. When did he join the Rémy network? I shall never know: the people who could tell me are dead.

When the possibility of making landings along the coast was being studied, they consulted him. When information was wanted about German movements of boats and camouflage, they asked him. He was in contact with Claude Francis-Boeuf of the CND (Confrérie Notre Dame), Colonel Rémy's intelligence network. Francis-Boeuf had been sent one day as assistant to Professor Legendre, director of the marine biology laboratory at the Collège de France in Concarneau, to help carry off the extraordinary coup of the Ouessant operation.[14] With him, my father was to take care of the adaptations to two trawlers, the *Papillon des Vagues* and the *Général Charette*. At his town hall they distributed clandestine ration coupons and maps. Eventually, in November 1943, his boatyard manager, Jean Garrec, persuaded him to join the Libération movement, and he became its leader after Dr Nicolas was arrested. "I am 'Monsieur Charles'," my father told me. Not just for Libération either, but for all the other movements.

He introduced me to Patrice, to the Le Flochs, and to two social workers with whom I started up an effective welfare programme. But my Resistance activities did not eat up all of my time as they had in Paris. There was time left over to make regular entries in my diary. And that 3 May, I would turn twenty-one.

"I am of age. I have just finished my last J3 chocolate ration for April.[15] What will my 22nd year bring? People are predicting the most dreadful calamities: the landings are expected everywhere, in

14. Operation "Pound": a US commando raid on the German radar installations on the Ile d'Ouessant (Ushant Island), 3-4 September 1943.

15. J3 denoted the official ration category for "children of 13 to 21". "J" stood for "*jeunesse*".

the middle of the country as much as on the coasts, as there's a lot of talk of airborne troops. If the Allies want to cut Brittany off, we shall be crushed like grain between millstones."

The next day I received a letter from Elisabeth who had returned to Paris:

My dear Mic,

I am writing to you after a fifth air-raid warning to end the day with. Distant bombings – or nothing at all – but these constant interruptions are a terrible impediment to daily life. So it's decided: if the railway line hasn't been cut again by then, I'm leaving on Wednesday morning for Tours, and Le Roncée. Had a letter today from Uncle Charles, who has offered to put me up until the end of June. And what finally made up my mind was that today the train was running normally again from Austerlitz, whereas in recent days you had to take the Sceaux line to Massy-Palaiseau, and then on to Juvisy, with a 1km stretch of sagging track where apparently you had to walk! I imagine your decision will be influenced by mine.

That was true. Until that point I hadn't given up hope of going back to join my group in Paris. But if Elisabeth was leaving Paris, there was no point in thinking about it. It felt like cowardly desertion, and it hit me hard.

I was alone in the garden, with Elisabeth's letter in my hand. The scent of the pinks and mock orange blossom filled the air, drowning out the more discreet fragrance of the white climbing roses on the wall. The road was deserted. Or not quite. Drawn by a bay horse at a brisk trot, an English dog cart passed by. It was driven by Ernest de Saint-Georges, very upright, his hair impeccably parted down to the nape of his neck in the old-fashioned way, and beside him his wife

Mathilde, splendid in a broad-brimmed hat trimmed with flowers, on their way from their estate at Kernével to Concarneau.

Gloaguen, of the Vengeance group, had told me a lot about them lately. I had needed to meet him, as ever to ensure the unity in action that my father and I sought, and that would be centred round "Monsieur Charles", who was universally respected and admired.

He had spoken to me about our friends at Kernével because their woods were sheltering young people from the Concarneau Resistance.

On Fridays before the war, we used to go there to savour Mathilde's famous gateau. On Mondays we would scoff another one at Pénanrum, on Wednesdays at Kerminaouet and on Saturdays at Portzou. Every day of the week during the holidays, and often in the winter, the same group of friends would get together at a different property.

Now it was no longer cakes that were served at Kernével, but potatoes and bacon, to assuage the hunger of the youthful "men of the woods". Gloaguen told me how they were preparing food supplies for the difficult days to come: on the farms they were killing dozens of pigs, to be preserved in tins, rolled into sausages or pressed and salted in barrels. Some of the farmers needed a fair bit of persuading, but by hook or by crook food stocks were building up.

New recruits for groups such as Vengeance, Libération or the FTP (Franc-Tireurs et Partisans) were numerous, as were arrests. Many volunteers had already taken to the moors and woods. Some took the decision with a cool head, like Lucien Hascoët, who said to his aunt: "Aunt Anna, I have to go to the Maquis at two o'clock this afternoon. I shall need food for two days."

"You must talk to your mother about it."

"She'd be too upset: when I signed my pledge I laid down my life, for France cannot save herself alone, and my life is my own to give."

Others came with the Germans hot on their heels, such as Albert Gloaguen. On 6 February 1944, two of the Le Guennec brothers, leaders of the Vengeance group in Quimper, had been arrested, with their mother, sister and others. Gloaguen thought he was safe. He was wrong. Six days later, he was in the back of his jeweller's shop in Concarneau when the young sales girl suddenly appeared, white as a sheet, saying, "They're asking for you." He didn't need to be told twice: it was the Gestapo.

The girl went straight back into the shop and said to the men: "No, I was mistaken, he doesn't seem to be here after all." Gloaguen just had time to race down the passage and hide behind a door. The senior Gestapo officer was suspicious. Pushing the terrified girl aside and leaving his men to guard the shop, he ran down the passage towards the glazed door that opened into a little yard at the side of the house. When he opened the door, it set off a peal of chimes. Amazed, he looked up, closed the door and then opened it again, repeating the little game two or three times more, so giving Gloaguen a few precious moments to dash out of the yard door into the street. "I'll go to the café opposite to see what's going on," he thought to himself.

But at that moment the German managed to drag himself away and spotted him. So he gave up on the café idea and turned into the lane leading to the church, walking not running. The German followed him at a good distance. He was a good deal shorter and heavier than his quarry. Gloaguen went down towards the Quai d'Aiguillon, with the man still at his heels. Clusters of onlookers had gathered. "Now I must do something," he thought, and he turned around. The Gestapo officer drew his revolver and took aim. So he took off and dived into the hallway of Carrière the chemist. Disaster! His jacket caught on the door handle. "I'm done for," he groaned. The German tried to fire, but his revolver jammed. As he made frantic efforts to clear the breech, Gloaguen unhooked himself and hurtled down the passage, slamming three doors behind him one after the other before emerging into the yard where a sixteen-year-old apprentice dispenser (they called them *mouches*, or "cabin boys") was chopping wood. "They're after me, you haven't seen me!" Gloaguen yelled in his direction as he raced towards the vegetable garden, scaling the wall in the blink of an eye and jumping down into the deserted road.

Meanwhile the German had been doing battle with one of the doors, which was particularly heavy and difficult to open; nevertheless he was now hard on the fugitive's heels. He spotted the young dispenser:

"Did you see him?"

"Oh! Yes!"

"Was he tall?"

"Oh, no. Small. Like this."

And he measured about thirty centimetres with his hands.

"What was?" the man asked, astounded.

"A rat," replied the boy...

At a loss, the great Gestapo chief, now reduced to an absurd little man in an apoplectic rage, headed back to the house and embarked on a top-to-bottom search, without casting so much as a glance at the garden, where, clearly imprinted in the soft earth, were Gloaguen's footprints.

• • •

I did not confine myself to Concarneau. I made regular trips to Quimper to liaise with the departmental HQ of the French Forces of the Interior (FFI) under Colonel Bertaud, or to visit Madame Vandamme, who formed part of an escape route for British and American servicemen. At that time she had a batch of clients to evacuate as soon as possible, but the route via Brest was no longer viable. She had therefore asked me to find a boat at Concarneau. I had found one, when my father announced one lunchtime: "No vessels can leave harbour anymore, for fishing or any other reason.

A warning poster was put up in town this morning." Terrible for our friends across the Channel, but such a good sign of our occupiers' growing anxiety!

My days in Quimper would begin or end at my Aunt Guite's house, my father's sister. We would talk for hours in the walled garden, sitting on the bench and watching the lengthening shadows of the cypresses and magnolias. The boys and baby Edith would come and go around us, always on the move. Anneck, her eldest daughter, was like a sister to me.

Aunt Guite had given up expecting the return of her husband, who in 1940 had set sail from Douarnenez on a tuna boat with a group of young people. From England he had set off for Syria, then Egypt, before being captured at Bir-Hakeim and put on board an Italian ship, the Nino Bixio. This was torpedoed by the British on 17 August 1942, and Uncle Edouard, my godfather, ended his war in the lukewarm waters of the Mediterranean. We knew nothing of his journey or of his death, the message from the Red Cross saying merely that he was missing. My aunt had known some dark times since that June of 1940 when she found herself on her own with seven children to bring up, including five boys and the infant Edith. My cousin Anneck had done all she could to support her like a man. Lots of women came round to console her; one in particular, Yvonne, told her over and over, month after month, what a noble choice her husband had made. My father, my mother and my aunt all loved each other very much. All my family in the Cornouaille region were very close.

I felt as though I was part of a whole, unshakeable as a fortress.

• • •

"Weapons, we need weapons!" they kept saying. At the end of April my father had gone to Pont-l'Abbé to ask Colonel Bertaud for arms in person, but he hadn't been able to find him. He'd knocked on other doors in Quimper, but no one had any weapons. The hoped-for parachute drops hadn't happened or had been intercepted by the Germans. Nevertheless, Patrice managed to recover a machine-gun, and on 29 April he brought back three more in the police superintendent's car. They had been dismantled and had begun to circulate in the district in food sacks hidden under potatoes. We had to keep the boys occupied at all costs, as having nothing to do was making them mutinous. "Don't make a move," said London. Waiting, always waiting.

"We've run out of money," the two welfare assistants would tell me practically on a daily basis. "We need more." I sent letter after letter to Paris: no answer. I would have to go back.

"Where are they going to send us?" the French parachutists at Auchinleck camp in Scotland were wondering. Geo and his friends were thinking in dots and dashes and wondered if they would ever know enough; but the chief radio operator Hoffman finally told them: "I'm pleased with you. You have proved yourselves as radio operators and I know that the missions you are entrusted with will be successful."

Transmitting and receiving radio messages held no further mysteries for them, nor did encoding and decoding. Like the other parachutists, they could survive on their own in the wild, locate any rendezvous, shoot accurately with a rifle or Colt, and kill a man silently with the sharp, slender commando daggers issued by the British army.

The quartermaster's stores were flooded with new equipment and materiel: they had never seen so much. "You must be at your smartest. Field Marshal Montgomery is coming to inspect you." The great British commander-in-chief in person? What could it mean?

He arrived in a jeep, short, wiry, determined, a bundle of energy, his black beret pulled down over one ear. He passed down their ranks and spoke to his "trusted men from Libya", then he climbed onto the bonnet of his jeep and the group gathered round to hear him speak; "I have the pleasure of announcing that you will be the first to go into action on D-Day," he said. "You are an elite unit, and I know I can count on you to carry out the difficult but glorious missions for which you have been chosen."

The first. They practised jumping again, once by day and once by night, from the Albemarle aircraft reserved for the parachutists, and then they went on leave. "For the last time," they thought. It was the end of April. The day after their return to Auchinleck they went south like thousands of others. They were stationed at Fairford, near Cirencester. Also like the others, they were virtually prisoners. The whole of the south of England was now just one vast, hermetically sealed military encampment.

CHAPTER 9

Waiting with the Family

My mother would have liked to keep her seven chicks under her wing, but my eldest brother, having sent his wife and his daughter Sabine to us, had stayed in Paris, Elisabeth had gone to the Touraine region, and Pierre was fighting or getting ready to fight, no one knew where. Arthur, whose school had taken the decision to shut, had suddenly appeared one morning after a dramatic journey. Only Françoise and my little sister Suche had stayed in Kerancalvez from the beginning of the war.

Consumed with anxiety, my mother had let me go back to Paris on 9 May. I had seen my OCMJ friends again. Jacques Nord had been arrested like so many others, and Frédéric had taken his place. Everyone was feverishly preparing for the Paris uprising, and I was thinking about staying there with them again. I decided to consult Hamon, head of the CAD (Comité Anti-Déportation) and one of the most important Resistance leaders: no one would have a better idea of where I could be most useful in the fight to come. We walked a long way together, from Boulevard de Port-Royal to Place Saint-Michel. He was wearing the nondescript raincoat I'd always seen him in, and it flapped against his threadbare trousers in the biting wind.

"Honestly, Marie-Claire, I tell you it would be better for you to go back to Brittany. You won't regret it. You'll have some very interesting work to do there, I assure you." He shook my hand, unsmiling. One war was ending, and another was beginning.

The symbolism of bridges: in my mind I was on a bridge, and I didn't know which bank fate would lead me to. It was on a bridge that I met Sylvie and Francis, the new western regional leader, one last time. This time I was leaving for good. Francis said:

"When the Allies have landed I'll go straight to Pontivy, to the Bruhats." He gave me their address. "Meet me there as soon as you can."

"If you don't come, what shall I do?"

Marie-Hélène Lefaucheux had given me a large sum of money and I had got home without mishap, even though the plan to destroy the bridges had gone into action on 6 May, and the Morbihan department had been given a blanket order to sabotage the railway lines in Brittany as a trial run. My parents had been hugely relieved to have me back in the nest, and there then began a strange, deceptively quiet interlude, the calm before the storm. There were already a few signs of what was to come: longer personal messages from the BBC, so delightful in their unfettered flights of fancy, and more particularly the transmission to my father of instructions for D-Day and H-Hour, with their "key" messages.

The precious envelope had been placed with my mother's notebooks in the cupboard under the stairs, which was crammed full of extracts from books, from Homer's *Odyssey* to the *Souvenirs de la Duchesse d'Abrantès*, and from Caesar's *Gallic Wars* to the novels of Loti and Barrès. We had read nearly all of them, Arthur and I, and the random selection of knowledge they contained had helped us to keep up with other children of our age who went to school in the normal way. For us it was different: our childhood had been one of freedom and independence, more about walks on the moors than poring over exercise books. My brother Pierre used to say that this unusual childhood had turned me into a great romantic. He was probably right. And Suche was following in my footsteps.

She had a strange passion for Greek and Latin, and was having lessons with old Abbé Delabar, on the Quai d'Aiguillon in Concarneau. Had her studies of ancient Rome and Greece and her passion for the classics already left their mark on her? We were astonished by her stoicism on the day the British bombed the port.

"Suche had set off by herself about half an hour before the British arrived," my mother recounted. "I raced after her. The people I passed appeared calm, even though about twenty planes were making a tremendous din and four or five of them had peeled off from the group to bomb the German boats near the turret. As I was going over the bridge, an old man who had taken shelter against the parapet shouted:

'Take cover, Madame!'

'No, I have to find my daughter!' I shouted back as I raced past.

In the distance, I saw a supply ship explode and sink. A second one was hit.

Still running I arrived at Abbé Delabar's house, only to find the old man and child immersed in their Latin studies on the third floor, quite unperturbed. The Abbé said admiringly: 'Madame, your daughter arrived with the sang-froid of a Roman senator! And just a few steps away, I could see the plumes of explosions in the harbour!'

'I wasn't frightened, Maman,' said Suche. As for the Abbé, oblivious like Archimedes to everything except his learning, he stuck his nose back into his Greek textbook and didn't deign to look out of the window again. When I told him I could see ambulances and German motor launches going back and forth with the wounded he seemed to feel that I was merely interrupting his lesson."

While she approved of my Resistance activities, irregular though they were, my mother tried to balance them out with other, more normal pursuits. She took me to an artist in Concarneau and asked her to teach me to paint in oils. In my classes at Rue de Seine I had only done sketches in pencil and wash or gouache. But as I painted fruit on a table or houses on the hillside, my heart wasn't in it, and I regretted it. War didn't encourage artistic creativity. The prime objective, winning it, cancelled out all others. And then the problems in finding turps or plywood and hardboard to replace canvases were discouraging, as was the mediocre if not downright abominable quality of the paints. Yet Françoise persevered, and she had painted some wonderful flowers. I often heard my father going up to her bedroom to look at them, happy that in spite of everything we could still find ways and means of self-expression.

My mother also made great efforts to keep us looking neat and stylish, with means that were ever more straitened. We managed to obtain a ration coupon for some wool fabric, which was used to make a skirt suit for me.

Françoise, Arthur and I took turns on the piano. I had started doing my singing exercises again: people passing on the road outside were treated to "Solveig's Song" by Grieg or Gounod's "Ave Maria", repeated ad infinitum.

And we both wrote, my mother and I. Sadly she no longer "thought" in verse. Her poems slumbered in envelopes without any new additions. Anxiety and fear had driven inspiration away. But as well as noting down the news bulletins, she wrote about our daily life. She would sit in her room looking out over the view, like me.

The reality of our lives is to be found in the pages of her diary, as in mine, a mixture of tragic grandeur, of everyday joys that crop up no matter what the circumstances, and of purely material obligations:

My mother:
13 May: Mie back (from Paris).
No electricity. We all wonder why. Bombing, water shortage? People

talk about a destroyed power station, but nobody knows anything. We go to bed with the sun.

14 May: Excellent sermon on Joan of Arc. The priest castigates pessimism. France will be reborn, as it was after Joan of Arc.

16 May: The dentist tells me that he cannot work any more for lack of water and gas. However, he finishes off what he was in the middle of by spraying my tooth with ice-cold water. Dentists who still have primitive equipment are the winners. But, he says, "We will soon see an end to our great penance!"

The Allies are fighting outside Cassino. For me, life is still a frantic hunt for food.

Some Germans asked my husband: "They have landed, haven't they? You of all people should know." It's a false rumour coming from Morlaix.

18 May: "And the people will cry: peace, peace!" A prediction from Saint Odile. A rumour "of unknown provenance": we will have peace in a fortnight. But nobody really believes it.

19 May: British and French forces have captured Cassino, and the Americans have captured somewhere too.

Me:

22 May: Not having the wireless, for lack of electricity, has really changed the atmosphere in the house, one of the biggest changes along with the lack of bread: our isolation is complete. At mealtimes, the absence of news bulletins has brought us back to the political and general discussions that we have grown up with since our childhood.

My father rises above the war that we are living through and considers the future upheavals that await us with the imbalance between the eastern and western worlds, so deeply divided in their standards of living. "There are fundamental laws that will inevitably come into play," he says. But we must find solutions, nevertheless. We must live with an atlas in front of us." We discuss the present situation; we talk about the memory of our cardinal uncle. He occupied such an important place in our extended family! We all think that his defeatism was due purely to his great age and that he would be as impatient as we are to see what is about to happen. Papa tries to stay calm, but sometimes he explodes in sudden bursts of anger that electrify the atmosphere like summer lightning, and above all he is always humane in his conclusions.

When war topics have been exhausted, we turn to problems to do with the weather or food supplies. Feeling relaxed, we watch the canary sitting on her eggs in the cage outside the window and slip scraps of food to the cat who is about to have kittens. Our meals are shrinking. Papa does not want to take advantage of his position as mayor to improve our daily fare. We are hungry. In the evening, after dinner, one or other of us will quietly slip out of the sitting room. We hear the squeak of the kitchen door, followed by the larder door and the door to the cellar, where the meat safe is. We go to see if by any chance there might be a little something that could be eaten without being too unfair to the others. In the morning Anna utters a range of exclamations as she discovers the disappearance of a leftover in the bottom of a bowl, or the shrinking of the butter on the plate.

The evenings seem longer without the wireless. Sometimes Papa, standing in front of the fireplace, picks up a book and reads a passage out loud. Yesterday he shared with us the intense poetry of *"Le Cœur innombrable"* by Anne de Noailles. He is starting to say again, "Soon we shall be going to La Villeneuve," his parents' property at Quimperlé which is now Aunt Guite's, but which remains a family home to which we are very attached. The Germans have turned it into a rest home for their airmen, even though the house is bright white and on a high point only twenty or so kilometres from Lorient. Why are they not tempted by Le Poulgwin? Perhaps because the old manor house is too out of the way on the Aven? So we still have one family refuge left unviolated, still magical, where we go very often; Papa likes to go there to share his worries and his hopes with his brother Arthur, while my mother and her sister-in-law Valérie speculate on which distant battlefields their sons Pierre and Xavier might be fighting on.

Order from the Germans: cows must not graze within a kilometre of the coast, because of mines. People say the Kommandantur have decreed that dogs must be taken in to be registered (but we only have cats).

This morning the Germans surrounded Trégunc and rounded up all the men aged between sixteen and forty.

You can hear the surf on the rocks, as though the sea is breathing. It's completely quiet, completely dark; tonight it's the spring tide, and there's no moon.

23 May: All night I imagined I heard the sound of planes and artillery. It was the new moon, and they didn't come! We are very disappointed and are already starting to make new predictions. I have put the "landings" suitcase away again, in its place between the fireplace and the wardrobe.

31 May: It feels like high summer. Desperate drought, such as hasn't been seen for years. The wheat is still good, thankfully. The scorching heat is an invitation to go swimming. But the signs with skulls and crossbones warning of mined areas have proliferated. The cows, undeterred by the notices and tempted by the beautiful long, uncut grass, are being blown up one after the other. The beaches are bristling with scrap metal of every description, and the Kommandantur has ordered Papa to plant 3.5-metre-tall stakes in the fields to stop gliders from landing. He is dragging his feet …

He is worried about our position, with its commanding view of the sea, and Maman has written half-heartedly to relatives inland to ask if we can seek refuge with them if we need to. Papa, meanwhile, wouldn't dream for an instant of leaving the house. It stands halfway between two very distinct areas of his commune, Le Passage and Douric-ar-Zin, with the market town of Lanriec, Le Cabellou and the surrounding countryside. Everyone is worried about the insecurity and living conditions that are getting worse by the day. Papa declares that he has been waiting for this moment for four years, that he is not the least bit surprised, and that we should take the greatest precautions in these final days, as no one knows what the Germans will do.

• • •

The waiting, like the drought and the heat, was reaching its climax. Not everybody was waiting in hope. For some people, their attitude towards the occupiers ensured that they were scared to death at the thought of what might happen to them if the landings were successful. People were being sent miniature coffins in the post.

Others were worn down with worry – even though they had been prudent enough to avoid compromising themselves in either one direction or the other – simply at the thought of the chaos that would probably, they said, accompany the liberation. To this they would almost prefer the order they detested, but order nevertheless, imposed by the occupiers. They pondered the places that stood a chance of remaining undisturbed and where it would be prudent to go and stay awhile, to wait and see.

And many others said to themselves: "War has to have victims. Let's just make sure it's not us!"

Arthur enveloped us in sublime music while we waited. The laments of Isolde and the transports of Parsifal drowned out the rumble of the bombers on their way to Lorient. Often my father would listen out for the bombers.

• • •

On 1 June, Michel's brother Jo arrived from Pontivy. He came to offer us some weapons. "We have a lot in the Morbihan," he declared mysteriously, refusing to give any details. "We could bring them to you, or else you could come and collect them," he insisted. My father thought that we had to try. We saw Patrice from the Libération group: he had a lorry, men and a hiding place. "OK," said Jo, "I'll go back to Michel, and I'll be back with more details and perhaps some arms." I begged him to hurry. The great day was surely very near. Afterwards, the enterprise would be extremely risky, if not impossible. As a precaution, I told him that he would find me at Le Faouët on 5 June. I was due to go there to see the mother of Jean-Louis Fraval, the envoy from London whom I'd met in Lyon.

Then the weather changed for the worse. As was his wont, Arthur scrutinised the sky and gave us his forecast, which matched my father's predictions. Neither was promising.

On 5 June, I bumped into my cousin Anneck, quite by chance, on the train: she was on her way to see another relative who had sought refuge near Le Faouët. The Fravals – Jean-Louis' mother, her daughter, son-in-law and grandchildren – all welcomed us like family. Since their electricity was back on, they listened to all the BBC bulletins. The four victorious notes of Beethoven punctuated the air throughout the day. We heard that Rome had been captured after a ferocious battle: Rome, Saint Odile's city of cities, had been declared an open city and was saved.

The evening bulletin contained a long litany of personal messages, which included the second line of the Verlaine poem: "*Blessent mon coeur d'une langueur monotone …*"

My father heard it and looked gravely at everybody around the table. After dinner, he went to join my mother in her room and said: "We are on the alert."

I shared a big bed with Anneck, sleeping between crisp, cool sheets. My sleep was disturbed by a muffled rumbling, like constant artillery fire. When I woke up, I could tell that the rumbling came from the north. No one knew what it meant.

• • •

We were sitting down to a copious breakfast, the farms inland being less short of food than those on the coast, when Madame Fraval's son-in-law suddenly appeared, overcome by emotion. He was listening to the bulletin in the room next door.

"That's it," he said. "They've landed. This time, that's really it!" We looked at him, stunned. We had been waiting for this day for so many months! Had it finally arrived? "They've landed …" Let them say it again! Let them never stop saying it …

I was thinking: "I have to get to the rendezvous: I have to leave Kerancalvez."

Everyone had had their own idea where the landings would take place: someone thought Holland, someone else Norway. "Come on, think about it, what port could be better than Antwerp?" Brittany was thought to be a possibility, but the Pas-de-Calais had more votes, particularly those of the Germans.

And they had landed in Normandy, between the rivers Orne and Vire.

Where was Brittany in all this? My father was rarely wrong: he predicted that the landings would be carried out with large numbers of airborne troops, and the Allies announced that they had sent 18,000 parachutists. There must be some nearby. But where?

CHAPTER 10

Arrival

The night was mild, the wind light. The parachute swayed a little as it slowly descended: the RAF Stirling had dropped him from quite a height. The full moon shed a bright, pearly light over the silent forest.

"Where am I?" Geo wondered. "I don't recognize the DZ[16] they showed us on the map at the briefing at all. The pilot's got it wrong. If the Germans are down there it'll be a clay pigeon shoot."

As the ground loomed closer he released his kitbag, attached to his belt by a rope some eight metres long. It was so heavy that the rope burned his palms as it slipped through them, despite his gloves. "It must weigh over 40 kilos with the radio set," he reckoned. He heard branches breaking, making a terrific din to his ears, followed by a muffled thump.

His descent gradually slowed right down, and he came to a gentle halt in the crown of a tree, or rather on one of its main branches, where he looked like some gigantic multicoloured fungus that had just erupted in the forest. The soft rustle of the nylon silk died away as the branches settled back into their places beneath the weightless dome. Geo was left hanging, beneath him a dark void of unknown

16. Drop Zone.

depth. For a few minutes he didn't move a muscle, every fibre of his being on alert. His eyes were becoming accustomed to the darkness of the undergrowth: he was surrounded by trees, his silent, numberless companions. Over an hour later, having tried in vain to grab the trunk of the tree with his legs, he started bouncing gently, over and over again, forcing the branch lower and lower until finally it was touching the ground. He was thinking.

He saw himself again with the others, back in the camp surrounded by barbed wire. A loudspeaker was playing *Sur le pont d'Avignon* incessantly, and they wondered why. Now he knew: it was their BBC call sign, which would send the coded messages for them to transmit in Morse code. They had named the battalion Pierre, and he was the chief radio operator of Captain Botella's group, Pierre 3. When Sergeant-Major Hoffmann had called him and eleven other radio operators together to tell them he had chosen them for the battalion's first mission, he could hardly believe it.

Where could the rest of his team, Le Cudennec and Renaud, have landed? They had left Madagascar together. When had they had that briefing in Captain Botella's tent? So much had been going on in the last few days that you got confused. Three days before the false start, yes, it must have been then. A blow, that business with the bad weather. Perhaps every night here in this forest had been as calm and clear as this one. Anyway, it didn't matter now. He didn't yet have his feet on French soil, but he was getting closer, centimetre by centimetre.

The Captain had been very calm and precise. In front of an enormous map of Brittany, that province where most of the population of Réunion had their roots, one way or another, and his forebears in particular, a second native land within the larger one of France. On Réunion they would say to French tourists: "Go to Langevin, it looks like the Finistère coast," and on Mauritius they'd send them to the beaches at Gris-Gris or Souillac to remind them of the Pointe du Raz. Well, he was going to get to know it properly now, this ancient Celtic land.

Captain Botella had told them they would be leaving in four groups of nine men each, a commanding officer and eight junior officers and men, two groups to prepare a drop zone in the south, and two in the north, to receive the rest of the battalion. "Why such odd names for the bases?" Geo wondered. "In the north we're to be Samwest, and in the south they'll be Dingson." The first thing was to make contact with the Resistance, about whom they hadn't really been told very much. Then locate a good spot to receive their comrades in the battalion and weapons for the Maquis. And pick up the men who would be leaving on eighteen sabotage missions two days later in groups of three, and who had ten days to get to their rendezvous: Agamemnon and Béatrice in the north, Charlotte and Dudule in the south.

"The day after tomorrow?" Geo looked at his watch, a beautiful Swiss one they'd given him when he left. "Over an hour. It's the 6th today. I must have arrived at about midnight, as I've been thrashing about here for ages. We took off from the aerodrome at about ten o'clock, the first of that incredible mass of aircraft lined up in serried ranks, just as Monty promised us. We were with Marienne's group, and Captain Deplante and Captain Deschamps were in the other plane. We'd had a friendly cup of tea under the aircraft wing and everyone had joked around to keep our spirits up. Colonel Bourgoin insisted on saying a last farewell, just before the plane took off. He was counting on us, he said: if we failed, the mission was doomed. In a nutshell, our acts of sabotage were to cut Brittany off from the rest of France and prepare for a second landing. A month – we had to hold out for a month at most."

With the tips of his toes, he could now feel the good, soft woodland earth with its mix of half-rotted autumn leaves. Another tug at the parachute ropes and he landed firmly on his feet. He heaved a great sigh. How stupid it would have been to be captured there, ready hanged! He undid the belt's circular lock, which the dispatcher had checked with care on departure, and got out of the harness; now free, he drew the British dagger that he had spent forever sharpening from its leather sheath, and cut half the ropes to free the parachute. In daylight it would be spotted from miles away. It was a difficult operation, and uncomfortable because it made so much noise.

He took off the cumbersome Mae West life jacket, which would have been a blessing if their aircraft had been shot down over the sea by enemy fire, or even if he had dropped into a pond or river. And he took off the thick khaki canvas parachute jacket that stopped the parachute ropes from getting caught up with all the indescribable paraphernalia that he had on him: belt, card holder, binoculars, water bottle, dagger, and the big Colt revolver attached to his leg by a leather strap. On top of his battledress he still had on a camouflage battle jacket. With luck it wouldn't get too hot as the day went on. Especially since lugging all this baggage around would be far from easy. Quick. Now he had to get it all together. The rope on his kitbag was still attached to the harness belt, so he just had to follow it to find the enormous bag, to which he had attached a haversack. Good: now to decant the equipment from one bag to the other. Gently with the radio transmitter, although nothing could have walloped it harder than the landing.

His wireless set, his responsibility. "Without your radio operators, the mission is impossible," they had been told. It was true: the life of the whole group was going to depend on the wireless set. He was to do whatever was necessary to prevent the Germans getting hold of it, not the pad[17] with lines of letter groups, with the duplicate copy in Britain; not the small piece of silk with the "grid". Renaud and Le Cudenec had another set, one carrying the transmitter and the other the receiver and generator; but his was complete, like the

17. One-time pad with key lists for sending encoded messages.

one belonging to Rameau, chief radio operator under Captain Deschamps with Devize and Sauvé.

He clipped the grenades to his belt, as a Colt revolver wasn't much protection by itself, and he'd never been able to pack in a machine-gun. And look, there was the little first aid kit. Kneeling among the ferns, he stayed stock still for a few moments: he seemed to hear their Syrian medic, Lieutenant Sassoon, telling them: "Stomach upsets can be awkward: take this pill to stop them. Careful though. If things go to the other extreme, take that one, which will have the opposite effect. And here's your morphine. Never inject the patient in the upper body: they could die. If they're in too much pain, inject them anyway."

"I don't need it for the moment," he told himself. "My landing could have gone far worse."

The haversack was full to bursting and he had to squash his sleeping bag on top of it. He could just hear a dog barking in the distance. "No time to lose," he thought. They had been warned that they would be facing formidable adversaries: paratroopers from the 5th Parachute Division with veterans of Rommel's Kreta division of the Afrika Korps, hardened White Russians from a Waffen SS division, artillery units, coastal defence infantry, and a Luftwaffe infantry division specially trained to hunt down parachutists, complete with dogs. Nearly forty thousand men. A strange coincidence, really, that a division of that magnitude should be deployed to hunt down parachutists. Did Rommel, so intelligent, suspect there might be an operation to cut off Brittany? There were only perhaps six or seven hundred men in the entire battalion. It wasn't going to be easy. For the moment, the first objective was to find Captain Botella, and there was no time to be lost.

He had disentangled his parachute. He rolled it up and stuffed it in his kitbag with the Mae West and his khaki jacket. He felt quite emotional as he buried his parachute: it felt like the end of something. They had been given them on 4 June, at four o'clock in the afternoon, the British had just the one; the Americans had a spare emergency parachute. But naturally British parachute packers would never make a mistake! The very thought! He dug as deep a hole as he could with his entrenching tool, but the ground was a mass of roots. Good riddance to the kitbag: it was so awkward that he'd hardly been able to move in the Stirling, and when it was his turn to jump the dispatcher had had to give him a hand to carry it to the gaping hatch. For a long time they'd watched the light: red, then suddenly green as the dispatcher yelled "Go!" The journey had taken forever. They had been told before they left that the two planes would cross the French coast east of Saint-Brieuc and fly over Brittany at high altitude to the south coast; then they would bear west and then north, dropping the two Dingson groups and then the two Samwest groups. The north and south groups had been split between the two planes, so if one of them came down the mission could still go ahead. Allied bombing over Saint-Nazaire would make the Germans think the planes were just bombers going back to base, and no one would come after them.

Squashed up together, a bit drowsy since they hadn't been able to sleep for several nights because of the intense excitement, they had allowed their thoughts to roam. The journey hadn't been a particularly pleasant one, despite the absence of anti-aircraft guns; but all the same, they shouldn't forget their comrades who had formed ranks to watch them leave camp, and who would have given anything to be in their place!

Now he had finished covering the freshly dug earth with leaves and ferns. "The British parachutists we met after that were as excited as we were. We were singing at the tops of our lungs. Leaving is something we'll never forget. I've never seen the Red Devils in such a state! Everyone we met gave us the thumbs up. Lorries rolled on endlessly as far as the eye could see, and I lost count of all the aircraft.

We really understood that the great day had come for the Allies. I'm glad to have been there."

He got to his feet at last and slung the haversack on his back, spacing the straps well apart. With compass in hand, he began to work out how to make his way to the coordinates of the rendezvous. They had had frequent training exercises in finding their bearings at night, no matter where: there was no reason why it should be any harder in the Forêt de Duault. But he must be some distance from the northern horn of the forest, where he should have been. He was much too far south. He climbed up a steep, rocky slope. His special felt-soled shoes made no sound, but he had to be wary of the stones. One rolled right down to the bottom of the ravine with a noise like thunder.

Geo stopped in his tracks: the whole forest seemed to have sprung to life. He could hear a cracking noise in the undergrowth. "Maybe it's foxes; they must love it here," he told himself; he was much more concerned about the barking dogs, which were coming closer. For a moment he crouched in a thicket, his revolver drawn. He had no idea where the others were, and he had never felt so alone. He had loved the mild summer nights he had spent camping with the scouts in the highlands of Madagascar: he understood the nights there. Everything about this one was unfamiliar, even the trees, which he couldn't have named. "Fine trees," he thought. Now a dog was coming straight at him. He searched in his pocket to find the stuff they had given him to put dogs off their scent. You had to be careful not to break the phial on you, or all the dogs from miles around would be on the attack. Basically, its risks outweighed its uses. You could strangle a dog or shoot it with your revolver, like a man. But this dog was in pursuit of a hare, and didn't come to flush him out of his thicket.

"Probably poachers out hunting," he concluded, since German dogs would be too well trained to miss him.

When the night was quiet again he carried on, now following a ravine that would take him in the right direction. Dawn was breaking, drawing scraps of mist along the valley bottoms. The birds were beginning to sing. Geo looked at the tender leaves of late spring, and the green grass fringing a stream (where he splashed his face with water to rub off the black grease that he'd smeared it with before leaving); after living on the bare uplands of Madagascar he couldn't get over all the greenery and foliage. France was very beautiful; he was glad to be there and to see the glittering sunrise. He forgot that he was in British uniform in a country occupied by the Germans, cutting an unfamiliar figure, the same colour as the forest. He unfastened the chinstrap of his helmet, covered with netting in which he had stuck some branches, and took it off so that he could feel the cool morning air. The earth and the dew-covered leaves gave off a pungent scent. "I'm free and alive, that's the best thing." He felt sure the others were thinking the same thing. He touched the epaulette of his battledress, into which he had slid his evasion kit: a map of France printed on silk and a tiny saw, tiny like his compass. He was wearing the rope as a vest for the moment; all he had to do was untie it at the bottom and everything would come. "Do what has to be done and stay free, that's what's asked of us," he concluded.

He walked for a very long time. Hiding behind a slope, he saw a farmer driving a big hay cart drawn by a powerful Breton horse. He hesitated over whether to ask him the way. Then he let him pass. Clever him. Someone else was coming: Botella. They had regrouped. The sabotage missions could take off from England the next night.

• • •

"All well," the north signalled, but from the south there was silence. Anxiety was growing in London, where the radio operators were working round-the-clock shifts in case there was a message. Nothing, still nothing.

Yet Captain Deplante and his stick had landed without incident. Nowhere near the appointed spot, although there was a river nearby, but it was flowing in the opposite direction from the way they expected. They waited in the hollow of a copse for dawn to break. Once they had got over their shock, the inhabitants of a hamlet had told them that they were now near Guchenno, a long way from Plumelec and the rendezvous with Captain Marienne's stick. They had two nights to get there. After that it would be assumed that anyone missing had been put out of action. They left in the evening, passing close by a tower that looked abandoned in the middle of moorland. Abandoned? It was a German watchtower, ringed by barbed wire, with heavy machine guns and a mortar, and minefields for defence. More than a hundred White Russians had been taken there as workers. It was one of the most dangerous spots in the entire region.

Marienne's drop zone was precisely this moorland with its old windmill: the pilot's aim had been absolutely accurate, spot on. He had dropped them at the designated location and then carried on to the Forêt de Duault with Botella's stick.

They landed close together, moreover, and – imitating a quail's call – they soon found each other. All that was missing was the trunk. A very large trunk containing who knew what for the secret agent Fernand, who had jumped with them. They left the bags with the three radio operators and went off in search of it. It seemed a peaceful spot, until they heard the sound of battle, and explosions suddenly ripped through the silence. They had only gone a hundred metres, but it was a hundred metres of open moorland. Under a hail of gunfire they threw themselves to the ground; Bouétard was wounded and fell: he was to have been their liaison with the Resistance, as the Plumelec region was his home. He was indeed coming home, as it turned out. He was the first soldier of all the Allied armies to be killed on D-Day.

The Germans or the Russians – impossible to tell in the dark – were trying to encircle them; there was gunfire from all sides. The group managed to get away, but the radio operators were captured.

"To the river," said Marienne. Three of them made it there. There was still intermittent fire from the enemy. They had no idea what had happened to the radio operators, but they were certain to have been captured, with the radios and everything else. In the night, around three in the morning, dogs were brought in. They had to run again, this time through the water to escape them. Dawn found them exhausted. A thin wisp of smoke was rising from a farmhouse chimney. "We'll go over there," thought Marianne. But then he heard the people inside talking an unfamiliar language, guttural like German. "They must be Germans," he thought, and abruptly pulling open the shutters he shouted: "Hands up, this is France!"

"Why threaten us? We're French too," said a woman from inside the room.

"Just as well," said Marienne, "I don't understand Breton," and he lowered his gun with a smile. The farmers of Le Pelheu were in the Resistance, and liaison with their leaders was rapidly established. They were soon able to track down the survivors of the stick.

Meanwhile, Deplante was sending his first message to England: "Out Station 2 to Home Station. Good landing 10 km from DZ – Stop – Marienne not at rendezvous – Stop – Area calm, will wait till morning of 8th, Deplante."

But while the parachutists were rejoicing at having got their message through so quickly and clearly, a herd of cows made an untimely appearance with their young cowherds. Astounded at the sight of them and in spite of promises *"aux Français"* to keep their presence a secret, the girls lost no time in announcing the tremendous news to their older brothers, lads who were "in it" too. It was not long before they arrived with bottles of cider to celebrate the encounter.

They wanted to join up on the spot with this regular army that had fallen on them from the sky.

"Hold on," said Deplante, "Could you first try to find our comrades?" and he explained what had happened. They went off, amid a flurry of injunctions to be careful. Deplante's stick settled down to wait again, thinking sombre thoughts. Another night passed.

In the early morning, they saw a group coming towards them. It was Marienne with some FFI, led by Jégo from the farm at Le Pelheu.

• • •

The first French parachutists had landed in Brittany. But what of the people waiting in the Morbihan? As they waited, they were unaware that on that night of 5 June 1944 a pilot was studying a map of their department. Yet Eisenhower was counting on them: "We were depending on considerable assistance from the insurrectionists in France. They were known to be particularly numerous in the Brittany area."[18]

During the month of May, the department's general staff had already established its HQ at La Nouette, an estate of some seventy hectares near Saint-Marcel. At the beginning of 1943, Emile Guimard had come to find the farmer, Monsieur Pondard, whom he knew well.

"Would you agree to allow parachute drops on your heathland at Le Pinieux? It's a good, open site."

"In such matters," the farmer replied, "it is impossible to refuse."

The parachute drops started, there and on seventeen other appointed sites. Emile was a fund of ideas for camouflaging the men, the arms, and himself in a variety of disguises. Everyone had their ideas.

---

18. Dwight D.Eisenhower: *Crusade in Europe*, William Heinemann Ltd, 1948.

At La Nouette, the farmer's daughters drove their cows back and forth five or six times along paths where the tracks of lorries and carts carrying weapons posed a danger, and they swept and rearranged the grasses and other vegetation on the verges. Often the containers would be scattered over a wide area as they fell. Packed with weapons and explosives, they were too heavy to transport. Instead they were emptied where they fell, and the girls would carry armfuls of machine guns to the waiting vehicles. Then the container could also be loaded. At the hiding place, the heaven-sent bounty of the night had to be stored with care, packed into the containers to protect it from the damp. This gruelling, exhausting business could sometimes go on until dawn. Sometimes the aircraft were delayed and daylight came too soon. Then everything was camouflaged where it fell, buried under the heath or in the earth. What was the meaning of all these fresh molehills? "You just wait and see," the farmer would say, "I'll sort that out for you." He would take his horse and plough and in two shakes he would have the DZ tilled. Better still, with noble, sweeping gestures he would broadcast buckwheat, and as the sun came up over Malestroit the birds would call and swoop over the freshly sown seed. Patrol away, *Messieurs les Allemands*, and search as hard as you like!

Comings and goings began between the villages and the farm. People would come to fetch weapons, seek orders, or see Emile who was often there. General Allard spent two months in hiding there. Madame Salles, the owner, a beautiful grande dame of eighty, would go to her summer cottage beside the farm to relax for the holidays, and was delighted by all this activity. A contingent of Maquis and saboteurs occupied the woods and were fed almost exclusively by the Pondard family. Eventually, three shacks were built in the woods, one for the radio team, one for the office and HQ, and one for personnel. But they would wait for D-Day before they started using them.

For the moment, the general staff had its headquarters at the Mallards in Saint-Aubin, and this was where they were all assembled

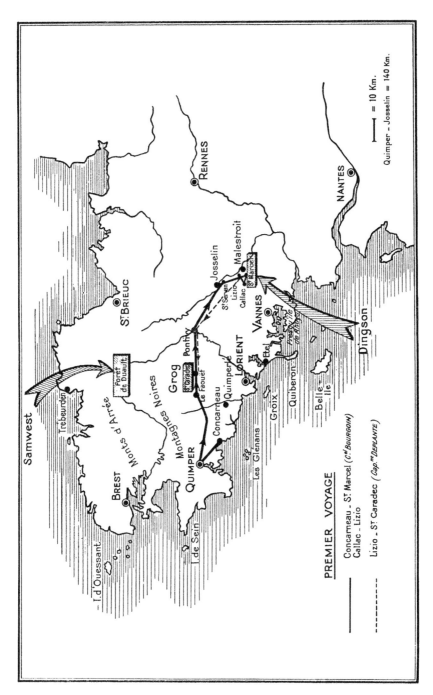

First trip: Concarneau to Saint-Marcel

on 5 June. At nightfall, all the FFI commanders who had been summoned arrived. They had brought out from its hiding place the bottle that contained the decoded names of the men on whom they could count. Each had his own password. Jeanne, the liaison agent for the general staff, had also been summoned. Commandant Morice[19] and Captain Guimard announced: "We have received the messages…" But they had all been waiting so long that they couldn't believe it.

"Yes, yes, we have," Guimard insisted, "I'm telling you, I'm quite certain, this time they're going to land." The messages announcing it and addressed to the whole of France arrived on 4 June:

Les dés sont sur le tapis
Il fait chaud à Suez

And for the Morbihan only:

La flèche ne percera pas

Arrangements for carrying out two plans, *plan Vert* for the destruction of the railways and *plan Rouge* for guerrilla operations, had been set in motion the day before.

While they were talking the air-raid warning sounded and the anti-aircraft guns started up. They put all the papers and listes they had brought with them into a suitcase. "Take this," Guimard said to Jeanne, "and go and hide in the fields until the all-clear." She hastened away. When they reconvened soon afterwards – Morice, Guimard, Carro, Hervé, le Coutaller, Le Garrec, Muller and Manceau – Guimard reassured them: "It's not for us. There's something out towards Plumelec." Marienne was coming.

He was going to Saint-Marcel and La Nouette with Deplante and would send the first two messages from base to the colonel in command of the regiment:

---

19. Code name for Commandant Paul Chenailler.

"Pierre 1 – Code 101 – Confirm message sent by FFI commander – confirm figure of ten companies poorly armed out of twenty-five – Send urgently all available officers, troops and equipment, especially Bren guns. Your presence here essential. Urgent. Am filled with enthusiasm about the organisation and its immense possibilities. Resistance HQ confirms able to help Samwest from now on. Charlotte and Dudule identified. Will be well equipped and defended. Inform all No. 43 missions. Have sent out a patrol. Mission currently at HQ will be informed and guided towards its objective. Confirm DZ 418 233 OK2. Also good for gliders. Expect from you eight D + 3 to D + 4. You will be guided by Eureka.[20] Site marked by beacons and defended. Recognition letter agreed. 50 lorries 3 tons. 50 saloon cars available. Have large reserves of provisions and livestock except flour. Send urgently petrol, medical supplies and uniforms with identification if possible. Await confirmation of your arrival. Will stay quiet for now."

Signed: PIERRE 1 Marienne.

And:

"Pierre 1 – Code 101 – Confirm message sent yesterday evening to Commandant Bourgoin – Situation re-established in admirable fashion despite bad landings. Have found Pierre 2 and Fernand – Have made contact with the Resistance – Am in HQ – Great success – 3500 men in regular formations await you. Your presence here essential (may give you details during the day) – Confirm arrival – Urgent – Equipment and men."

And so it was that the heathland of Le Pinieux, known as La Balcine, was to become a strange theatre for eerie nocturnal ballets.

• • •

20. A ground-to-air short-range navigation system that could signal the letter to the pilot to indicate the precise location of the drop zone.

On the morning of 6 June, the Allies were landing on the Normandy beaches, with more serious losses on some than on others, the US Army Rangers had scaled the Pointe du Hoc, and the airborne troops who had flown just after the Brittany SAS groups had already taken Sainte-Mère-l'Eglise. Deplante's stick was waiting until nightfall to go to their rendezvous, and Marienne's was regrouping, depleted in numbers; Geo was still looking for Botella. Young men everywhere were leaving to join the Maquis, and the sabotage campaign was beginning. At the Fravals' the news bulletin had just ended on a triumphant note.

"Anneck," I said, "let's go and see what's going on in the street," and out we went.

There were masses of people outside and women were leaning out of their windows shouting the news to each other as if the Germans didn't exist. Excitement, joy, a degree of apprehension. It wasn't happening here precisely, but what would happen "afterwards"?

"What's my father doing this morning," I thought. "I'll try to get back to Concarneau today if I can." But when I reached the main square I was stunned: there, parked up by the pavement, was our car! Hadn't the Germans forbidden all circulation of traffic when the landings were announced? Which wasn't hard for them to do, considering how few vehicles were still capable of being driven. And yet my father was at Le Faouët …

He was waiting for us with Patrice in the Fravals' dining room. "Well, yes," he told me, "we came to fetch weapons. There wasn't any other way; in a few days it will probably be impossible. Nobody stopped us on the way here today." On that, Jo arrived, thinking his brother Michel would be there.

"If he's not here," he decided, "he must have gone back to Pontivy. To get weapons we'll have to go there." Did we have enough petrol? My father lowered the dipstick into the tank: there was just enough left to do the trip.

We lashed Jo's bicycle to the front of the car with a rope. I asked Anneck if she wanted to come or stay: of course she wanted to come with us, and she climbed in the back with Patrice and Jo. I got in the front beside my father.

I looked at him. He looked a little strained. I felt incredibly close to him and wanted to be like him, not just in his dedication and determination but also in the way he looked: to have his fine nose, straight and narrow, the clean lines of his mouth and the firmness of his chin.

Then I leaned forward a little, my eyes fixed on the road, which was still clear. My thoughts rushed by as quickly as the telegraph poles on either side of us. Here and there the lines were cut. Would I stay at Pontivy? Would Francis be there? But what about Maman? How could she bear it if I left her at a time like this? I wanted to see her again. I didn't know what I wanted any more. What about the weapons? Where would we put them? The car boot wasn't big. Would there even be any? Sometimes Michel had a tendency to exaggerate his capabilities. I was gripped by doubts again.

At Pontivy we waited a long time for Michel at the Bruhats' house. The couple only had one son, Jacques, aged about twenty and a friend of Michel, and they feared for him. Night was falling; we were just about to leave when Michel suddenly appeared, but with disappointing news. The weapons he had planned to get had just been found by the Germans. That long journey, so much petrol, so many hopes, all for nothing. I was furious. And I was amazed by my father's equanimity as he said, simply, "Let's go home."

No news of Francis, but Michel was expecting him at any moment. "Marie-Claire," he said, "even if he doesn't come, you do realise that I'll really need you for all the other liaison work." I knew that. I persuaded my father to leave me in Pontivy, but he made me promise to return home the following day, whether Francis arrived or not. After that we would see.

The next morning, still no sign of Francis. To our amazement the trains and buses were running, and I headed back to Concarneau. Would my father have been arrested? It was a constant fear. No, he was there with Maman, but he looked worried. The acts of sabotage planned for D-Day were scheduled for the following night in the commune of Lanriec, particularly the destruction of the German telephone lines. As mayor, might he not be taken as a hostage afterwards? However, I told them that I had to leave again. "Wait a little," was their response, "think about it." And the day passed in a state of unbearable anxiety.

I started my diary again:

6 June 1944: We hear a lot of artillery fire. Aircraft flying over en masse, heading towards Plomeur, the aviation base near Lorient.

I wonder more than ever where my brother Pierre is.

The battle in Caen is ferocious. Nothing will be left of it.

Elisabeth will have no more letters from Paul until victory comes.

The sun was about to set behind Beg-Meil when Maman came into my room. She sat down on the bed beside me. She had brought some peas to shell. Anna was often tired and weary; we had to help her, which we did, but Maman didn't like making us do household chores, as she wanted so much for us to enjoy being together as a family. She never stopped working, which sometimes made us feel guilty.

My father came up too, and stood in front of the open window, watching the last glimmers of the setting sun over the sea.

"Darling girl, think carefully," they said. "This is extremely serious."

"I know," I replied.

"I shall need you here," said my father.

"I know," I replied again.

"And Marie, you know, with this sabotage about to happen tonight, I should prefer ..."

Oh yes! I understood. I understood only too well. Was it allowed to be so pulled in two directions, to feel so torn? Did I not have a paramount duty towards my family, especially if my father was arrested? But I told myself: "Françoise is here. She can do exactly what I can do. She will do it."

Maman was dropping the peas one by one into the saucepan: the regular reverberation punctuated our silences. Now my father was pacing up and down between the wardrobe and the window. The air was very mild, the earth smelt lovely.

"I'll tell you what I decide tomorrow," I said eventually. They embraced me with great tenderness and went out of the room.

I had the night to make my mind up. I was gripped by a visceral fear of making the wrong decision. I felt sick. I had to decide. Every hour of that night was spent weighing up the pros and cons. Happy are they who allow themselves no time to choose, or who are forced by circumstances to make an immediate choice. Better to be thrown into the terrifying chaos of the landings, to not be able to think any more, or just to think, "I have to destroy that blockhouse, I must put that gun out of action." To be mortally afraid, but not to think any more. But that was absurd: right up to the moment of death or the annihilating wound, we have to choose. We can crouch behind the metal defences or advance up the open beach. The dangers surrounding my father and others locally could only increase, but I had promised Francis. I knew he needed me and that there were weapons in the Morbihan. Perhaps by going there I would be helping people in Finistère.

I paced up and down my room in the moonlight. I gazed tenderly at everything I loved. If only my grandmother could speak to me from her picture frame! But she kept her aloof expression and her wry smile. If only Christ on the cross would lift his head and tell me what I should do! But he said nothing. Very well, doubt would lurk in the depths of my heart like a snake, sometimes slumbering, but venomous. I would never truly know if I had done the right thing: God had not given us the gift of certainty.

"Take care," they had kept saying earlier. Prudence: so fine and admirable! One way to be prudent was to just live quietly at home, leaving the rest of the world to muddle along as best it can.

But that would be impossible at a time like this! As that endless night wore on, so did my thoughts: "My parents have to tell me to be prudent. That's how it works between parents and children: a certain kind of prudence. One they know well, one they practise, the genuine thing, which is to weigh things up carefully and then take risks to achieve the better outcome. I shall go."

Morning had broken. I went to find my parents and told them I was setting off straight away. Then Maman gave me some advice: "Go straight to your friends in Pontivy. If you go anywhere else, send me the addresses. You know the risks a young woman runs: be very careful." I reassured her and told her that I knew how to defend myself. My father always went to the boatyard at about nine o'clock. I kissed him at the bottom of the stairs. The front door banged shut, then the garden gate.

All that was left was to get my things together. What should I take? "Basically," I told myself, "it's like going to camp." I took my "army" rucksack, made of quite loosely woven canvas that I had lined with an old waterproof; in it I put some spare underwear, a new checked blouse that Maman had just had made for me by the dressmaker in Concarneau, a blue cotton skirt, my sewing kit, my picnic box, a beaker, a water bottle, a mess tin and my *Manuel du chrétien*. On top of it all I folded my bulky khaki raincoat. By about ten o'clock I was ready. Right up to the last moment I was still hesitating. I tidied my room carefully, dragging my heels. Impossible to tear myself away.

Eventually I went out onto the landing and said, "Maman, I'm leaving." Without a word, she followed me down the stairs to the garage. She watched as I stowed my rucksack carefully on the luggage rack of the bicycle I had borrowed from Le Faouët, as mine was out of commission. We barely spoke, trying to keep at bay the tears that neither of us wanted to show.

A small girl from Le Passage appeared, coming to borrow some books. She was one of Suche's friends. I wished her a thousand miles away! Perhaps it was better like that after all. I hadn't said anything to anyone at home, except that I was going to Quimper. The small girl just stood there, waiting. She above all mustn't know anything. I gave Maman a hug and went out through the gate. I heard the same sharp snap as when my father had shut it behind him as he went off to work, as usual.

Part II

Into Action

CHAPTER 1

Rendezvous with Francis

I left Quimper the day after I'd left Concarneau, parting from my family once and for all as I said goodbye to Aunt Guite and Anneck on the quayside outside their house. A thick mist enveloped the town and the surrounding countryside. I was going to my rendezvous with Francis at Pontivy, with Le Faouët splitting my journey into two manageable stages. There were not many people about: everyone was waiting with some trepidation for the Germans' reaction to the numerous sabotage operations of the previous few days. There had been no telephone call at Quimper, which meant my father had not been arrested. My parents had let me go, but what did they really think about my decision, deep down? What were their thoughts?

If I'd only been able to read Maman's diary: "I think of Mie from dawn till dusk. And in the night when I wake. Perhaps my imagination runs away with me. A kind of fatalism continues to get the better of me, and the feeling that I too, were I in her place, would have wanted to do the same thing. And that we should not stand in the way of a fine and noble thing."

I was coming up to the level crossing at Saint-Yvy when a boy sitting on the bank shouted: "Hey, mademoiselle! Have you got papers?" I'd gone past him, swept along as far as the level crossing by the momentum I'd built up from the top of the hill. Putting my foot to the ground, I turned back: I didn't much appreciate this cross-examination and was deeply wary.

"Yes, of course I have."

"You'd best not carry on, even so. The Germans are arresting everyone further on. They've piled the political prisoners from the Saint-Charles prison in Quimper into buses and are putting them on the train to Germany. They didn't dare do it at the railway station."

All the prisoners from Saint-Charles? If there was any chance of rescuing them, it was now or never. The first thing would be to cut the railway track to gain time; the next thing would be to contact a Maquis group. Who to turn to? I didn't know anyone in the local Resistance. People said the gendarmes were against the occupiers. The gendarmerie in Rosporden was my only hope. There wasn't a second to lose.

"Do you know how many buses there are and if there are many Germans?" I asked the boy, "And do you know another way to Rosporden?"

"There are two buses and I don't think there are many German guards. You can get to Rosporden by that road there. Only it's a bad road and tough going, all steep climbs …"

So I set off on a mad dash, racing up the steepest of hills, speeding downhill without so much as touching the brakes. At last I careered through the little town at top speed, coming to a halt outside the gendarmerie, red-faced and dishevelled, still thinking only of my prisoners. I asked for the commanding officer, addressing one of the gendarmes who was slow, methodical and completely uncomprehending, but who nevertheless took me to his sergeant, who also took a while to believe me and take me seriously.

He looked at my Michelin map to see where exactly the buses were, not saying a word. I could sense his hesitation and I found it exasperating. I insisted:

"This is a one-off chance, I tell you, and we can't miss it. We must do something for them. Even if there are risks, they can't be worse than deportation. Not one of those prisoners will come back. You must know the best place to cut the railway line!"

"Yes, yes, of course," he said, without conviction. Disheartened, I was on the point of leaving when he suddenly made up his mind and issued orders: one of the gendarmes put on a leather jacket, got his powerful motorcycle out of the garage and roared out of the yard, making an infernal din. He set off in the direction of Bannalec, the next station on the way to Quimperlé. The sergeant shook my hand and assured me: "Don't you worry, it will all be fine." I put away my map, which had been a source of wonder to him. All we could hope now was that the operation would be a success. I was hungry and headed to the Hôtel de la Gare: from there I'd be able to see if the train... But surely that was the train, the one in the station now? I asked a waitress: yes, that was the one. So far I hadn't been fast enough. If it could just stay long enough to give time to blow up the tracks further on! First course: the train was still there. Second course: still there. Third course: still there. I got my hopes up again. The tracks must have been cut. Dessert: it was leaving, alas! And so was I, heading towards Bannalec.

At the crest of a hill I spotted my gendarme coming into view on his motorbike. He gave me a brilliant smile and a victorious thumbs-up. "So they must have pulled it off," I thought. At Bannalec the train was in the station, however. People were looking at it in distress, for they knew some of the people on board. After that I didn't follow the railway line any further, and I didn't know the fate of the train, but I didn't have much hope. Not fast enough, I hadn't been fast enough. Exhausted, I sat down by the roadside, running my hot hands through my windswept hair, then squeezing them together so hard that my knuckles turned white. I was furious that such an opportunity had been missed, I knew it had; I was in despair at the thought that the men and women in the railway trucks could have been free by now, and that they weren't because it takes too long to convince other people when the only thing you have going for you is the strength of your own conviction. I longed to go home, but then despised myself for being so discouraged after just one setback. So I got back on my bicycle to ride the thirty-five kilometres that still lay between me and Le Faouët.

At the Fravals' house, Maria from Lorient was pressing Breton headdresses. The hot iron on the damp fabric filled the room with a clean smell. Pressing the headdresses takes a lot of patience: you have to take each section separately, dip it in the starch, and then start again. Maria's fingers were nimble and quick. Beside me, a single rose in a vase was just opening, crimson, sumptuous and regal, and it enveloped me in its fragrance. It was raining outside, a drenching, heavy downpour. The day before, the Fravals had given me hope of seeing Michel, and I'd waited. He didn't come.

As the day wore on, I decided to continue on my way, however unpromising the weather. It was already 11 June. They let me keep the borrowed bicycle for "such a noble cause". The road was even more deserted than the road to Quimper. Telephone wires were dangling from their posts.

Before reaching Malguénac the road ran straight through interminable pine forests, and in the distance I could see a man watching me through field glasses. What could I do in this lonely spot but carry on? Behind the leader stood a group of young men as badly shod as they were shabbily dressed, with helmets from the Great War or scarves knotted round their heads like pirates. Thrust through their belts were antiquated pistols and great butchers' knives. Some of them were holding old shotguns and perhaps a couple of tommy guns. Were they going to stop me? After all, they could only be in the Resistance, like me; that wasn't much comfort though.

I was coming up level with them. The leader, a tall dark man with the air of a condottiere, brought me to a halt:

"Where are you heading? What are you doing? Show me your papers."

"I'm in the Resistance, and I'm going to Pontivy."

"Who are your leaders?"

"Michel."

"Don't know him. You're lying."

They had all come up close and were surrounding me, looking ferocious. "So here's the danger Maman was talking about on the day I left," I was thinking. "You always think that you'll be all right, but what can you do against such strapping and determined fellows? They'll roll me into a ditch in this sinister spot, and I'll find myself all alone by the side of the road."

The leader took me off down a sunken path. He gave orders for my bags to be carefully searched in case I was carrying weapons: they had initially thought that the water bottle in one of the pockets was a grenade. He examined my papers. Meanwhile I looked at them all one by one to see if there were any who looked sympathetic. On inspection, I found there were several. They were taking an age to copy down all the details of my identity card. "They're going to check them out," said the chief. Did they want to take me with them? Not on your life! But I could feel that things were calming down. Stories that I'd heard about some Maquis groups had taught me to be wary, but it wasn't in my nature to be distrustful for long. I ended up thinking they were almost nice. They told me proudly about their leaders Pierre and Thierry. "You'll be stopped further on," they told me finally, "by another Maquis. Mention Pierre's name and they'll let you pass." But I'd had my fill of drama for the day, and really could do without any more. I arrived at Pontivy without further mishap, and Michel informed me that I'd been stopped by an FTP group.

Monsieur Bruhat had put on heavy leather gloves and a mask, and I watched him catch an agitated swarm of bees on a tree at the bottom of his garden. The buzzing of the panic-stricken bees, the heat of the magnificent sunshine and the fragrance of the strawberries and raspberries that filled the air around me kept my immediate thoughts in this magical world that enchanted all my senses. Several times a day I would move between this enchanted world and that of the war, a contrast that was strange and disturbing.

The BBC was saying: "The Allied navies have complete control of the Channel: no submarine interference so far." They broadcast a warning to fishermen: "To all on the coasts of western Europe: from 9.00pm on Thursday 8 June to 9.00pm on Thursday 15 June: those at sea should return to port immediately. Those on shore should stay there. Any who contravene this order will put themselves and the Allied cause in danger."

"Why?" we wondered. "Are they planning a landing somewhere else?" Whatever the case, they seemed pleased with the advances made by the troops in the landings sector. They spoke of the "suddenness of the breakthrough" and added: "It is not a dream. It is an unhoped-for reality!"

Eisenhower proclaimed: "It is the dawn of the Liberation. I am proud to have under my command the valiant French troops who never stopped fighting. I ask for prompt obedience to my orders [...] Victory is on the march."

On 10 June the Allies were at Isigny and Sainte-Mère-l'Eglise and we heard there were fierce tank battles in Caen. On 11 June, Montgomery announced: "After four days of fighting, the Allies have taken a firm hold on French soil." They had announced the day before that French parachutists had taken part in the operations, and with every bulletin we were hoping that they would specify which ones. What the German radio was telling us also added to our rejoicing. General Dittmar himself admitted: "We have entered the first phase of a battle in which the decisive turning point has become fearsome. We have been taken by surprise. The Allied Command has only thrown in half its forces against Normandy. We must therefore expect further landings."

Never before had I listened to so many news bulletins; never had I read so many threatening notices, appearing in rapid succession on the Kommandantur walls; never before had I pored so often over the map of France; never before, finally had I felt such impatience to do something.

With each passing day, it was becoming increasingly clear that something had happened to Francis: he would not be coming. I caught only occasional glimpses of Michel, on edge, unshaven, tired, his plus fours falling down to his heels, spending most of his time with the boys in his Pontivy Maquis, who had absolutely no need of me. His brother Jo was there too. I kicked my heels in town, helped Madame Bruhat pick the fruit in her garden, and began to wonder what I was doing there. I'd be better off going back to Concarneau.

I had reached this conclusion when the simmering conflict between the FFI and the FTP[21] heated up. Michel thought it wouldn't be long before they came to blows. I was appalled. Of course there weren't enough weapons for everyone and maybe the FTP had reason to hope for more supplies than the FFI. They had carried out more operations and had been active in the Maquis much longer than the FFI, but they had not followed the orders from London. Nevertheless, Michel said, "Pierre is a good chap. I know him well. We have to find a way for him to come to terms with the FFI."

Finally, a highly agitated Michel said to me one night:

---

21. The FTP became part of the FFI under the command of General Koenig, but as they always tended to keep a degree of autonomy within the Resistance, they continued erroneously to be referred to as the FFI and FTP right up the Liberation.

"Things are really bad."

"What things are really bad?"

"Weapons. The FTP have decided to attack the FFI over them, and they will."

"We have to do something, Michel."

"Yes. Apparently there are some parachutists over near Malestroit. The best thing would be to go over and see them."

"Definitely, Michel, they're the mediators we need. Let's go!"

Michel hesitated. I went on: "Let me go on my own. A girl doesn't run any risks. The Germans are only stopping men. Anyway, don't you remember? Hache anticipated this in his orders to us. I know it by heart: 'On D-Day, women and girls are more likely to be exempt from the draconian measures imposed by the Germans. They will therefore be called upon to supply liaison agents for the different sectors of the Resistance.' You see? I should be the one to go."

Michel gave in. He would make the FTP wait, and I would go and find the parachutists.

CHAPTER 2

"La Petite France"

One of Michel's relations, a shopkeeper in Vannes, agreed to take me by car for part of the journey: as a precaution he would only pick me up two kilometres outside Pontivy. He would drop me at Saint-Servant, very near to the Chantier de Jeunesse[22] where a certain Colette, informed of my arrival by Michel, would take me to the parachutists.

The chateau taken over by the Chantiers was magnificent, its grounds beautifully kept, its sandy paths neatly raked, its lawns perfectly manicured. From a flagpole in the middle of the courtyard flew a large French flag. Further off, the gardens led down in a succession of terraces to dense woods overlooking the Guillac watermill and its millstream.

I asked for Colette, but he wasn't there. Good start! Would anyone else there know the way? I didn't know quite what to make of this establishment, in principle more pro-Pétain than pro-de Gaulle, but the presence of Colette seemed to suggest otherwise. The mission undertaken by Jean-Louis – our "man from London"– to petition

---

22. Introduced in July 1940 to replace military service, Chantiers de la Jeunesse Française were compulsory paramilitary work camps for young men, strongly imbued with the values of Vichy and Marshal Pétain.

General de la Porte du Theil, High Commissioner for the Chantiers de Jeunesse, had perhaps produced some tangible results. I was advised to wait for Quinquis, one of the leaders, who was expected soon. He turned out to be the cyclist in short trousers who had just passed me near Saint-Servant. "I'd like to speak to you alone," I told him as soon as he arrived. He led me down one of the garden avenues. I explained why I was there. Not questioning my word for an instant, he assured me straight away:

"I know the way. I'll take you tomorrow morning, but whatever you do don't breathe a word to a soul. The head of the Chantier is out there with them. Yes, the head of the Chantier in Saint-Servant, Captain Villars. You wouldn't want the war to be fought without us, would you!"

"What am I going to do tonight?" I asked anxiously. "It's getting dark. Is there a hotel in Saint-Servant?"

"You must be joking! You can sleep here. You can be a troop leader who's just done a training course in the Côtes-du-Nord and wants to visit our camp. Don't go and blow your cover."

As soon as we were back with the others, Quinquis made a big song and dance about me being a troop leader. I stuck out my chest and put on a serious and resolute expression, while keeping any conversation deliberately vague. When the team who had been clearing away the bomb damage in Ploermel and taking care of the victims came back, we went into the wooden hut they called the dining hall. There was much talk about the British bombing of Ploermel, which had been heavy and there were many casualties. Opinions differed as to the adjectives to be applied to our Allies across the Channel. The hubbub stopped dead for the *Chant au Maréchal*, in honour of Marshal Pétain. I was guest of honour on the high table, up on a dais with the leaders and bang opposite an enormous photograph of Pétain. It was deeply worrying that I didn't know the words. For a Chantier troop leader this wasn't going to look good. I redeemed this grave deficiency by standing perfectly to attention and casting a look of pride over the long wooden tables below, flanked by a hundred or so young men singing at the top of their lungs: fine-looking lads with shorn hair, clean and neat, strong in their beliefs and good sorts. "Splendid future soldiers," I thought.

Quinquis led me up a medieval spiral staircase to the infirmary where I could have the nurse's bed since she too was "over there". "Well," I said to my new friend, "I'm going to find a whole town over there!"

"Pretty much," he answered. Bidding me goodnight, he said he would wake me up at five o'clock. We had to leave before the Chantier's flurry of activity around the morning muster.

Sleep? Can you sleep when you're living a dream? The next day I would be in a camp of French parachutists, parachutists who had come from England, who had arrived during the very night of the landings, as Quinquis informed me. Not only was I going to see them, but I had to talk to them. What solutions would they suggest for the FFI/FTP infighting? By the fading light of day I looked at myself in a little mirror above the washbasin. What would they make of me?

I was up and ready when Quinquis knocked on my door at dawn. There would never be enough hours in this extraordinary day of 15 June. I was hungry, but he seemed to be spending ages making a full square meal in the dark kitchen. "Dig in", he said, "It's a long, hard walk, I can tell you, so eat up." Forthright, stocky and kind, he looked at me, amused at my impatience. The steam rising from his cup of ersatz coffee, a concoction of ground acorns or sunflower seeds, obscured his strong features. He dug out some stale bread from a cupboard and cut it into chunks with a camping knife, then dunked small pieces in his coffee. I liked him. "Here's someone with his feet on the ground: I can trust him." He cut the end off a dried sausage – a rare luxury. "Some days you have to treat yourself," he said, offering me a few slices. I laughed. He could read my thoughts!

Along the way, Quinquis explained what I would find at the Saint-Marcel camp, as it was called, after a village near the command post of the FFI and parachutists' HQ. To be more precise, he said, the CP had been set up at the farmhouse of La Nouette, more parachutists were arriving every night, and since his last visit to the camp the battalion commander should have arrived.

"He's called Bourgoin," he said, "and he's only got one arm."

It looked as if it was going to be a beautiful day, and as the sun rose great forests of blue pines emerged from the mists of night. Spiders' webs glittered with dew. "I couldn't have wished for better weather," I kept saying to myself as I struggled along behind my guide, "it's all just perfect."

We skirted the market town of Sérent and came to a road that veered off to the left. "Here," said Quinquis, "we are entering *la petite France*. That's what the local people, who are helping us, call this favoured spot. Here you can say anything you want."

The path wound its way under pollarded trees at first, and then we were in the wilderness: wild hilltops virtually bare of vegetation, with just a few strips of heather or sandy heathlands. Here and there were slate screes or scattered boulders. The view stretched into the distance as far as the high moorlands of Lanvaux, rising blue and violet on the horizon. Overall, the landscape had a melancholy atmosphere that I had only ever come across in small corners of the countryside at home in Cornouaille.

"We're here," said Quinquis finally, leading me down a muddy track to a farm called Clairefontaine and to the camp's guard post, or more precisely the garage. Liaison agents left their bicycles there in a lean-to, and we added ours to the top of the pile. The ground rose behind the house, and it was there that the woods began. I followed Quinquis along a narrow track. Pine needles scrunched underfoot, resin scented the air and birds called from tree to tree.

A loud "Halt!" stopped us in our tracks. A young man rose before us, his machine gun trained on us. "Turenne – France!" cried Quinquis. Satisfied by the password, the sentry lowered his weapon and let us pass, sitting back down beside a hut constructed from branches in the ditch.

Woods, more woods and several repetitions of the password before we reached the camp proper, coming upon it as we rounded a bend in the path. In the shadows I could see a great many men, some in uniform, coming and going as if they had a lot to do. There were shouts, and the clatter of mess tins; you could almost have been in a scout camp, but instead of tents they had built huts. Greeted first on one side and then on the other, Quinquis took me further and further on. "Here is our company," he said at last, his voice swelling with pride. They had made their camp beside the path, half in the woods and half in the ditch. There the men had built a veritable house of branches, the interior lined throughout with blue parachutes. They lay down on silk, they slept on silk, they cleaned their weapons with silk. The cabin roof glowed like something out of the *Arabian Nights*. They had parachute silk in blue, white, red, green and black, but to line their commander's hut they had used blue silk alone – regal and sumptuous!

Quinquis introduced me to Captain Villars. He had put on his uniform from 1940 again and looked magnificent. I saw the nurse from Saint-Servant and some other young women. A tall lad with a brick-red complexion and a face as round as the moon said to me: "Well? Have you signed up? Here we take everyone, girls and boys. There are quite a lot of us, you know."

The girls wore Red Cross armbands, but they also did the cooking. I was offered coffee in an enormous tin mug, and a slice of bread and jam. Meanwhile Quinquis explained to Captain Villars that I was to go to the CP. They spoke of the CP in solemn tones, which did nothing to reassure me.

Captain Villars called one of the men in his company over and instructed him to take me there. The man slung his machine gun over his shoulder and off we set. All around, men were busily cleaning weapons. So many weapons! I thought of the men in Concarneau and Quimper who would have given anything for just a few weapons like these. This was where they needed to come to get them. By contrast their kit wasn't so good. Some of the men still only had clogs. We came out of the woods, then crossed a stream and a marshy meadow. In the shade of the willows, radio operators were at work, parachutists, the first I'd seen. In the next field, I passed some Senegalese in French uniform. "From Ploermel; they took advantage of the bombing to escape and join our camp," said my companion; then he stopped, indicating a farmhouse: "I'll leave you here," he said. "You've arrived."

It was La Nouette, the command post.

• • •

"You're in the OCM? It's of no interest to me: it's full of Gestapo."

I was stung by the injustice of the remark.

"You shouldn't judge the OCM harshly just because we've had so many arrests. We hate traitors, real triators, just like you do, and we hate the Gestapo, who might have been able to make some people talk. How can we be sure we wouldn't have done the same in their place?"

Major Morice loomed over me from his great height. He stood bolt upright in the middle of the farmyard, feet slightly apart, so sure of himself! Even less agreeable than Captain Guimard who had been rather irritated by my story about the FTP, but who had nevertheless agreed to seek out the regional chief of staff. The latter observed me for a while in silence before going on: "We are about to have a staff meeting with Commandant Bourgoin. I shall bring up your FFI and FTP matter. We'll see. Just wait here. OCMJ? Not a name I know.

Still, I'm inclined to believe you." Captain Guimard had arrived to join Commandant Morice and now looked at me, smiling. Evidently he found me amusing.

I sat on a tree trunk in front of a pile of firewood. It must have been nearly eleven o'clock and it was starting to get very hot. The men who went to and fro in front of me kicked up wreaths of golden dust. Would the farmers still be hoping for rain? Just to my left was the entrance to a sunken path, its shadows in stark contrast with the dazzling brightness of the farmyard. The men who emerged from it seemed to come from another world. Suddenly a noisy group appeared in front of me, to be greeted with enthusiastic shouts. Several parachutists came out of the farmhouse: "Skinner, it's Skinner!" With that they rushed towards the man at the front the group and plied him with a barrage of questions:

"Well? How did it go? Any mishaps? The Vannes-Redon line? Did you manage to cut it?"

"Job done," Skinner replied. "Happy to be back though."

"Another mission completed," said a boy beside me.

"What kind of mission?"

"Sabotage. Some men blow up electrical transformers; some blow up petrol tanks; others blow up underground cables or power stations. They parachuted in eighteen groups of three men, just after the landings. I've been here with Captain Guimard for a good fortnight, and every day I've seen more arriving. All dirty and tired, and so happy to be successful. But you should just hear them talking about the training they made them do! It was something else. And their kit is fantastic. Apparently we're going to get some stuff too. Even shoes. Not like we couldn't do with them."

He pulled his bare foot out of his clog and observed it pensively.

"I see you haven't got anything much to do at the moment. Me neither. It's great watching them, isn't it? Hard to believe, all these fellows in British uniforms, with their camouflage jackets. No two ways about it, they look terrific. Don't you think?"

Yes, I did. I pinched my arm hard and it hurt: I wasn't dreaming. From the black hole of the path a Renault emerged filled with gendarmes, spick and span like the car. "Probably from Quimperlé," remarked my companion. "We were talking about it yesterday. Think we can say they're all in the Resistance."

They disappeared into the CP where Skinner had already been taken. With all these new arrivals, my meeting wouldn't be finishing any time soon!

"Are you staying with us?" asked the boy.

"No, I have to get back to Pontivy as soon as possible."

"But you'll be back?"

"I hope so."

There was a constant stream of patriots coming and going in front of us.

"These guys come to collect weapons and then go back to their sectors. Some stay on. Anyway, good luck! Grub's up. My mess is a good way off: I'll leave you now," my neighbour concluded, and he went off, hands in pockets, happy and fulfilled. On the other side of the farmyard a queue was forming. A cook was busying himself around an impressive cast-iron cooking pot, stirring the contents with a long wooden spoon, then ladling it into the mess tins being held out to him. In the fields further off I could see more queues, and more cooking pots. It was unbelievable to see such an organised and disciplined camp so close to the Germans, on what could still be called "their patch". How long would it go on?

The powerful silhouette of Commandant Morice was framed in the farmhouse doorway. He cast his gaze over the surroundings with a satisfied air, then saw me. "Come," he said, "Commandant Bourgoin wants to see you." The man himself appeared behind Morice in his parachutist's uniform, just as tall, just as solid, just as strong.

They ushered me into one of the ground-floor rooms, on the right-hand side of the main farmhouse. It was Monsieur and Madame Pondard's bedroom. A table flanked by benches had been placed lengthwise in the middle of the room. It was covered with ordnance maps, their whiteness gleaming in the half-light, which took me aback. The shutters had been half closed to keep out the midday sun and a shaft of light cut the table in two. I sat down on one side of the table and the two commanders on the other. They leaned towards me attentively to hear what I had to say. This was no time for shyness; I had to win my case. I forgot that Bourgoin was the famous "Manchot", the one-armed hero. All I could think of was the conflict between the Pontivy FFI and FTP, and I spoke at length. When I'd finished, Commandant Bourgoin said: "Right! Tell this Pierre to come and see us and we'll discuss it with him." They were forgetting Michel. I added: "If Pierre comes, Michel must come too."

"O.K. bring him too," and he added: "You are a determined young lady. I like you." I could feel that I'd finally convinced him that what I'd told them was important. This was the moment to plead the cause of Finistère, and of Concarneau, and I did so with a passion. "Don't worry, we'll arm them all," and with that the parachutists' leader stood up. "Come with me. You can have a look at what we can give them, your friends."

He took me to the east of the farmyard, along a path that led up towards the moors, a path bordered by high banks planted with oak trees whose branches met above us. Some thirty metres from the farmyard, where the banks opened out more widely, he showed me a pile of assorted weapons that had been placed there after the last parachute drop: tommy guns, Bren guns, bazookas, grenades, and rolls of plastic explosive. "Every day men are given arms here and go off again," he said, "and every day new arms and ammunition arrive from England." I thought of the single machine gun that Patrice's boys had in Concarneau, and of my father's fruitless journey to

Pontivy, but I said nothing. The parachutists did not appear to really grasp what could have been set in train by the Resistance; it was up to us to teach them.

• • •

"Have something to eat before you go," said Commandant Bourgoin in a fatherly way. It was true that I had seventy kilometres to cycle before nightfall. I wanted to reach Pontivy that night so as to come back to the camp next day with Michel and Pierre. So I went into the enormous kitchen at La Nouette where there was a great bustle of people. Madame Pondard, vivacious and smiling, as fresh and gay as her five daughters, who she introduced to me, made sure that nobody wanted for anything. She gave me a big bowl of soup. I sat down at the end of a very long table where the new arrivals from Skinner's stick had installed themselves, with other parachutists and several girls who eyed me with curiosity. Madame Pondard introduced them to me too: Jeanne, Micheline, Anne-Marie and Marie-Thérèse.

"Here we're one big family," she told me. "And if you come back you'll soon be part of it." Everyone was congratulating one of the girls, Jeanne, for the action she'd taken during the Le Garrec battalion's skirmish in the woods at Billy. The battalion had not been able to leave Saint-Marcel as planned, since there had been fewer parachute drops over the past few nights because of bad weather over England and the Channel. There were so many questions I'd have liked to ask. Why had such a major camp been established in this corner of Brittany? Why were the Allies sending so many parachutists? What operations did they have planned for the future? I didn't dare ask all these questions today, but I would tomorrow, for certain. I contented myself with gazing at these young soldiers. Many of them were the same age as Charles, Richard and the others, but there was something different about them, something I couldn't quite put my finger on yet, an air of being from "somewhere else", possibly just because of their slight English accents, which it took them a few weeks to lose. At the sight of the French insignia on their shoulders, I kept saying to myself: "This is the new French army, the one we've been waiting for, our very own."

The Commandant said: "Till tomorrow then," and I went back to the 8th Company in its pinewood. Quinquis was staying for the time being. "Not for long," he said. "I'm liaising between the Chantier and Captain Villars. Go back via Saint-Servant and tell them all's well here." Many of the others came running up to me, asking me to pass on messages to those outside, like boys at boarding school, in particular my tall ruddy-faced friend. "Drennec at your service, mademoiselle," he said, before imploring me to stop off at his aunts' shop in Josselin. "They will tell my parents that I'm well and very happy. The poor old things will be relieved." I promised I would. "Wait, you must take something beautiful with you." He disappeared into the Arabian Nights cabin and came out again with two pieces of parachute silk, one blue and one white. They would be the loveliest scarves I had ever had – but not to be worn until after the Germans had gone! In the meantime it would be better to hide them. I mulled this over as I followed my new guide through the woods. When he left me, in sight of the Clairefontaine farmhouse where my bicycle was waiting for me, I hid behind a bush and put them on like petticoats under my skirt, tucking them tightly under my belt. I hoped that if I encountered any Germans they would behave like gentlemen!

Captain Villars and Quinquis had advised me to head for the Nantes-Brest Canal at Le Roc Saint-André, and then to take the quiet towpath straight to Josselin after stopping off at the Chantier. I didn't stop off there, as I was worried that I might be caught out by the curfew while on the deserted road between Josselin and Pontivy. There were Germans all over Josselin. They had made their local headquarters at the chateau that belonged to the Rohan family.

CHAPTER 3

The Last Days of Saint-Marcel

As soon as we got back to the camp the next day, Morice grabbed Pierre and left me with Michel: with the sparse numbers of our OCMJ in Brittany we didn't carry much weight. However, when the long discussion with Pierre was over, Michel obtained permission to go and fetch a company from our movement.

"Stay here till tomorrow, Marie-Claire, and I'll be back within the day with my brother Jo and my boys." He was as delighted as I was to see Morice, the local head of the FFI, come to an agreement with Pierre on the question of weapons and on the FTP more generally. I didn't know where all this would lead, but for the moment it was at Saint-Marcel that I stood the most chance of being useful. While waiting for a proper task, I was thrilled to watch all that was going on around me. Lorries and cars would draw up in the farmyard, load up with weapons and head off again, leaving clouds of powdery yellow clay dust in their wake. With each arrival and departure a veil of fine dust would fall on the leaves hanging from the trees and the parched grass. The weather stayed hot and cloudless and everything was parched, grass, animals and people.

A girl came running up, the daughter of the station master at Questembert, on the main Quimper-Paris railway line. She announced that a convoy of troops had passed through, heading for Normandy. The parachutist who was head of intelligence was summoned and noted down what she told him. The convoy would soon be attacked by the RAF: a message would be sent straight away. Her young cheeks were pink from running and her eyes shone with happiness at transmitting such important news. On the off-chance, I spoke to her about my train of deportees. Had she seen it pass through? Yes, sadly! Who could save them?

The lorries were succeeded by cattle, herded in to become tomorrow's steaks. Skilled butchers dealt with them on the spot. Every trade was here: mechanics, bakers and cobblers among many others. Emile Guimard tried to find solutions to a huge range of problems, one of which – to judge from the number of our patriots pestering him for shoes – seemed particularly intractable. Men clamoured for him on all sides. I watched him from a distance and took care not to approach him.

I was intrigued by a tall, thin man who wore round glasses. I asked Anna Pondard, who was sitting beside me on the stone bench outside the farmhouse, if she knew him. Yes. He was Captain Cyr, who had been parachuted in at the same time as Commandant Bourgoin. He was the American liaison officer. There was one peculiar thing about him. When he dropped onto the heath he wasn't wearing his glasses, he was wearing contact lenses, directly against his eyes. Apparently, these were already quite common in America and were replacing spectacles. She had watched fascinated as he took them out and put them away in a little box. He had explained to her in his strong American accent that he kept them for "moments of danger when things might kick off".

"He looks like the British liaison officer, Major Smith,"[23] Anna went on. "You can see him over there, by the gate to the vegetable garden, he's not that young and he doesn't have much hair left! And he wears round glasses, but not contact lenses. Both of them are creatures of habit and take regular baths in my mother's washtub in the washhouse. We heat pots and pots of water for them on the stove. Look, here's Captain Fay: he's English too, and he knows lots of things."

Night was falling, and Monsieur Pondard had come out to take the cool evening air on his doorstep.

"Well, Monsieur Pondard, what do you think of your farm now?" asked Captain Fay.

"It's changed a lot, that's certainly true, but we're glad to see so many soldiers around us! Only we can't help wondering what the Huns are going to do at the end."

"Don't worry, they're going to start sending us jeeps, which will mean we can get down to Sarzeau to be there on the night of the landing. Because there's going to be a second landing on the Rhuys Peninsula, which will create a diversion and completely tie up the Germans that are in Brittany - 150,000 at a conservative estimate - and who must at all costs be prevented from reinforcing the German defences in Normandy. It's tough over there. The Resistance and parachutists have cut a lot of routes of communication for the moment, but that might not be enough: they're soon repaired. It's also likely that the two artificial harbours the Allies have built on the Normandy coast, and even at Cherbourg when they've taken it, won't be enough to disembark the divisions that are still waiting in England and America. Quiberon is a good bay. You'll see, Monsieur Pondard, very soon we'll get the message announcing the landing, and then we'll understand the true purpose of Saint-Marcel. If the

---

23. P H Smith (4th SAS – Wash) was in fact an RAF Squadron Leader. For more details on "Major" Smith see: https://fflsas.org.

Germans would just leave us in peace for a few more days. Let's hope they do."

"Let's hope, but last night they had searchlights sweeping the sky. They can't possibly have missed the planes coming in. Thirty-two this time. Imagine!"

I listened. A veil was lifted: all was now clear. So that was where the second landing was to take place: on a deserted beach on the Rhuys Peninsula, near Suscinio and the market town of Sarzeau. That was why yesterday Commandant Bourgoin had said to a liaison agent in front of me: "You come from that part of the world, son, go and see what's really happening around Rhuys, and then come back at the double to tell us." Suscinio, with the ancient chateau of the Dukes of Brittany beside its beach, renovated by Jean Le Roux centuries ago so that he could spend a few holidays there, and still majestic, even in ruins.

• • •

Supper time brought all the parachutist officers back to the CP from places scattered all over the camp where they had spent the day initiating young recruits in the handling of weapons, and trying to make something resembling a regular army out of this motley collection.

My place was between two of them, the one as silent as the other was voluble. He couldn't stop talking about how much he admired the potential of the camp and its general organisation. "When we were in England we could never have imagined this," he kept saying. "The Germans will have their work cut out in Brittany, and I hope we'll see them before long!"

Many of the parachutists were feeling frustrated as they waited for the battles they were expecting, and for which they had prepared with such meticulous care. The only fighting going on was in Normandy, and they were starting to wonder whether they wouldn't be better off there. In the end this second landing about which they had been told before leaving England, but which was kept a virtual secret here, was probably going to unleash the real battle. The expected jeeps sounded promising, and my neighbour was counting on having one, which for him would be as good as a tank.

Occasionally my neighbour on the other side looked at him, and then he shut up, as you couldn't tell what was going on behind the fiery glint of his dark eyes. He was very dark, very tall and lean, his face almost emaciated, a few white hairs at his temples despite his youthful air. He looked determined but distant at the same time, as if he was following some inner dream. He looked stern but was interested in those around him, all with the same intense gaze, the same passion and concentrated ardour that he didn't make a show of, but that you could sense. When they spoke to him people didn't use rhetorical flourishes but were clear and precise. Disconcerted at being so close to him, I thought: "This is a leader." My right-hand companion leaned towards me:

"His name is Marienne. He was parachuted in on the first night, on 5 June, in the south, with Captain Deplante."

In beds lined up against the walls were the wounded who had made bad landings in trees or elsewhere. Madame Pondard came and went with pots of soup and potatoes with bacon, helped by her three grown-up daughters, Geneviève, Anna and Henriette.

The conversation was becoming more general when they started talking about Samwest: it was the first time I'd heard this name and it took me a while to work out that it was a second base like Saint-Marcel, but in the Forêt de Duault on the Côtes-du-Nord, near Callac. They had received the worst possible news from there on 12 June, four days earlier. The Germans had attacked in force and the parachutists had had to retreat after a battle about which little was known. That same day, Commandant Bourgoin had sent Captain Deplante to set up a new base to collect the men who were coming down from Samwest and to continue the work they had begun: receiving the huge parachute drops to provide weapons for the patriots and organising sabotage operations to keep Brittany cut off. So I wouldn't see this Deplante who my neighbour had just mentioned. The fate of the parachutists travelling in small groups or cut off in the south of the province seemed rather tragic to me, and I wondered about what had happened to the wounded. I remembered how vicious and jumpy the Germans at Concarneau had been after the landings and more recently at Pontivy. They would be merciless.

"Come and see tonight's parachute drop with us," said a pretty dark girl with heavy plaits wound round her head like a tiara. "It will be particularly good; we're expecting some jeeps, and they'll have at least four parachutes each." While we waited for the appointed hour, I sat on the stone benches with her and the other girls and a few of the parachutists. "We sit here in the evenings," said Marie-Thérèse. "The days are very long. The parachutists talk to us about Britain and we tell them all about Brittany. They're so nice!" She laughed. We all laughed. We felt so young and invincible there. And happy, despite our worries beneath the surface about one or many of our own, and despite the thought, which you had to push to the back of your mind, of those who were dying and who had been happy like us.

On my right was Jeanne, who told me how she had come to be in the Resistance and how Micheline, who she pointed out a little further off, had taught her how to handle and use explosives. "We've been all over the place," she told me, "often to schools and pharmacies, hiding our formulae in our bicycle saddles, and teaching Maquis leaders how to make bombs in cheese boxes and bottles. Micheline is a chemical engineer. The British parachuted her into Brittany a few months ago, because there were far too many accidents with the explosives and detonators that were sent to the Maquis, with most of the boys making silly mistakes out of ignorance. Micheline did a very intensive training course in England."

As we listened to these fascinating and sometimes very funny stories, it seemed like no time before a warm voice came out of the darkness that had finally fallen: "Girls, it's time to go if you don't want to miss the start." I recognised Captain Guimard's voice, but now relaxed and gentle, calm and light-hearted. Dark-haired Marie-Thérèse, who seemed to have adopted me as her new friend, took me by the arm, and we made our way up to the heathlands of Le Pinieux.

The other girls had gone on ahead, but I stayed on the side of the path with Marie-Thérèse and Captain Guimard. I asked him if by any chance he had known Agnès de Nanteuil,[24] whose arrest I'd heard about the last time I was in Vannes. "Agnès? You knew Agnès?" he said. "She was my liaison agent, one of the best I've ever had. Really, you knew her?"

"Yes, we did our scout leaders' camp together, we were in the same group of six." There was a silence. Then Captain Guimard told me how Agnès had been arrested. I could feel something had changed between us. After that he told me all the details I wanted to know about the camp, "his" camp. He spoke for a long time.

The planes had still not appeared and our impatience was growing. It was childish; I should have kept calm. After a pause, he went on: "I can tell you something, Marie-Claire, friend of Agnès, I worry about all this: all these men, all these comings and goings, all these planes, all this activity. This camp wasn't intended for eight thousand men! I'm not happy about it and I don't like that business in the Forêt de Billy at all.

"The other night a plane no one could identify flew over the drop zone. That's really not good. We'd be better off getting out of here quickly, tomorrow if possible, going somewhere else, spreading

---

24. Agnès de Nanteuil, liaison agent for the chief officer of the Morbihan department and General Audibert, was arrested with her sister on leaving church at Vannes on 14 March 1944. The train taking them to Germany was bombed at Langeais on 3 August and Agnès was gravely wounded. She died in great pain ten days later. She was twenty-one.

ourselves out between several different spots. With so many young men, it's difficult to impose the strict safety measures that are essential. It's difficult to stop people from talking." He was about to go on when a distant hum rooted us to the spot, suddenly tense. They were coming. Until you could be certain it was British planes you could hear, fear had you in its grip. What if it was the Germans? The radio operators working the Eureka beacon were close by. And then there were the torches laid out in the shape of the prearranged letter. The huge beasts were almost upon us. Marie-Thérèse let out a cry of fear: "Their wings are going to touch! Oh, Marie-Claire, we were so frightened the night Commandant Bourgoin arrived! Two planes suddenly appeared, flying towards each other and it seemed to us they were at the same height. A collision would have been terrible. They just managed to avoid each other by a whisker, but it was only by a miracle that the lower one didn't slice through the harnesses of the dozens and dozens of parachutes that were already swaying in the sky, with men dangling below. Now I'm always frightened: but how can I even think that when the British pilots are so accurate!" The planes had made a wide circle and were coming back. "Let's hope they drop the jeeps!" said Marie-Thérèse. Huge flowers suddenly blossomed above us, like gigantic jellyfish. We lost count of them, but we couldn't see any groups of four. "What a pity!" said my companion. "You should have seen it when Commandant Bourgoin arrived! It was magnificent. They'd given him a big tricolor parachute, red, white and blue."

The night was still, and thousands of stars glittered in the sky. "This is one of the most extraordinary sights I shall ever be privileged to see," I said to myself, enraptured. A light breeze blew one of the parachutes over towards us. "Look out!" shouted Captain Guimard. "You don't want a container landing on your head." But what fell into a bank of heather was a man. Marie-Thérèse rushed over to help him disentangle himself and see if he'd broken any bones. Some of the parachutes twisted into a torch shape, and the containers broke up when they hit the ground, occasionally exploding. The parachutists and the French patriots were silhouetted against the flames as they struggled frantically to put them out. We watched as some of the parachutes, dropped too early or too late, disappeared into the woods or far away over the neighbouring moorland. Men were running everywhere. The booty had to be collected up as quickly as possible. Further waves of aircraft followed the first one and the spectacle was repeated, as thrilling as before. The new arrivals went past us as their comrades took them to the farm. Madame Pondard was waiting for them in the farmyard with pitchers of mulled wine. They couldn't get over it.

We left the drop zone too and made our way back to La Nouette. I climbed up to the attic by a narrow spiral staircase between the two front doors. A partition of a decent height divided the attic into the "women's quarters" and the "men's quarters". After crossing the first room, where some parachutists were already asleep alongside Monsieur Pondard and his son, we reached our own domain. Marie-Thérèse had brought a Pigeon oil lamp from the kitchen, and it shed a soft light over some forms wrapped in brilliantly coloured parachutes. "You will never sleep in softer or finer sheets, or under lighter or warmer covers," said Marie-Thérèse, showing me a spot to lie down, next to her own. I plunged fully dressed into this snowy, velvety whiteness. Some of the men were joking and laughing in their corner on the other side of the attic. Several of the girls were quietly saying their rosaries. They were youngsters from the convent at Ploërmel. We joined in with the responses.

• • •

Abbé Guyodo said Mass every morning at eight o'clock in an orchard behind the farmhouse. I went with Marie-Thérèse. The portable altar was set up against the wall of the cottage belonging to the owner of

La Nouette, the very elderly Madame Salles. When we arrived, she was descending the wooden steps in front of the house majestically, before going to sit in an armchair. The orchard was the only place that was still cool. I knelt in the dense grass, damp with dew, beside Loïc,[25] one of the six children of young Madame Bouvard, from the neighbouring chateau of Sainte Geneviève. She lived there with her mother-in-law, her husband having left for England. Loïc was about fourteen, but still seemed like a little boy. Somewhere or other he had found a pair of German boots that gave him an air of Puss-in-Boots, and the confident look in his dark eyes reflected a deep contentment. He walked with a serious air, and he talked with a serious air, like a special envoy on a mission, like someone "who-knew-things-that-you-didn't". One of the parachutists served Mass and there were others around us, but only a few. It was Saturday. From dawn everyone was at work, distributing arms, settling in the new squadrons, issuing instructions, doing training and PE, preparing food and I don't know what else!

When I got back to the farmhouse it was bustling with activity. I decided to join in by making some armbands, having noticed some women sewing dozens and dozens of them in a corner of the main hall the night before. They cut sheets into long strips, hemmed them, drew the Cross of Lorraine in a triangle in Indian ink, then attached hooks and eyes. It would make an embryonic uniform for all the motley assortment of boys to whom enlistment cards had been issued. Jeanne bade me farewell: she was leaving on a liaison mission.

"If only I could do the same!" I thought. "It would be so much better than sewing!" Had Commandant Bourgoin not said to Michel only yesterday: "Let me have Marie-Claire …" The door of the CP was wide open. He saw me.

"May I have a word with you, Commandant?".

---

25. Loïc Bouvard survived the war and was awarded the Croix de Guerre. His account of the battle of Saint-Marcel can be seen here: http://lesamitiesdela.fr/lien23/138-saint-marcel.pdf

"Yes, come in," and he shut the door behind me.

"Would it be possible to find a mission for me – today? And every other day too, as Michel will be back here with his group and he won't have any use for me. I've been getting my hand in for a year now: it seems a shame not to make use of me when I'm fit for service. At least I think I'm beginning to be." He laughed. I found him less intimidating: he had such a good-natured air about him, with his eyes of palest blue and his mane of thick fair curls! A gentle giant.

"You've come at the right time, young lady! I was just looking for someone to go and see Captain Deplante at the Grog Base near Saint-Caradec. I'll show you on the map." He leaned over the Michelin map that lay open on the table and showed me the two coordinates. The directions were pretty vague, it seemed to me: a proper paper chase to find a spot that was right out in the wilds. I had a hundred or so kilometres to cover. I worked it out: "Leave as soon as possible; sleep at Pontivy, where I can pick up the rest of my things; tomorrow at Saint-Caradec; back here on Monday."

Bourgoin went on: "Ask Captain Deplante for a detailed report on the situation over there: manpower, liaisons, recovery of the Samwest parachutists, etc. Tell him I'm going to send him a group of paras from here and he will tell you the best itinerary for them; tell him to set up a rendezvous with a guide for me, say twenty or so kilometres from his camp. Then come straight back to Saint-Marcel."

Just as I left the house a van drew up outside, and out of it there emerged an odd little man and a pale and tired-looking young lad shabbily dressed in a threadbare, ill-fitting suit that was white with dust, like the van. Bourgoin grabbed him by the shoulder with a joyful cry: "Metz! Is that really you? I'm so pleased to see you! Come and tell us how you got away and what happened with Samwest."

Meanwhile the little man, who was the driver, parked the van against some bales of straw, bales of which not much remained, a little less each day, as everyone helped themselves to the straw on a daily basis for one use or another. The driver told one of the patriots that he was leaving that evening with the lieutenant, taking with them a cache of weapons for the Maquis to which they belonged, which had virtually none. This gave me an idea. "Could you give me a lift to the Pontivy road?" I asked him.

"Yes of course, as long as the lieutenant agrees."

He did. They would put my bicycle on the tarpaulin that was to cover the weapons. These they chose one by one, from the heap on the path. Not bazookas, even though there were so many of them, but machine guns, Colts and ammunition. Marie-Thérèse wished me luck: "See you on Monday!" She was sorry I wouldn't be there with her to witness the arrival of the jeeps, which had once again been announced for that night's parachute drop.

CHAPTER 4

Operation "Grog"

I had the Michelin map spread out on my lap and was looking for the roads that were most discreet; they were also the worst. As the van jolted along, I was flung now against the little man, Lieutenant Metz. "Where exactly are you heading for?" he asked. "We might be going in the same direction after the Pontivy road."

"No, because I want to get to Pontivy this evening so I can reach Captain Deplante in Saint-Caradec tomorrow."

"You're going to see Captain Deplante? Well, I am too. I just have to go back to Plélauff, in the Côtes-du-Nord, to drop off these weapons. Why don't we join forces and try to track him down together?" As soon as he'd said it I agreed. I would go with him to distant Plélauff: it would be late before we got there, after nightfall.

We emerged on to the main road at Pont-Hamon. The sudden roar of an engine. A car? A plane? Our driver slammed the van into reverse and put his foot down, and we found ourselves concealed in a sunken track. A couple of paces away from us, a German truck drove by. "No need for them to see us looking like this," muttered the little man. There was no denying it: all three of us looked a fright, white from head to foot. The state of my hair was particularly mortifying.

We'd been hurtling along at top speed through clouds of dust, and our driver's throat was dry. He took us into a roadside café for a glass of cider.

The owner sidled up to us, giving us a suspicious look. "Bless me! Wherever can you have sprung from, with all that dust! It's getting late now, soon be time for curfew." Silence.

"The things they're saying round these parts! Seems there's a whole lot of parachutists up on the moors somewhere round here. But you know how people talk! Some people are also supposed to have spotted a whole load of boats over Penmarch way. Other people are saying there's a British fleet cruising off Saint-Nazaire, and that's where there'll be another landing. Even the Germans don't know any more than what we do. Sometimes they stop off here for a drink: I was a prisoner during the 1914 war so I can understand a bit of what they're saying. They say you can't believe the wireless anymore." He went on and on and wouldn't leave us alone, and I could just see him asking Metz for his identity card. Did he have one? So I started prattling on about the weather, and the awful drought we'd been having, and the terrible famine that would doubtless follow. How people were saying that the peas had shrivelled in the pods in the fields and there'd be nothing to make any preserves this year. We had to drive the conversation on, rather than waiting for someone to put a hand on our shoulder and say: "Right my friends, off we go to the Kommandantur." That would be an idiotic way for such a promising adventure to end.

The café owner let us go on our way, eyeing us with deep suspicion as we left. The little man set off on the nearby road to Rohan, put his foot hard down and kept it there. There were German weapons and munitions stores at Le Gueltas, on the edge of Forêt de Branguily, but there was no way of avoiding this dangerous spot. The sentries didn't move a muscle as we sped past. Still going at a furious pace, we raced through vast forests and across wild moorlands. The little man knew the lie of the land here intimately and took paths that looked highly improbable. Bare hilltops, steep gullies and enormous boulders towering against a red sky like molten lava made for an apocalyptic landscape. This was the Pays des Korrigans, our little driver's home turf.

Metz spent this hair-raising journey telling me about the battle of Duault. He told me about his first combat, about having to leave Captain Botella behind in the forest, and about retreating with fury in their hearts. A fiery sunset enveloped us in its flames. As I watched them spreading over Metz's lean features I thought: "Are they all going to fall, one after another? What about Metz? How will he die?"[26]

We'd arrived in a farmyard, as far as I could tell, since it was now dark. A parachutist in uniform came running towards us: "Well, have you got the weapons, Lieutenant?" When he saw me getting out after Metz he looked stunned. He had a lot of decorations. "He's going to tell me he's come from Libya," I thought. And sure enough he did. Then he added:

"We'll give you something to eat, mademoiselle, and then find you somewhere to sleep."

Metz cut him short: "I'm taking mademoiselle to Plélauff. She will stay with someone in the town. We don't have anything suitable here."

So I went on for another few kilometres across the fields with the lieutenant, and we soon found ourselves sitting opposite each other at a table that the café owner had laid in a matter of seconds, despite the lateness of the hour. We were starving. The woman watched us as she cracked the eggs for an omelette, hesitated, nodded her head, and then cracked one more, and then another one, saying to herself: "Young people like that, they have to eat." She had laid a proper tablecloth and beautiful plates for us and had put an oil

---

26. He was killed in action in Indo-China in 1947.

lamp on the table, gleaming from a recent polishing: electricity was becoming increasingly patchy. We wouldn't have the BBC bulletin that night, but the good woman was thrilled to regale us with a hotchpotch of the latest news: General de Gaulle's visit to France and his triumphant welcome in Bayeux, the Russian breakthrough in Finland, the advance in Italy, the French capture of the island of Elba, and the latest diabolical weapon deployed by the Germans, a sort of pilotless aeroplane that dropped like a bomb and was causing terrible devastation in London. "There's no end to the things they'll invent, that lot," she concluded.

Metz and I were getting to know each other better, and the soft glow of the lamp and the elegance of the table carried us away from the war. I asked him how old he was: twenty-two, the same age as my brother Pierre, who could have been there in his place, who might have landed somewhere else in France: when would we know? Metz's family lived in Paris in the same district as my own. I learned how he had made it to England with his father and why he had chosen to join the parachutists. He had just graduated from the Ecole des Cadets.

"I really thought I wouldn't finish in time!" he said.

He confirmed with the woman that she really did have a room for me, and then left to go back to his hideout, dubbed Ker-Lapin. We arranged to meet back at the café at dawn to travel on to Saint-Caradec. The people at the café said they could lend him a bicycle.

• • •

Our guide, a young FTP from Duault, left us at the junction with the road to Ploërdut. "The Germans requisition bicycles there," the farm workers warned us along the way, "and they also ask for identity cards."

"Have you got one?" I asked Metz.

"Yes," he said, "but only one for FFL parachutists!"

"You'll have to have another one made," I said, "if you want to go on moving around as a common-or-garden civilian."

"That's exactly what I don't want to do. The sooner I can get back in uniform the happier I shall be, and I hope this time I'll be able to hang on to it!"

We skirted round the village and were relieved when soon we saw a milestone saying "Saint-Caradec". Deplante was around here somewhere, but where? All the tracks looked the same: there were little woods everywhere and our map wasn't detailed enough to plot coordinates to the nearest kilometre. There was nothing else for it, we'd have to ask. I scrutinized the faces we passed, trying to guess who might know. But after hazarding a few questions here and there we drew a blank. We studied the map again. Deplante had to be a little to the south, in that direction, and off we set on a new route. We passed close to a farm. I went in.

A woman was busy sweeping the yard.

"Madame, can you tell me where the patriots are? I have to find them without delay."

"Patriots? Dunno. None hereabouts."

I insisted.

"Like I told you, haven't seen none," and she carried on sweeping outside her door, all the while throwing me furtive glances. I had the impression that she knew something, all the same.

I waited a little, then I risked it: "Madame, this is very serious, I have a parachutist with me." Would she betray us?

The woman abruptly looked up: "That's not true."

"You may not believe me," I replied, "but he has his papers." Then she called her husband, who stuck his head out of the window. He scrutinised me grimly while his wife explained what was going on, but consented to come down. I could make out Metz's silhouette outside the gate, where he was following our exchange with a certain amount of anxiety, not understanding everything because of the thick local accent.

I called him eventually, and he propped his bicycle against the fence and came over. He produced his papers. This time they believed us. Their tone changed: "OK," said the farmer, "I'll take you to the village." He didn't deign to elaborate, but we knew we were on the right track.

He took us to a café where he said a few words in a low voice to some men who were having a drink. They made us wait while they whispered among themselves and looked at us, and then two leaders of the Liberation movement arrived. They knew where the base camp was and would take us there.

When we got there I kept in the background, but Metz beckoned me over and introduced me to Captain Deplante. "Marie-Claire has come from Saint-Marcel, I can vouch for her. We travelled down together. She has been sent by Commandant Bourgoin, moreover."

"Very good," said Deplante, and he shook my hand. He was a broad, well-built man with smiling eyes. "Very different from Marienne," I thought. He talked very fast and never stayed still. He had the infectious self-confidence of those who are lucky and know their luck will last.

The command post adopted as the new base was that of the 5th FFI, commanded by a schoolmaster assisted by two elderly captains and an inexperienced lieutenant, but all of them very willing. This general staff, with the parachutists and Deplante himself, gathered around the table in the farmhouse at Kerusten. I was at one end, next to Lieutenant de Carville,[27] a very young man with perfect manners who said very little. In any case, Deplante dominated the whole

27. Gérard Gaultier de Carville was wounded at Rosporden, near Concarneau on 6 August 1944 and died the same day at Quimper hospital. He was twenty-one. On 28 July he had escaped the terrible tragedy at Rosgrand, near our family home of La Villeneuve, when the Germans killed André de Neuville, one of the FFI leaders in the region, and captured General de Torquat de la Coulerie, who with twenty young *résistants* was shot at Kerfany on 30 July.

proceedings with his strong personality. He laughed expansively, and his gestures and words expressed an intense vitality.

After we'd eaten, he took me some distance away from the farm so that I could tell him about my mission. We stopped near the radio transmission post, where a Tarzan-like figure in his underpants, with a shock of wild dark hair, was furiously cranking a starting handle while his companion transmitted a message, tapping away at top speed. The two men had constructed themselves a shelter out of ferns in a corner of a field formed by two embankments, and had installed the aerial above them. The Tarzan character was talking, groaning and swearing in a strong Parisian accent that Deplante clearly found hugely amusing: "You see here in front of you his lordship Bailly," he said, "his gift of the gab will cure any low spirits!"

He stretched out on the grass, first on his side, then on his stomach, then a different position again, but failed to find one that suited him. I'd told him as we walked what Bourgoin wanted to know and he summarized it on a piece of paper: FFI numbers; FTP numbers (best kept separate); parachute drops; rescued Samwest parachutists; sabotage operations carried out since his arrival; German troop formations in the area. I learned in detail about his eventful journey from Saint-Marcel to Saint-Caradec. The first chosen spot had turned out to be unsafe, so he'd decided to make his base where we were now. Nevertheless, he'd been informed of troop movements in the area and artillery had arrived in the town. They should move, but would stay long enough to receive sufficient weapons to supply the needs of the local FFI and FTP. He noted down the main points of his report: I would memorize the rest.

Finally, having had enough of lying on the grass, Deplante took me back to the farm, first giving the radio operators a new message to transmit regarding the next day's parachute drop. All that was left was the question of the Saint-Marcel parachutists proposed by Commandant Bourgoin. Deplante spread out his map in a grassy meadow: a British parachutists' map with its beautiful greens and blues and its surprising of what I felt were often not the most important farms and villages. This time he wanted to sit on something. We tried a rock, which wobbled, but a tree trunk proved the perfect spot. We carefully traced the safest routes for the four or five parachutists who would come, preferably at night. Crossing the canal would be risky, but Deplante would find good guides who would wait for the parachutists for four successive evenings near the mill at Bieuzy-les-Eaux: he showed me the spot on the map. Then I took the little scrap of paper on which he'd written his pencil notes, rolled it up like a cigarette and put it in my turban. I'd decided to wear one all the time: it was the only headgear that made me look half-decent on a bicycle, and it was perennially fashionable. All I had to do now was set off for Pontivy.

I sped along, feeling elated: I loved the unfolding, golden warmth of June. I sang to myself, saying over and over: "Well my girl, are you happy now? Parachutists' liaison agent, will that do for you? Could you think of anything better? Hamon was right. Look where that meeting in Rue d'Assas has brought you."

Who knows? Perhaps I would finally find Francis at the Bruhats' house. But there was just Michel, struggling to herd his boys together to leave for Saint-Marcel. Once again, he suggested that the shopkeeper who had brought me to Saint-Servant should give me a lift, only this time he would drop me in Vannes. That suited me perfectly, as the weather had broken: it was raining.

CHAPTER 5

Where are They?

Rain lashed against the windows all night, and by the following morning a violent storm was unleashing its full fury.

As before, my shopkeeper gave me a lift; a strong, capable type, he was a man of few words who treated me like a child. He kindly bought me a hearty lunch in Vannes before he drove off. I strapped my bag on and tied my handkerchief over the sodden bicycle seat so as not to stain my skirt and raincoat too much. I had forty kilometres to go, taking the Elven road. The wind was pitiless, bending the tops of the trees and smacking me sideways. Leaving Vannes, the climb was endless.

"Why do things have to be so hard? Why, why, why?" I kept asking myself.

"Hold fast, resist, keep on going," my father would have said if he'd been with me. It's all a matter of willpower, he'd assured us forever. It was a good moment too to call to mind my outdated philosophy book that had been my bible when I was about fifteen. I knew the chapter on free will by heart. At that time I'd jump out of bed when the alarm went off to do my exercises. There were better things to do now. I was spurred on by pleasing images of my imminent arrival at the camp:

I would go into the welcoming kitchen and Madame Pondard would bring me a bowl of piping hot soup. Afterwards, I would slumber on amid the silk parachutes for twelve uninterrupted hours.

I passed the Tours d'Elven, lashed by the rain, and cycled through the deserted town. The rain was trickling up my sleeves, down my neck, everywhere. My bicycle was squeaking, my bag was leaking and my things were getting soaked. The never-ending sunshine had made us long for rain, but perhaps not in such quantities. Behind the roaring and whistling of the wind, I imagined I could hear the crash and din of the Allied army as it hurled itself at the coast of Normandy: the splendid man-made harbours at Arromanches and Saint-Laurent smashed to pieces; the boats smashed against each other, and the Germans having a field day firing from their indestructible bunkers. And it was true. Fate hung in the balance. England was cut off from the bridgehead. The Omaha Beach harbour, which had finally been abandoned, had yielded enough debris to fill the large breaches in the harbour at Arromanches, but it still meant there was one harbour less at which to land the waiting divisions and the thousands and thousands of tons of equipment. Quiberon had a good bay and a harbour. I couldn't stop thinking about the new landing that had been announced. Wouldn't this weather put everything in jeopardy?

The weather, always the weather: the wind was against us, as it had been against the Veneti: I knew the story of this Gallic tribe well, and their situation seemed strangely similar to ours: they were defending their land, their property and, most precious of all, their independence against that mighty army that was marching inexorably up from the south, with at its head a very great general: Julius Caesar. But Caesar was very different from our Corporal Hitler, with his hysterical speeches. His fate too was hanging in the balance, in those distant grey vistas that I was looking out over at last, outside the entrance to the Gulf. Caesar had sat down on the tumulus at Thumiac, not far from Suscinio, from which he could follow the battle between the two fleets, the Veneti with their large, powerful ships, and his general, Brutus, with light galleys with oars, built in haste at the mouth of the River Loire. On that magnificent August morning, a stiff north-easterly gave the advantage to the manoeuvrable, high-sided vessels of the Veneti, but in the middle of the day the wind dropped. Caesar felt his luck returning. With scythes that he had fixed to the ends of long boathooks, Brutus slashed all the shrouds securing the Veneti masts, and cut the rigging and the great leather sails, now hanging loose and limp. The sea became as smooth as glass and the Veneti began to die. Too much wind or not enough. Whatever the weather, Bretons have fought, resisting against the Franks and putting Charles the Bald to flight on the banks of the Vilaine River. Winning or losing, like the royalist émigrés who landed at Quiberon and were shot. Pray heaven that the parachutists' mission would not end like that! The royalist "Whites" had landed on 27 June 1795, the same month as the landing, and perhaps the same day. My imagination, running as wild as the storm, went from Caesar to the tough Breton chiefs, from the young royalists full of illusions to the strange army I was now serving. I fancied I could hear their calls and shouts in the trees twisted by the wind that bent towards me.

I was nearing Sérent. Not before time: at night the sentries concealed in the bushes would fire on me, for I didn't know the password and would have to talk my way out. I heard a few gunshots. Was there going to be fighting?

Gunfire meant that the Germans were not far away. I thought up a plausible story for them: I was going to see my sister, a refugee at Ploërmel. When I got to the turning for Bovrel, I asked at the corner café. And I was told:

"There was a battle yesterday. There were huge numbers of Germans. The French left during the night: we heard lorries. That's all we know: we were so frightened. What a tragedy! To think, mademoiselle! They say there were so many young lads around Saint-

Marcel! Where are they now?" But I couldn't bring myself to believe this terrified woman. Come now! I'd left the camp on Saturday, and everything had been so quiet. She had to be wrong: it was just a skirmish. She was exaggerating. She'd been too frightened. I'd go and see for myself.

I took my bicycle and started walking along with three women wearing black hooded capes like widows. They looked weary and sad and hardly spoke.

"We're going to that farm you can see over there," they told me. "Don't go any further, it will be the worse for you." But I still couldn't see any Germans, and I wanted to be absolutely sure. "Well, try as far as Trévero," murmured the grim-looking trio. As I had now left the Ploërmel road, I would tell the Germans I was a refugee, that I had just come from Paris and didn't know anything.

I was on my own. Gunshots. Bursts of machine-gun fire. They were getting closer, but there was still nobody in sight. I carried on along the narrow muddy road to Saint-Marcel. I was frightened, terribly frightened. Would the Germans believe me if they came? What if they searched me? I had Deplante's report in my turban. It must be very wet by now; thank goodness it was written in pencil. I would only destroy it as a last resort – not yet.

I was alone and out in the open, visible from all sides; I would be shot, it was idiotic. I had passed a sunken path on my left, full of brambles and boulders, where the water pouring down the banks had made a stream; I dragged my bicycle down into it and stopped, my heart pounding. It felt like something was moving above me, where the trees were like a ceiling overhead. No: it was the wind. Going back a little along the track, I came out onto a heath. The sky wept in anguish. The whole landscape was hostile, grim, terrifying. What was I to do? I went further up on to the low-lying heath that scratched my ankles: I had to find the parachutists. If the Germans were still firing, it meant that there were still some of our men left; I couldn't get this thought out of my head. But they wouldn't be up on high terrain like this, exposed to the four winds. I'd be better going further on along the road. Here I would be killed.

And suddenly I realized that all the risks that I'd taken over the past year hadn't been enough to instil a feeling of detachment: I was still attached to my skin, my good sound skin. I put my bicycle on the ground and I felt very alive, very intact.

But I could be damaged ... for good!

How long did I stand there, motionless, lost in my thoughts, with danger all around? I couldn't say. I was gripped by fear and thought that I would never really shake it off; that I would never again be at peace. It was a heavy price to pay.

The Trévero farm lay below the road in a dense quagmire, and only a fire in the vast fireplace shed light on an old man, a woman and a little girl, who stared into the flames in silence; and so did I, a stranger. But I had spoken with such sincerity that eventually they had to believe me, and the woman brought me some bread, butter and some fat bacon, took off my coat and draped it over a chair in front of the fire. Just like in the café, she told me about the noises they had heard. First the sound of the Germans arriving in ever-increasing numbers. Then the battle: artillery fire that shook the farmhouse walls; then around midnight a tremendous explosion that had plunged them into the depths of terror. They thought everything over towards La Nouette must have been blown up. Opening the shutters a crack, they had seen patriots and parachutists go past, some on foot, some on bicycles, many of them wounded. Ambulances and lorries had driven off towards the west. Some of the boys had said: "It's in flames over there, Saint-Marcel, La Nouette and the chateau of Sainte-Geneviève."

"But the night was so dark you couldn't see a thing and the rain soon put out the fires. There must still be some men hiding nearby:

the Germans thought they could see them everywhere and were firing randomly into the undergrowth."

The old man shook his head, saying over and over again: "So terrible, so terrible!"

What about Clairefontaine, had they burned that down too? No. Right, I'd go there. I might find a straggler who could tell me what had happened, or the farmers themselves could. What about the message? Should I still keep it? I hadn't seen any Germans. I merely pushed it a bit deeper into one of the turban's folds.

"You say it's too dangerous to cycle on the road? Is there a way of getting there on foot, along the ditches?"

The little girl looked at me like a hunted animal as I went on:

"I could go there with her, carrying a milk can." More machine-gun fire ripped through the storm. What should I do? On my own I'd get lost. How many people had I had to convince already! I ought to know how to do it by now!

"You must understand, it's very serious, I have to find Commandant Bourgoin, the parachutists' commanding officer."

The old man got up and took his *pen-baz*,[28] and said in the local patois: "I'll go."

"Be careful, grandfather Vincent," said the woman. "The longer it goes on, the worse they'll get." She gave me an empty milk can, and I followed the old man, who walked with the long, regular strides of someone used to travelling on foot. He took paths that were invisible to me, through the ferns and skimming the banks. Bursts of gunfire came closer and closer, and strewn across paths and in ditches we could see machine-gun cartridge clips, a motorcycle with its wheels in the air, the clear signs of a retreat. I was overwhelmed with the certainty of it. The Veneti had been beaten, the royalist émigrés had been beaten, had we been beaten too? No. My fear melted away; the spirit of all the Breton warriors stirred within me. I wished I had

---

28. Breton for a stout, knobbed stick.

164

a weapon and an enemy in front of me. But there was no one; the storm had abated, and between the shots the silence was devastating.

• • •

At Clairefontaine they welcomed us sadly, as if they'd had a bereavement. Two hours earlier, the Germans had come, had searched the house and found some parachutes.

"We told them there was nothing we could do about it, the parachutists were too strong. Then they left." At first they said there was nothing useful they could tell me. I was sitting on a bench, listening to old Vincent talking to them in Breton. We drank cider and then more cider: harsh and bitter, but I was determined not to leave without finding out something. And at last I heard that the last fifteen patriots and parachutists from the camp had passed by Clairefontaine that very morning and that they had spoken about Callac. Finally, finally, a name. The sky, still threatening rain, was darkening. I said to Vincent: "Quickly. Let's go."

They wanted to keep me at Trévero for the night, but now every lost second seemed disastrous to me. "Do you know what's happened to the Pondards?" I asked on the off-chance. They had been taken in by relations at Ville Guizio, a little further on. If only I had known earlier!

Madame Pondard and her daughters were exhausted with grief, but nevertheless ready to take action. They embraced me emotionally. "Could one of you come with me to Callac?" I asked. "You know the area." Anna detached herself from the group and said to her mother: "We can go to Gamber's place: he'll be able to put us up." It would soon be nightfall, Anna's bicycle had a flat tyre, we had to find another one; I was dying of impatience.

Gamber greeted us gloomily, as he had just buried his weapons in the garden. Did he at least know where the parachutists were hiding? "Hereabouts, in the woods and copses."

"Which woods? Which copses?"

"All right then, go and see at the chateau at Callac. They might still be there."

It was a grand chateau. The courtyard stretched like a very broad avenue up to the main building with its beautiful Renaissance façade. Dilapidated buildings flanked it to left and right. It was overgrown with grass and moss. Most of the windows were shuttered. Some of the shutters hung wretchedly from their hinges and clattered in the wind; roof slates littered the ground.

"Do you really think they're here?" I said to Anna. With a vague feeling of anxiety, we went towards the far end of the courtyard. I knocked on a little door: a parachutist opened it.

A bundle of firewood was burning in the vast fireplace of what must have been the kitchen. Patriots and parachutists whom I'd never seen before filled the room. They had put their weapons on the furniture and looked exhausted. I learned that Commandant Bourgoin had spent most of the day with them but had left a few hours earlier. Commandant Ollivier[29] would tell me where. Would this chase never end? One of the parachutists took us to the kitchen garden, on the other side of the courtyard. Two men were there, eating strawberries. At the sight of us they stood up, embarrassed, and one of them said: "We haven't had any in England, you know; and we've been dreaming about them for four years!" I didn't blame them! I thought back to Richard's cinema outing the day before his arrest and the need to relax. Commandant Ollivier embraced Anna Pondard, whom he knew well, having joined Saint-Marcel early with Tinchebray,[30] the head of the BOA,[31] and shook my hand. As I told him about my journey and Captain Deplante's camp, he assured me that he would tell me later where Commandant Bourgoin was.

---

29. Commandant Anatole (Alain) Willk, also known as "Olivier" or "Ollivier". He and Captain Cyr were near Nantes by 28 June 1944 immediately after the destruction and dispersal of the Saffré maquis.

30. Dominique Tinchebray, code name for Edouard Paysant, probably executed on 18 July 1944.

31. BOA: Bureau des Opérations Aériennes.

"He doesn't trust me," I thought.

"In the meantime," he said, "you will dine with us."

The Comte and Comtesse de Lignières received their guests in impeccable style. The menu was good: I remember the excellent leg of lamb to this day. Madame de Lignières was petite, dark and sporty-looking, and wore her straight jet-black hair tied back. She'd kept her beret on and wore it pulled right down over one ear, which gave her a very 1920s look. She was decisive in the way she took the lead over the meal, the conversation and everything else, while Monsieur de Lignières deferentially sought her opinion or approval. I was disappointed that not one of the parachutists I'd known at La Nouette was there. Anna had told me a few details about Sunday's events, but our chaotic, headlong journey had made it impossible for her to give me a very coherent account.

Feeling too intimidated to join in the conversation, I looked around at the antique furniture in the dining room and the beautiful silver on the damask tablecloth, in contrast with the dilapidated state of the walls. Monsieur de Lignières noticed my curious glances and said: "You must come back and see the Renaissance part of the chateau, the most beautiful part. You can see the Napoleon window there."

"Napoleon?"

"Yes. He came here two summers in succession, for the September holidays, to visit the Comte de Marbeuf, then owner of the chateau, who was governor of Corsica for several years. There he had been a close intimate of the Bonapartes, and especially Laetitia. For a long time Napoleon wondered if Marbeuf might be his real father. That would have made him half Breton. Everyone in these parts believes it. And for this twelve-year-old boy, the count had a window punched through the thickness of his bedroom wall in order to let in more sun. Astonishing, don't you think? You know, mademoiselle, the region must have made an impression on Napoleon, and he lauded Brittany for producing a race of soldiers and sailors."

Napoleon, the young schoolboy from Brienne, spending his holidays on these wild moorlands, what an extraordinary story! And the story of Callac didn't end there, as I also found out that this was the rendezvous that had been given to the parachutists before the camp was evacuated. A good part of the records of Saint-Marcel had been buried under the flagstones of the chateau stables. Soon the Germans would come, and its story would turn to tragedy.

We had barely finished dinner before the parachutists gathered up their weapons to leave: a patriot had warned them that the enemy was quite close. Madame de Lignières wanted to take them to the Moulin de Callac on the River Claie. I still didn't know where Bourgoin was, and I went with them. As we crossed the kitchen garden I noticed there were a few strawberries left: "When will they be able to eat them again?" I asked myself. Some rustic steps made from slate flags led down to the orchard, surrounded by a high wall into which a rusty door was set. Madame de Lignières struggled to turn the key. On the other side was a wood of beech, oak and pine trees above a tangled undergrowth of brambles and ferns, which sloped steeply down to the valley bottom. It was raining even harder, nearly dark and almost curfew time. Anna Pondard left us, as she was determined to sleep at the Gambers' house.

"Come with me" she said; but I was resolved not to leave Commandant Ollivier's side until I had some definite information.

"I'm sure I'll find a bed or some straw in this great chateau," I told her. "Don't worry about me. I'll see you tomorrow morning."

They all halted to say goodbye to Anna: Commandant Ollivier, and Captain Cyr, wearing his round glasses, "as things aren't kicking off", and five or six others. One group had already gone further down into the woods. When Anna had gone, Ollivier said:

"Show me the message, and I'll see if I can tell you where Commandant Bourgoin is."

I couldn't find it, so I had to take my turban off. My poor wounded vanity ... The scrap of paper was in such a state that the Commandant could barely read it. Folding it up again, he looked at me:

"It's true, you have to see Commandant Bourgoin. He is on the moors at Meslan. That's all I can tell you." Madame de Lignières knew the area well and said she thought I should look around Lizio.

She urged the parachutists to follow her, as she feared the Germans might arrive at any moment. Then the American gave me a handshake that rattled every bone in my body. His little cap, battered and waterlogged, was in a sorry state, but he still had style, with his head held high and his handsome gold-rimmed glasses. Ollivier had brought several machine guns, which were proving an encumbrance for a march through the woods. He kept one and put the others in my arms, saying: "Hide them if you have time and try to remember the spot." Then he bade me a warm farewell and ran to catch up with Madame de Lignières and the American, already some distance away. That left just me in the dark woods. The sounds of the undergrowth crackling underfoot had faded away, and now all I could hear was the rain. I had three submachine guns and cartridge-clips, and they were very heavy. I hid them carefully under the brambles and ferns, put some stones on top and noted a few distinguishing features. I wondered what would become of these men. What would they do? How would they continue the struggle? What sitting ducks for the Germans!

I didn't know that it would be a Frenchman who would be chosen to lead the hunt: Maurice Zeller. A Frenchman who had become their creature. He had earned his spurs in Finistère, where he arrested Abbé Cariou, who had been in charge of departures for England from Douarnenez, and the head teacher of the Le Likès lycée in Quimper, among others. But then he was called to the Morbihan and sent to Pontivy, where he was to become one of the most active members of the *Front Aufklärungstruppen* (FAT), which would decimate the Resistance. Who would he ensnare?[32]

It would be my brave Bruhats, the mother and father, Jacques having managed by some miracle to escape by jumping over the garden hedge. Zeller didn't catch Michel, but he ransacked his house. He didn't need to worry about Michel's brother Jo, because he had already been arrested on his way to Saint-Marcel. They hadn't succeeded in arresting the parachutists and the patriots all together in their camp. They would catch them one by one.

I was lost in thought, and I didn't know if it was the rain that was pouring down my cheeks, or tears.

· · ·

As I knocked again at the little door in the courtyard, I was hoping that Monsieur de Lignières would be able to put me up, but this time it was firmly shut. I headed for the feeble light of an oil lamp winking in the window of a lodge building at the entrance. Through the window I could see men and women sitting at a table, who turned when I knocked. A man got up to open the door. It was the chateau farmer, who lived there with his wife, their large brood of children and one or two farmhands. There was just a single whitewashed room with a beaten earth floor, its walls lined with box beds. They had made a big fire to dry their sodden clothes. The usual custom, once the stew was cooked, was to keep just a few glowing embers under the ashes to rekindle the fire first thing in the morning.

If they wouldn't let me sleep in the barn, I would sleep in the woods. I didn't even care about the rain anymore, all I wanted was to sleep. They put their heads together. Finally the farmer's wife, a comely young blonde woman, made the decision: "She can sleep in

---

32. Forced by the Allied advance to leave Pontivy on 3 August 1944, Zeller fled to Germany. Arrested in May 1945, he was put on trial and executed on 17 July 1946.

my bed." So, after putting my skirt, jumper, socks and shoes in front of the fire, I lost no time in nipping smartly between the coarse sheets in my underwear. Everything here was a family affair. The children shared the box beds, while the farmhands slept up above. A few hens, perched on the cornices, were already asleep.

Then Monsieur de Lignières turned up too, uneasy in the solitude of his too-large chateau, even though he occupied only one part of it, most of it being given over to the wife of a Forces Françaises Libres man, who had remained there with her three children. The kindly farmer's wife made him up a makeshift bed on the sofa in front of the fire, near our bed, then came back to bed with me. She spent a long time talking to me soothingly, and I was half-asleep when I heard her comparing me to Joan of Arc. What a joke! But, I thought, no one could possibly ask for anything more precious than the goodness of that heart of hers, more precious than the fine intelligence so worshipped by men, so wondrous and often so cold.

As I drifted off to sleep in that farmhouse bed, I kept saying to myself: "Without goodness, without human fellowship, intelligence isn't worth a bean, not one brass farthing, nothing." I slept a long sleep in those rough, clean sheets, dreaming of peaceful holidays and sunshine. A small boy was eating blackberries in the bushes: his name was Napoleon and his accent was not from these parts.

CHAPTER 6

After the Battle

He was asleep. His large form was stretched out on a messy bed. You could barely move a step in the room without banging into a crate or a pile of boxes. Some rudimentary straw mattresses had been piled up against the walls, and old newspapers and crumpled-up papers littered the floor. "He must be wounded," I thought. "At any rate he's not dead, and his old parents will be happy." I'd recognised the young man from Josselin. He moved, and still half-asleep murmured: "Drennec, at your service." Then he opened his eyes, propped himself up one elbow and looked at me, bewildered.

"Has Commandant Bourgoin left already? They told me I'd find him here," I said. "I've been looking for him for a long time."

"Yes, he's not at this mill anymore, but he hasn't gone far; he's at a farm further up the way."

He had recognised me and spoke with confidence. "We're going up there at about eleven o'clock; you can come with us. You'll have to wait a bit." Resigned, I sat down on a crate and asked Drennec exactly what had happened at Saint-Marcel. He opened some British tinned meat and set about spreading it on a piece of bread before beginning his story.

"Have one with me. All those kilometres make you hungry," he added. The bowl of milk I'd had at Callac at dawn already seemed a long time ago, but the sun had come out again, which had perked me up.

"On the Saturday, as you'll remember, everything was still going well. Captain Villars' company was part of the Caro battalion, with a thousand men, and we were covering the north and west of the camp. General de la Morlais' battalion was in the north-east with five-hundred men. Those were the two battalions that had been brought in from the very beginning to defend the CP. The Le Garrec battalion had only arrived on the 14th and would already have gone off again to the coast with its thousand men if it had been able to muster enough weapons. It was guarding the south and the south-west. The parachutists were between the Le Garrec and La Morlais battalions, at least two hundred of them, with more supervising the men elsewhere."

"What about the jeeps? Did they finally arrive on the night of the 17th?"

"Yes, we got four, with six parachutes each. I was at the drop zone. But the containers of the Vickers machine guns that should have been mounted on them got smashed when they hit the ground. Le Gall, the gunsmith, worked through the night to make the only salvageable one useable again and to fit out a second jeep with an automatic rifle, but nothing else could compare with a Vickers. I saw one in action afterwards. Thirty-two planes came, and dropped over six hundred containers. When we added it all up we worked out that over a hundred and fifty planes had done drops at La Baleine since 6 June. Quite a record, although now we wonder if it was such a good thing. The German observation post at La Grée in Plumelec had evidently spotted those planes, and on those last evenings we could see the powerful searchlights at Meucon.

"Anyway, that night an aircraft was duped by false signals sent by the Germans and confused by the lights of the railway station at Roc-Saint-André, where a convoy had halted. It dropped its containers on top of it – no weapons, but they say there were parachutists. Poor chaps. I wonder what happened to them. So that last parachute drop at Le Pinieux turned into a pretty good fireworks display.

"The camp would have had a few more days of peace if two Traction Avants full of German military police hadn't managed to get lost on the road to Saint-Marcel at the Hameau de l'Abbaye, near Bohal and the Hardys-Béhélec manor. We had a small guard post there, and that's where Captain Marienne was. A shell pulverised one of the cars and its occupants. The Germans in the other one abandoned it and ran. We caught three of them, but lost the fourth. Of course the Germans would have guessed something was up when their men didn't come back, but we'd have had more time if it hadn't been for the one that got away. He didn't take long to sound the alarm at Malestroit.

"If I'd stayed with the Villars' company I couldn't have told you much, but I was liaising between the battalions and the paras. I'd had a superb submachine gun for three days. You remember how we wanted to fight: we'd put up with it all and kept quiet for too long!"

I interrupted him: "Did many of our boys die in the fighting? How many do you think are left?"[33]

"We won't know exactly for a while; not too many, except I fear for the wounded who we had to hide all over the place. And I fear too for the ones who weren't wounded, as the Germans will move heaven and earth to get us now: because we killed a lot of them, hundreds, I'm pretty sure."

"Worse than at Duault. What happened next?"

He went on:

---

33. About 30 French combatants were killed, including 6 parachutists; 60 were wounded and 15 taken prisoner. Between 200 and 500 Germans were killed.

"We were on alert and we were prepared. I met men asking how to use a sub-machine gun or even a Colt! Abbé Guyodo said Mass that Sunday, peacefully under a dome of parachutes. The Germans arrived soon afterwards, at the same spot where they'd attacked at dawn. The Le Garrec battalion was alerted as soon as they arrived at Saint-Marcel, and this time there were two companies. I was at the Bois-Joly farm when they started firing on the FFI post from a hundred metres. The five boys there were killed on the spot, along with the little girl who was watching the cows in the neighbouring field. Then all our positions took aim at the Germans who were advancing under the coverts. You should have seen it! They flung themselves down in the wheat fields. They were advancing steadily, making furrows through the expanses of golden wheat: all that greenery on the march through our wheat! You could pick them off, one by one. They didn't give in. They've got guts, there's no two ways about it. By throwing smoke grenades they managed to reach the farm at Le Bois-Joly. They must have thought the CP was in the chateau of Sainte-Geneviève next door. Madame Bouvard was in the garden with her children, ready to attend to the wounded. A first-aid post had been set up in the chateau itself.

"What about Löic? What was he doing?"

"Captain Puech-Samson, Commandant Bourgoin's chief of staff, had made him a liaison agent. He had his rifle and went everywhere, along with his little thirteen-year-old brother.

"We fought furiously, but the Krauts took the Bois-Joly farm and got as far as the Sainte-Geneviève pastures. Reinforcements came up to double their numbers and they also had mortars that pounded the edge of the woods hard. But we still recaptured the farm. Soon the chateau was full of the wounded, who were given first aid and then ferried by jeep along the sunken lanes to La Nouette.

"Commandant Bourgoin and Commandant Morice had asked London for orders, as they were pretty sure the enemy wouldn't stop at small local skirmishes. Was the landing they talked about still going to happen? If so, when? That was what we needed to know. By midday, the Germans had suffered a lot of casualties but hadn't fallen back, hunkering down where they were instead. I went back to the CP at La Nouette. You remember the radio operators' position? They were listening to the BBC. It was 18 June, and they were broadcasting General de Gaulle's *Appel*, his speech from 1940: 'Whatever may happen, the flame of the Resistance must not be extinguished, and will not be extinguished,' and, 'Many French patriots will never accept capitulation and bondage.'

"That was what we were fighting for so furiously! And they talked about our military college in England, the Ecole des Cadets, as they call it. The last cadets to pass out had paraded in front of our own FFI chief, General Koenig: the year of Bir-Hakeim. Bir-Hakeim, Saint-Marcel, you could see the parallels.

"At the farm the women were leaving on the commandants' orders, but very reluctantly. They'd spent all morning caring for the wounded or going on liaison missions within the camp, and they wanted to stay to the end. One of them had always refused to leave the battalion. Captain Guimard installed Madame Salles in Monsieur Pondard's farm cart, and Madame Pondard with her daughters and other women followed along behind, each carrying a small bundle. We were all optimistic still and we called out: 'Don't worry! You'll be back tomorrow!' It's fair to say the Pondards have lost everything, because what there was in those little bundles amounted to nothing. The west was free, and a lot of other paths were too. I saw Jeanne and Marie-Thérèse heading across the fields, and Andrée and Suzanne – the girls you know."

"I haven't told you about Captain Marienne's four jeeps, but they were everywhere. I saw one of them coming out of the road to the abbey and into the full sunlight of the courtyard. Standing up in it was Marienne, a bloodstained strip of white parachute silk tied round his head. Everyone called him 'The Lion'."

Drennec was silent for a moment, as if he could see him again. I was sorry not to have witnessed this burning passion, not to have seen those men giving their all.

I'd been aware for some time of a couple of openwork crates full of baby rabbits. When I arrived they'd hidden at the back of their cages, but now they were watching us, pushing their noses up against the slats and wriggling them. We wondered how they came to be in this abandoned old mill, and who fed them.

"It would be better to let them go," I said. "They'll have a chance of surviving on the heath, but they'll starve to death in these cages." We prised the planks apart and sat down on the crates again. One by one they came out. We crumbled some bread and they nibbled it around us. I put one of them on my lap. It had long, fine fur, soft to stroke.

Drennec carried on: "Heavy German reinforcements arrived. Yesterday at Callac they told us they came from as far away as La Baule and the Coëtquidan camp, with armoured cars and artillery convoys. People had seen all that rolling past and were terribly worried for us. At two o'clock they attacked hard along a two-and-a-half-kilometre front. Germans and Russians. There are quite a lot Russians round here. From Georgia, apparently, but I don't know much about all those countries out East. They broke through as far as the chateau of Sainte-Geneviève. The parachutist Sergeant Navaille, who was on the roof and had been wounded twice, defended it as best he could with his Bren gun, holding the avenue with his fire. But some of the Germans managed to get into a big bedroom below him. He sent a grenade down the chimney, and the chateau held out until the evening. But in other places we'd started to fall back, and deep down we were scared, because we didn't know how it was all going to end.

"We'd called for help from the RAF, and they arrived at about four o'clock. Four fighter-bombers dive-bombed the German lines that were converging on the camp, attacking us with cannon and rocket fire. But by the end of the afternoon, the Germans were in the thickets and coverts of Sainte-Geneviève, we were fighting largely with grenades and the woods were ablaze. At about five o'clock, we had to abandon Le Bois-Joly and withdraw again, although the Le Garrec battalion held well. Those men from the coast, around Vannes and Auray, are a tough breed: all their lives they've battled with the sea. The Caro battalion was champing at the bit because it still hadn't seen the enemy in its sector. We were beginning to think that we would have to leave by night, and this is what the chief of staff decided when he received confirmation from London that the landing had been cancelled for the time being. But if we wanted to take as much equipment as possible, and blow up what we left behind, the camp had to be relieved, so at around seven we mounted a counterattack, which was successful.

Things could have turned nasty when fresh troops arrived from Coëtquidan. They were using incendiary bullets. We were being told about new troops coming from all sides, but not from the west, luckily for us, and the general staff made sure the withdrawal was well organised. Our orders from London were clear: spread out as widely as possible and carry on the guerrilla campaign. It had clouded over and was starting to rain; we were going to have a moonless night. There was still a hope that we might get away without too much damage, as long as the Germans didn't completely encircle us. That was what we were really afraid of. And more and more so, as darkness fell."

The baby rabbit had curled up into a ball on my lap. Was it afraid of the dark? It can feel so menacing – and how terribly menacing it must have felt on Sunday night at Saint-Marcel. For the many wounded and the unwounded alike.

"Some local men had agreed to take the lightly wounded to safe hideouts around Trédion, and the more seriously wounded to the clinic run by Augustinian nuns in Malestroit. We put them in a gas-powered lorry that was broken down but could be towed by a jeep, and covered them with sacks of flour. At about eleven we began to withdraw towards Sérent. Some of the troops continued to engage the Germans, crack SS troops, and every battalion mounted a rearguard. The leaders had got their orders and the rendezvous was at Callac. Captain Marienne personally made sure everyone got their orders and I didn't stop running. The chief of staff had left too, and the BOA leaders, Tinchebraye and Commandant Ollivier. I stayed with Captain Marienne until the end. At about half past eleven an aircraft circled over the camp, the one that was due to drop ammunition for us. The radio operators hadn't been able to send the message to cancel it. SS troops had already infiltrated close to La Nouette by seven o'clock, so it was a miracle that they managed to get away.

"The rain was bucketing down. The Germans seemed very close and there were only a few of us left. I'm no more chicken than the next man, but I didn't particularly enjoy that night. The lorries had gone, the light vehicles too, and we'd taken what arms and ammunition we could manage. Some provisions too." Drennec cut himself another chunk of bread.

"But there were still enough weapons on the path to arm hundreds of men – thousands, as many as five thousand they said. Loads of bazookas. Captain Puech-Samson, the tall, very fair chap you must have seen at the CP, was to stay behind to blow everything up. He'd been shot in the thigh but didn't pay it any attention. We were still quite close, being guided away in the dark by Jégo, when he set off the firework display at midnight. I thought my eardrums were going to burst. I wept to see the arms we'd wanted so much going up in smoke! So that's it. That's all I can tell you about Saint-Marcel. I made it to Callac at daybreak, and our orders were not to hang around there.

Commandant Bourgoin asked me to carry on with him. I didn't want to go back home."

Some other boys had appeared from an adjoining room and chimed in: "No, we don't want to go home, and we can't anyway." One of them went on: "We can't go home, any more than the refugees from Lorient who were living here can go back to their town. I don't know where those poor people have gone. As for us, we've got our work cut out to regroup after being so scattered. I know the Le Garrec battalion has gone down to the moors at Lanvaux, above Vannes. We'll all have our own sector, apparently. So we'll need you more than ever now, mademoiselle! There are a few radio sets, but not many. It was all going so well, and now there are men out in the wilds being hunted down by the Germans. Such a mess! 'Go back home,' that's what the FFI said to us, 'and we'll get in touch with you later.' That's what a lot of them will do. What's the point in staying in the Maquis?" They'd sat down around me, looking drawn, miserable, unshaven. No more was said. It was eleven o'clock. I got up and asked Drennec to take me to Bourgoin.

• • •

He stood before me, large as life, unshaven too, his features etched with the experiences of a single day, like all those who had been at Saint-Marcel, including Émile Guimard and Morice, who stood on either side of him.

"Where have you sprung from?" they exclaimed.

"From the Grog base, via Clairefontaine and Callac…"

I extracted Deplante's message from my turban. It looked the worse for wear but Bourgoin managed to read it, and I supplemented it with more information.

"Sit down", he said. "I must look a sight. I'll have a shave, haven't been able to since Sunday morning. We've had a couple of rough days, not to mention the nights. When I'm done you can tell me what you've seen."

I sat down in the dark little room while, lathering his face liberally with soap, the commander started his transformation in front of a tiny mirror on the wall. Every now and then he stopped with his hand in mid-air to say, "There were so many of them," or, "If only they'd been quicker with the landings." Morice, sitting beside me, filled in the gaps: "We put up a good defence. We'd taken some prisoners, but we let them go; we believe in the rules of war. But will they consider parachutists as bona fide soldiers? London thought they would; we're less convinced. En masse they're brutes – and they're fanatical. We've just heard they've torched the village of Saint-Marcel and all the farms and manor houses round about. They've arrested large numbers of civilians in Plumelec, Sérent and other places. And they know all about torture.

"The retreat was well prepared, but many of the men got lost in the dark and we still haven't made contact with all the parachutists, far from it! We've got to stay in small groups of course: there's no alternative. The parachutists will be split up to finish training the twelve FFI battalions."

Bourgoin added: "If only the Allies were advancing more quickly in Normandy! But if they've had the same weather as us it can bring everything to a standstill. To think they dropped us a week's rations. Who knows how many weeks we'll have to stay here like sitting ducks?"

He had shaved half his face and the other half was still covered in soap when I heard someone running along the path. A boy appeared in the doorway, breathless and crimson in the face, and gasped: "The Germans are fifty metres away!" We all leapt to our feet, Morice, Guimard, who hadn't said a word, and me. Bourgoin quickly wiped his face with a towel and stuffed some things into his American kitbag

– razor, shaving brush, towel – and we set off in single file down the sunken lane where I had left my bicycle.

Emile Guimard came up beside me, saying: "I was right to be worried, and the parachutists will have a tough job escaping from the Germans, like us. What a business it will be to reorganise this mess!"

I picked up my bicycle and said to Bourgoin: "Commandant, what should I do now?"

"Well, go home."

"But surely you'll still need liaison agents, Commandant?"

"OK. You're right. Go back to Captain Deplante and tell him what's happened to us. Tell him to break up his camp too." Then they gave me a wave, and I watched the three men in civilian dress as they disappeared around the corner.

I was at a junction where the lane joined the main road again. A German bicycle patrol rode past, possibly the ones the boy had warned us about. Just my luck! And they stopped me. Thank heavens I didn't have the message anymore.

"Have you seen any terrorists, mademoiselle?"

My "no" was so categorical that they didn't persist, but added:

"Be very careful, many terrorists here!" They had just been slaughtering them in an orgy of killing, some of them in the most terrible way,[34] and they would carry on killing; but they smiled at me and they too gave me a wave.

As I headed once more for Pontivy, via Josselin, I thought about all the other girls who like me were criss-crossing the countryside that day in search of the lost men, and to whom German patrols would also be counselling caution!

---

34. Among them was the wounded Sergeant Navaille, who was killed in bed in the farm where he was being nursed.

Louis Krebs, my father.

Concarneau in 1944, still with its sailing tuna boats.

Jean-Marie West. Arrested in April 1944, he was deported and died in Stassfurt concentration camp on 16 March 1945.

My brother Arthur playing the piano at Kerancalvez.

At the helm of the *Marsouin*.

Maman, my sister
Suzanne ("Suche") and
my niece Claude.

Our last family walk.

Kerancalvez.

A French parachutist of the Special Air
Service during training in Britain.

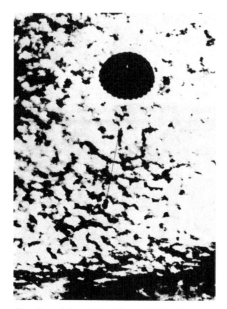

On the night of 5-6 June 1944, Geo parachuted into the forest of Duault.

Geo.

Left to right: Colonel Bourgoin, Captain Deplante, Second Lieutenant Gaston Autebi and Captain de Mauduit.

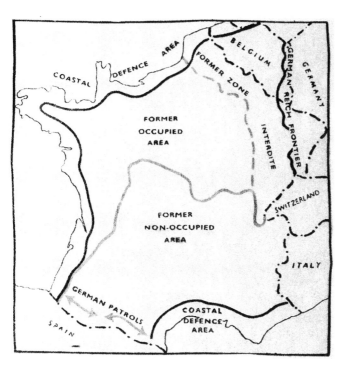

Detail of the map of France, printed on fine silk, that was part of the parachutists' escape kit.

Silk code chart used by the parachutists to encode messages they sent to England and decode the messages they received back.

The chateau of Callac, the parachutists' rendezvous after the battle of Saint-Marcel.

Captain Marienne.

Coët-Bigot farm, Captain Deplante's command post.

My message. Note how the messages alternate between French and English.

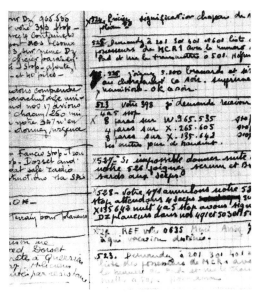

One of Captain Deplante's last messages before the Liberation.

The church bell tower at Quelven, from which the Germans searched for parachutists and the FFI.

Our guide Le Pen and his wife at Guern.

The killing of Captain Marienne and his fellow FFI parachutists by the Milice and the Germans.

Major Cary-Elwes and his batman Corporal Mills.

Colonel Bourgoin, Captain Guimard and the Mayor on the day of the Liberation of Vannes.

Men of the Breton FFI outside the town hall.

The Coët-Bigot parachute ...   ... and the wedding dress.

Our first departure for Concarneau, in the Mercedes, with the
parachutists Devize and Deves.

Lanriec church.

Le Treff farmhouse, where I learned
of my father's death.

My sister Françoise's studio.

The boat under construction …

… that was to be named the *Louis Krebs*.

General de Gaulle decorating the flag of the Free French SAS parachute regiment with the Order of the Liberation.

The parade on the Champs-Elysées.

François d'Humières ("Frédéric"),
one of the finest of the OCMJ
leaders, killed in action in Alsace in
January 1945.

In November 1944, the British Government invited 200
men and women of the FFI on a visit to Britain.

AVANT LE DÉPART, CES QUELQUES MOTS !

Puisque vous avez eu l'honneur d'être choisi parmi vos milliers de camarades pour participer à ce voyage, le premier organisé en territoire allié et ami depuis la libération, vous DEVEZ prendre conscience de l'importance d'une mission dont le retentissement à l'étranger va faire de chacun de vous, dès votre départ, un véritable ambassadeur de la Jeunesse combattante française.

Ce n'est pas un voyage touristique que vous entreprenez. Ce déplacement, vous le comprenez, se situe sur un plan beaucoup plus élevé et comporte, par son caractère même, des responsabilités auxquelles vous ne sauriez échapper.

N'oubliez jamais que vous représenterez, en Angleterre les F.F.I. et que c'est sur VOS PROPOS, sur VOTRE ALLURE, sur VOTRE TENUE que beaucoup d'Anglais ignorant des conditions réelles de notre lutte, jugeront de ce grand élan de volonté nationale qui, des maquis aux barricades, a remis la France à la hauteur de son destin et doit lui rendre demain sa place dans le monde.

N'oubliez pas non plus dans vos rapports avec nos alliés d'Outre-Manche, l'héroïsme dont a fait preuve le peuple anglais alors que, seul en 1940, il a tenu tête à l'ennemi commun et fait face à de terribles bombardements. Dites à nos Alliés toute votre gratitude pour la part glorieuse prise par les Armées Britanniques à la libération de la France.

Dites leur aussi que la volonté unanime de la France est de participer, chaque jour davantage, à la guerre et que, là encore, pour équiper nos troupes, leur donner des armes et assurer leur ravitaillement, nous avons besoin d'eux.

Pensez à nos milliers de tués, camarades déportés qui n'ont connu ni la gloire de la libération ni la joie de ce voyage et soyez digne de votre mission.

Ainsi, vous contribuerez à faire connaître, en Pays Alliés, la vaillante union de la Jeunesse Française et à rehausser encore aux yeux du monde le prestige des F.F.I, c'est à dire celui de la France.

Lt. Colonel CÉVENNES

PROGRAMME DU VOYAGE

13 Novembre Lundi A 9 h. très précises, rassemblement du groupe à la station de métro INVALIDES (extérieur).
A 9 h.30, le contingent sera passé en revue sur le terre-plein des Invalides.
A 10 h.15, départ en autobus pour le port d'embarquement - Déjeuner froid en route - Arrivée au port pour le dîner et le coucher.

14 Novembre Mardi Toute la journée, voyage à Londres - Dîner et coucher en Hôtel à Londres.

15 Novembre Mercredi Toute la journée, réceptions officielles et constatation des dévastations commises dans Londres par les bombardements de 1940 et par les V-1.

16 Novembre Jeudi Réception officielle des 8 Sections par les Municipalités de 8 grandes villes de Province.

17 Novembre Vendredi Dans la matinée, séjour libre à Londres.
Dans l'après-midi, départ de Londres pour le voyage de retour.
Dîner et coucher au port de débarquement français.

18 Novembre Samedi Voyage en autobus du port de débarquement à Paris - Déjeuner froid en route - Arrivée à Paris vers 16 h.

Noubliez pas de vous munir de vos cartes de pain et M. G. pour les repas qui seront pris en France, à l'aller comme au retour.

Au cours du voyage vous vous joindrez **obligatoirement à la Section N°** 5

Programme for the visit to Britain of 200 men and women of the FFI at the invitation of the British Government. "Cévennes" was the *nom de guerre* of Jean Pronteau. I was on this unforgettable trip.
See appendices for translation.

THE EARL OF SEFTON,

LORD MAYOR.

16th November, 1944

Aux membres des Forces Françaises Libres de l'Intérieur

Nous vous souhaitons la bienvenue à Liverpool: Nous sommes
très heureux que vous ayez pu venir visiter notre ville: des
paroles ne sauraient exprimer le profonde admiration que
nous éprouvons pour le rôle héroïque que vous avez joué dans
la libération de votre pays et pour la cause commune de la
liberté.   Nous espérons que vous emporterez un souvenir
agréable de votre court séjour dans notre ville.   Quant à
nous, nous nous souviendrons toujours de votre visite, et ce
souvenir contribuera à resserrer les liens d'amitié
indestructibles qui désormais uniront nos deux pays.

LORD MAYOR

Letter to the FFI delegation from Lord Sefton.
See appendices for translation.

Paris, le 25 Mars 1965
51bis, Bd de Latour-Maubourg

Madame,

     Vous voudrez bien m'excuser de ne vous
remercier qu'un peu tardivement du livre que vous
avez eu la gentillesse de coeur de me dédidacer et de
me faire tenir. J'ai voulu, en effet, au moins le
parcourir avant de vous en accuser réception.

     Vous dirai-je que, flatté tout d'abord de
constater que vous aviez pensé à moi, j'étais en même
temps un peu inquiet.. La veine de la littérature fémi-
nine n'est pas fort abondante dans la tradition française
et la Résistance a été si souvent trahie - mais par la
plume des siens ! Et je suis heureux de vous dire en
toute sincérité que je n'ai pas tardé de m'aviser que
mes craintes étaient vaines : votre livre, Madame, est
excellent.

     Excellent d'abord parce qu'il est écrit dans
une belle langue souple et vivante, exempte de toutes
mièvreries. Il est excellent surtout parce qu'en contre-
point, on sent battre un coeur, un coeur qui a su et
osé choisir. Or, j'aime les gens qui ont la Foi et qui
savent choisir.. Si la vie quotidienne est toute tissée
de petites lâchetés, de petits mensonges - quand ce ne
serait que pour ne pas chagriner qui nous entoure ! -
j'aime par contre, et je le redis, ceux qui ont la Foi
et savent la confesser. Vous êtes de ceux-là.

     En vous redisant toute ma gratitude et toutes
mes félicitations pour ce beau livre, je vous prie,
Madame, *de bien vouloir agréer l'hommage de
mon profond respect*

Madame M. CHAMMING'S
Editions France-Empire
68, rue Jean-Jacques Rousseau
Paris 1er

Letter to Marie Chamming's from General Koenig.
See appendices for translation.

Paris, le 30 Avril 1965

Madame,

Vous avez choisi de servir la France lorsque c'était particulièrement difficile et méritoire et de ce choix, de ce qu'il vous a conduit à faire, vous nous donnez un récit alerte et vivant qui est à la fois un témoignage et une leçon de courage.

Laissez-moi vous en féliciter et vous en remercier sincèrement. Sachez aussi qu'en lisant votre livre, j'ai eu une pensée pour la mémoire de Monsieur Louis Krebs, votre père, dont vous évoquez de façon émouvante l'action courageuse et le sacrifice.

Veuillez agréer, Madame, mes respectueux hommages.

C. de Gaulle

Madame CHAMMING'S

Letter to Marie Chamming's from General de Gaulle.
See appendices for translation.

CHAPTER 7

Deplante's Group

"Go home." He wouldn't have said that to Jeanne or the Pondard family. True, I wasn't a native of the region. Apart from Michel and his brother, of whom I still had no news, and the Bruhat family at Pontivy, I didn't know anybody there. What did it matter? I had written to my parents telling them that the choice I'd made still seemed to me to be the right one, and the disappearance of the camp at Saint-Marcel had only stiffened my resolve.

But Maman lived in a permanent state of anxiety. The Germans in Concarneau kept saying to anyone who would listen: "*The terrorists, alle kaputt!*" Reports of the battle must have reached them too. She was also anxious because after the second sabotage of the telephone lines and cables the Germans had imprisoned three hostages in the Maison Blanche, above the town, and my father had negotiated endlessly for their release, or at least for an improvement in their conditions. He was constantly going to see Otto, the German Kommandant – a man of a certain age who had not been completely dehumanised by the Nazi ideology and who had grown attached to the region. Well-disposed though he was, however, this did not prevent him from being zealous in carrying out orders from above. Eventually the three young people were released, nonetheless, in return for an agreement to mount a guard on the lines at night. Living conditions for the Maquis and for local people had deteriorated, but were no better or worse than in the rest of the *zone interdite*, the no-go area along the coast, which is to say that it was a daily struggle to find food, and there was a constant danger of falling victim to reprisals or a spasm of fury on the part of the occupiers.

I was still out of touch with the OCMJ, and any report I could give to Charles and Richard, if they were to come back one day, would be about my personal activities in support of the parachutists. Wasn't this what we had planned, to help the regular army? It was no longer a question of dealing with dozens of departments, as it had been with Charles and Richard, but with just two. Missions no longer had to be planned for months ahead, but for days. I was no longer part of an army that was disputed by many, constantly being decimated, and always having to replace good leaders with less good ones. Now I was supporting the French parachutists of General McLeod's brigade of the Special Air Service, a unit of the regular army in which everything was regular. In this I found a peace of mind that no one in the Resistance had known before the landings.

• • •

I found Deplante in the farmyard at Kerusten: "The base camp at Saint-Marcel has been destroyed," I told him. "I've just left Commandant Bourgoin. He asks you to disperse."

He gave me all his attention. The day before, he had received an alarming message about Dingson from London, but without any details; these I supplied. I had hardly finished speaking when he issued an order: "Meeting of officers and NCOs, now." The order went out, and they converged from all directions. Deplante went into a small room, a sort of outhouse on the same level as the farmyard.

He spread out one of his maps on a workbench. His finger moved precisely between the blue, green and red dots.

"What we had intended to do in the next few days, we will do immediately. The last of the Samwest group whom we've been expecting has arrived; last night's parachute drop brought us the additional arms we needed. After the business at Saint-Marcel, the German threat will become a reality: they could be here tomorrow. We shall split up. Each of you will take a sector, with the FFI and FTP, or 1500 men, as you know. We shall request parachute drops for each sector. There are eighty of us parachutists to divide between the four FFI and FTP battalions: five per company. You will leave immediately with the one that I assign to you. It is essential that the sectors of activity of each battalion should be perfectly defined and absolutely respected, and the zones of activity of the three companies within each battalion must be decided immediately. We need to be agile. We have to coordinate, but in small groups. Carville, you will go to Langonnet, here, and control the area from this river to this town. Golder, you will go to Glomel…" The litany of names continued. The men leaned over the map, forming a compact group in the half-light of the lean-to, at the foot of the ladder that led up to the loft. I had been pedalling furiously and now I leaned against the door frame, exhausted. Deplante carried on: "Metz, you will come with me, but we'll leave separately. I shall be, let's see, hang on … here at Ty-glaz, look, take down the coordinates. Go and get packed and leave as soon as you're ready." Then he added some details about the weapons to take, the precautions to follow, the contacts to make, the traces of their stay at Kerusten to expunge.

What was I to do in all this? A lot of parachutists came and went in the yard, and some spoke to me. Most of them had been at Saint-Marcel and wanted to know details about the battle. I didn't say much. Others were survivors from Samwest. One of them, leaning against the farm wall like me, was looking straight ahead, lost in thought.

He had just arrived, after a long series of night marches. He was slight and slender in his camouflage jacket, caught in at the waist with his broad canvas belt; his head was bare and he had a mop of thick black hair. At his feet he had placed his bag, helmet, and submachine gun. He was thinking of Madagascar, where he came from. We didn't exchange a word. And yet, it was Geo.

• • •

I felt unnecessary among all these men. It was best to maintain an attitude of reserve, like a young girl in a drawing room, or even to appear slightly aloof as a precautionary measure.

Out of place and infinitely alone.

Until then, I had been aided and supported while I was working out who I was – by my parents, Elisabeth, my friends, and then by Richard, Sylvie and the others. Now I had lost my supports, slipped from my moorings like a boat being launched: I was at sea, alone in a storm. We were all alone, scattered by the winds of war, and I was filled with a deep sense of loneliness. I decided to go and see Deplante:

"What should I do, monsieur," I asked. He looked deeply perplexed.

"Go home, mademoiselle."

"Are you really sure I can't be of some use to you?"

"Yes, of course you can. But it will not be a comfortable life. What will you do about sleeping arrangements?"

He looked at me as I stood before him, hesitant despite what I'd said and thinking of Charles in the Rue d'Assas: "Will you be free on D-Day?" So I would have to decide once again: home or the war, here. No permission to ask: I was truly free.

Standing in front of this man, I felt as though I had no past, no family, no home. I appeared to him and everyone around him exactly as I was, with my blue cotton skirt, scout leader's belt and big misshapen shoes, quiet, private, very short, a bit plump, neither pretty nor ugly, but with lovely eyes, so my mother used to say, always wanting to know everything and to understand everything, coming from who knew where and still without a future. They accepted me as I was, influenced by nothing other than my physical appearance, my actions and what I said, from that day on. This changed everything and demanded much more of me, since there could be no explanation or indulgence for what I was going to become. I could create any impression I wanted. I had a chance to be reborn, in fact, and the same was true for everyone in the Maquis, whether from Britain or from Brittany: we were all newly minted.

Our exchange went on:

"I'm used to putting up with no comforts: I've been camping and sailing."

"Of course if you really want to you can come with us. Since you're on your bike you can go ahead by road; we'll go on foot across the fields." He took out his map again and I got out my Michelin. "You see Ty-Glaz, here. We'll meet there tonight." Ty-Glaz: a name lost in a wilderness of moorland with a handful of little tracks that would all look the same …

• • •

At Ty-Glaz, when I got there after any number of wrong turnings, I found a grumpy farmer and no parachutists. Why was there a café in such a wild and lonely spot? But here it was, and nothing would be better than time to think in front of a glass of cider. I was about to open the door when I saw three boys arriving who looked shabby enough to be patriots. It didn't take them long to tell me about their adventures. The Germans had attacked their FTP group in force near Saint-Maudé. Their leader, Charles, had been wounded, might be dead. Since they knew that some parachutists had just arrived at a farm a little further on, they were going to join them. Mine, doubtless. I drank my glass of cider with them, feeling serene.

How could I ever forget Coët-Bigot? It was there that Geo and I exchanged our first words! A poor farm, all the same, remarkable only for its poverty. The main farmhouse and the barn stood to either side of a stony courtyard, approached along an avenue of handsome trees.

Night had fallen already, and Deplante immediately started worrying about my accommodation. We climbed a ladder into a loft above the barn, which was divided into three rooms. He took me to the far end of the third one, put some straw down in one corner, and then put the rubber cover of his sleeping bag on top. Some parachutists were also settling down in the other rooms. He asked the assembled company if anyone could spare a blanket for the new liaison agent, and I was soon spoilt for choice. When my bed was ready, he said: "Are you really sure you'll be able to sleep here, mademoiselle?" I assured him that it would be perfect. "Good. I'll soon have some work for you. Goodnight." And he left.

But the next day, since missions were slow to materialise, I had to make myself look busy. It was going to be imperative, I thought, to find things to do during my "off-duty" hours. Since it certainly looked as though we were embedded in a war that threatened to be long drawn out, and my fate was going to be linked with that of Deplante's group, I had better get to know its members: so I did a recce of the premises, and had a good look at those around me.

I was keen to see Metz again, the only one I knew well. He was shivering with a fever in the loft of a building set a little apart from the other two, from which there protruded the antenna of the radio operators, who were also there. Nothing could have been more ridiculous than going down with tonsillitis at a time like that, and the poor fellow, his neck swaddled in cotton wool, was champing at the bit. He barely recognised me. In the next room, I spotted the Saint-Caradec Tarzan, with another man whom I vaguely remembered meeting, but I didn't know where or when. He intrigued me. And then suddenly I saw myself leaning against the wall at Kerusten, beside him.

I watched the two men working. The unknown man was sending a message while Tarzan cranked the handle of the generator: "From Smith, stop, Pierre 5 has difficult situation well in hand here, stop, please do not send jeeps tonight, stop, a hitch at present, stop, send planes with maximum Brens, stens, carbines, Colts 45, grenades 36, Hawkins 75, gammons, stop, send camouflage clothing and boots but no food, stop, local Resistance very numerous and morale excellent, stop, possibility arms at once 2 FTP battalions total 200 also 1 FFI battalion, total 1100 stop, men young, keen and good." So read the message from Commandant Smith. When they stopped, I asked them to explain to me how their radio worked. The taller one, whom Tarzan called Geo, gave me a clear explanation. He had a slight English accent and I thought he was English. He said no, he was definitely French, and he came from Madagascar.

Madagascar … The island in the Indian Ocean had fascinated me since my childhood, along with Reunion and Mauritius, ever since my grandmother gave me a book called the *Journal de Marguerite* by Victorine Monniot. Coconut palms swaying in the breeze, with their clusters of enormous coconuts nestling among the leaves, banana trees with their brilliant green foliage, trees laden with golden grapefruits, rickshaws, witch doctors, canoes … I remembered feeling that victory was in the bag when the examiner for my baccalaureate oral exam said: "Tell me about Madagascar."

I asked a thousand questions. He told me about a duel between a cayman and a shark, about hunting wild boar in the dense forest in the east of the island, about the scents of cinnamon and cloves from Tamatave, where he had lived for a long time, about the heady fragrance of ylang ylang, and the incredible flavour of juicy lychees. A soft heap of bran had given us a comfortable seat. His shift, as he called it, was over, and we had time to ourselves. He told me that in fact he could only transmit at certain times, except in an emergency. He had been the head radio operator of Pierre 4. He would have liked to know what had happened to his Captain, Botella, who had been seriously wounded at the battle of Duault.

"One of my friends from Madagascar, Pierrot Thonnerieux, stayed behind with him. I always have to put saving the radio set first. Sometimes it's really difficult …." We went on talking like this for a long time, eventually touching on more personal subjects, like our childhoods and families. I felt wonderful, relaxed, happy.

When I went down into the farmyard again, I noticed an elegant young woman wearing high-heeled shoes and a broderie anglaise blouse, cool and attractive. She was talking in English to a tall young man with a pink complexion and fair hair, who looked deeply unhappy in an ill-fitting pale blue suit that was far too small for him. Deplante introduced me to her: "You will be working with Antoinette," he told me. "The Resistance holds no secrets for her; Allied airmen have hidden in her house for months, and here is her new protégé who will stay with us until the liberation – or the right opportunity! I think you'll get along with Marie-Claire," he added, turning to Antoinette. I had asked him to call me by that name at Saint-Caradec, but it was the first time that he he'd done so, and it made me feel I'd been accepted as "one of the family".

Antoinette was a schoolteacher, but in fact, although she was married, she wasn't much older than me. I was delighted to think that this woman was going to live with us, as the Germans had found her out and they were searching for her. "If you can speak English," she said, "Billy will be happy to chat with you: he doesn't know a word of French and is dreadfully bored." I laughed, and joined in their conversation.

At lunch, which I ate with Antoinette, Deplante and the other officers, I met Major Smith, whom I had first seen at Saint-Marcel, still as tall, thin and bald, with his round glasses perched on his nose. He spoke our language well, though with a strong English accent, and I was amazed at how well he knew our literature. He was fascinated by our country. Certainly more than he was by America, as he made quite clear to Billy, who although only twenty-five was also a major, commander of an Airacobra shot down over Morlaix a couple of months earlier. But it was hard to compete with the dignity and authority conferred on Major Smith by his superior age, being well into his forties; or that's what I thought at least.

We were sitting at the farm table, the sort of table that opens like a chest. I had seen the way local people would open them up to bring out huge buckwheat crêpes, stiff and hard as cardboard. They would make two enormous piles of them every fortnight, cooking them over an open wood fire. With potatoes and sometimes a bit of bacon, this was the staple diet of these impoverished people. They would cut them into tiny pieces and put them in a bowl of milk. Fortunately for us, British tinned food considerably improved the menu. Major Smith would not have been happy to go without his porridge and his marmalade. He had taken a patriot from the Duault camp, who had retreated to Kerusten, as his batman, and you would hear: "Amile, make me my breakfast … Amile, iron my trousers …" Emile would run hither and thither at his beck and call, for the Major was a good man and he was fond of him.

We stayed at Coët-Bigot for some time, and every day I saw Geo, while also getting to know his two Madagascan friends, Renaud and Le Cudennec, who had left with him and made up his first radio team. At last, Deplante started to send me on missions. To a variety of places, particularly Lieutenant Gérard de Carville's sector, near Langonnet Abbey. The abbey was one of the "emergency rendezvous" that had been given to the parachutists before they left, in case things turned out badly. There were others at Boquen, Timadeuc and the Augustinian convent at Malestroit, among others.

De Carville wasn't there, but Rayack, his second-in-command, also from Madagascar, was. Parachutists and patriots were enjoying a merry lunch in a wooden hut. Gorgeous sunshine, delicious aromas. The battles seemed so far away! But when the wind was in the right direction, you could hear the low rumble of the battle for Normandy. We thought they were dragging their feet over there and were only advancing in dribs and drabs. What good was a bridgehead if you couldn't broaden it? And if the enemy managed to regroup sufficiently, the Allied position would not be an enviable one.

The operations that had begun at Saint-Caradec carried on: parachute drops, distributing weapons to the FTP and FFI, training sessions by the parachutists, gathering of information that could be useful to London for potential aerial bombardments, or simply for our protection, organising a few operations, especially the cutting of cables. But their fervent desire to go into battle had to be put on the back burner as they made preparations for another D-Day, the second landings, or at least the day when the order would come to attack in broad daylight. Deplante and his battalions covered the whole of the north of the Morbihan and overlapped with the south and the Côtes-du-Nord, where other parachutists had been posted to lead groups of Maquis, though these were less thick on the ground than in the Morbihan. I wanted to go there and see.

In the meantime, I decided one night to go and watch the parachute drop that was expected. Geo had operated the Eureka transponder for the previous drop, so this time it was Tarzan's turn (though we should give him his real name, Bailly), but he was happy to pass the job to Geo, who suddenly wanted to go with me to the show. I was delighted. A mysterious understanding was growing between us.

Carts had been concealed on the sunken tracks around the drop zone, and several FFI and FTP companies were standing look-out, ready to load the containers. The zone was a large fallow field stretching out over the heights, and from the bank where I was sitting

I could see the hills rolling into the far distance. The night was clear, although the moon was just a slender crescent. Ferns, long grass and cow parsley surrounded me on three sides like a moving curtain. A gentle breeze occasionally brushed them, heavy with dew, against my face. A couple of paces away from me, Geo was waiting with the mysterious Eureka beacon, the new device that enabled the aircraft to locate us with more accuracy than any light signals. The transmission letter that night was "Y". The flexible antenna fixed inside the box vibrated like the antennae of a dragonfly. Major Smith had come over and was talking to me in a low voice, more aware than I was of the need for caution. I laughed. "Sshh, Marie-Claire, don't make a sound," he said. How could I not laugh at such a perfect moment? I was always laughing.

At the appointed time, two enormous, roaring black birds filled the sky, and the Eureka beacon started to signal its "Y" at top speed, setting them invincibly on course. Their trajectories were converging. "Lights!" yelled Deplante, and the four torches described a giant "L" on the ground. The aircraft were to fly over the drop zone following the long leg of the "L", so as to avoid collisions when there were several of them. I blocked my ears. At two hundred metres, those planes made a din that was earth-shattering. Each of them dropped twenty-four containers. Two searchlights scanned the sky. They seemed to be very close. Were the Germans going to appear? Were they going to shoot the planes down before our eyes? We would have to be quick to get the booty away, and we'd be better off looking for another drop zone. Where could we find a spot where we'd be safe? Heaven knew that area was remote enough. But Hitler's henchmen were everywhere, from Cap Nord to the Pyrenees. No time to think about Hitler or anyone else: the black boxes were dropping on all sides, like stones if the parachute "candled", or swaying prettily under their black or white corollas. The Eureka beacon was too accurate: two containers at least were heading straight for us. I leapt up from my bank and ran, with the beast at my heels. I turned round. The parachute was as white as the moon, transparent, pearly, wonderful. "That one's for me," I said to myself. The container plunged to earth two metres from me and I ran to undo the suspension ropes. There were lots of people looking for parachutes. In many a discreet bedroom sewing machines were tirelessly at work, stitching shirts for men and blouses for women, to be worn, soft and invisible, under a thick jumper. Several of the boys were already surrounding me, but when Geo came they went away again. He carefully rolled up the heavy silk. "You'll be able to make yourself a very beautiful dress," he said in a very definite tone.

Another container had fallen almost on top of the Eureka beacon, and yet another had caught fire a little further off. Everyone was frantically trying to put out the flames, as the spotlights were still circling above us. The moon gazed down on us with serene indifference.

At last, and in record time, everything was piled onto the carts, which jolted and creaked into motion. Our route took us past Ty-Glaz and the café beside the lane. The owner proudly welcomed the parachutists into his dining room and gave them a drink. They were joking around, happy to be there and pleased that the operation had gone well, on my left the little Canadian, with his old-fashioned French, cherubic pink cheeks and innocent blue eyes, finally in the old country that his family had held so dear since the time of Champlain, and further off, Sergeant Golder, with his splendid red beard, the serious and methodical Alsatian, the parachutist from Ker-Lapin "who had been in Libya" and, on my right, Geo. He had put the white parachute in his bag, next to him.

Wrapped in its innumerable folds, I had wonderful dreams at Coët-Bigot.

The containers had been temporarily stowed in a gully close to the farm, and in the morning I set off to see what they had in them.

Emile had said to me: "Come with me, I know where they are and I have to get some things to bring back – Major's orders." Major Smith had asked him to go and find "a few little things for snacks". The containers had already been opened, under the watchful eye of those responsible for them. It has to be said that the temptations were great, and that strict authority and even punishments had to be imposed to prevent pilfering. But let there be no illusions: whatever measures were taken, there were always light fingers. Spurning the rolls of plastic explosives, the pencil detonators, the Bren guns, the Colts and the ammunition, we came upon the riches of Albion: rice pudding, marmalade, tea, chocolate, sweets, bars of soap and cigarettes. The levels had already gone down. A guard appeared and we explained about the Major's "mission". After making a considered selection, we went off with our arms laden. It was like Christmas morning, I thought. This war certainly provided some strange contrasts. Then we ran into Major Smith, who was fuming. He too had made a little trip to the containers, in quest of a mysterious package. When at last he found it, he was observed triumphantly brandishing a bottle of vintage Scotch whisky. But then his smile suddenly froze: what recklessness! The bottom of the bottle had broken clean across and the contents had spilt all over the container. "I'll send a message to my blithering idiot of a cousin," he declared, "and tell him to treat such precious items with more care in future!"

Ugly rumours were circulating. The Germans were occupying some hamlets in the surrounding area: getting supplies was going to become impossible. We caught a member of the Milice who confessed he was looking for parachutists. The arms had been more or less distributed: the sector had received its share. We could leave the remote Kerguzul countryside. That same day Deplante said: "We leave tonight."

• • •

I put all my belongings in my bag and looked at the neatly rolled-up parachute in its canvas bag, perplexed. Impossible to take it with me. "Could you hide it somewhere?" I asked the farmer and his family. No one spoke for a moment. "The parachute means a lot to me, but if you don't have a hiding place that's safe enough and it might pose a risk for you, let's burn it." I gestured to the fire in the grate. A little old man suddenly hobbled towards me, unsteady on his feet, hoary and decrepit with age, but with a crafty look in his eye. "Well now, you give it to me, that bag. I know a good spot." He took it out of my arms: "You just come and fetch it whenever you like," he said, as he went out of the door.

"As soon as I can," I replied.

It was raining and the night was black as ink. We were walking in Indian file, within touching distance of each other, so as not to get lost. The tracks were steep, rocky and treacherous in places. I could make out the tall outline of Major Smith in front of me, and I was endeavouring not to fall headlong, either forwards or backwards. Most of all, I was afraid of slipping on a toad. In this weather they would all be out and about. Geo brought up the rear and was dragging my bicycle along. He'd insisted and I'd let him. I felt safer "disengaging" as part of the group this time, as I had bad memories of the hours I'd spent searching on the moors of Ty-Glaz.

The hamlet of Kerguzul bordered the road that we would have to follow for a while. The Germans no doubt preferred to play cards or do choir practice in the dry rather than mounting patrols in the rain: our luck was in. Splitting up into two columns, we advanced along both verges so as to make less noise. Antoinette was with us. I was dozing as we marched, and realised that we'd left the road when I felt the raindrops were further apart and bigger. Beautiful trees were weeping over us.

"Halt!" ordered Deplante. I collapsed at the foot of a tree trunk and the parachutists fell in heaps on either side of the path. The

Major was looking for somewhere to sit, as befitted his great height and dignity. He chose the stone wall edging the fields, bent his long, weary legs a little, and vanished as if in a conjuring trick. All that was left were two feet pointing tragically at the sky. Everyone rushed over. But the Major remarked imperturbably: "I'm perfectly comfortable, really. It was just the little wall that gave way …"

After five minutes of deep sleep, I had to get back on the march again with the others. We were arriving at Saint-Nouay, at the home of Monsieur de la Roncière of the 4th Chasseurs infantry regiment.

In the morning I found a general staff who were bright-eyed and bushy-tailed and a remarkably spruce Major, all doing justice to a hearty British breakfast: porridge, eggs and bacon and marmalade. On rising, the Major had asked for a bath. After looking at him as if he had asked for the moon, the farmer's wife thought for a moment, took him into the laundry and suggested he take a bath in the wooden tub in which she rinsed her milk bottles, which was certainly deep but not exactly suited to the Major's long limbs. But Major Smith had accepted, with good grace and a kettle of hot water. Meanwhile "Amile" was carefully pressing the creases back into his rumpled trousers with an iron heated in the embers of the fire, so restoring the Major's battledress to its typically British crispness. I felt ashamed of my drooping jacket, still damp and steaming from the heat of the fire. Smith had settled himself in an armchair and was quizzing me about seventeenth-century French literature, from Molière to Racine and from Boileau to Bossuet. He took pleasure, he said, in pitting his old brain against my young one. He also talked to me about Pierre and Thierry, the FTP leaders who had been with us since Saint-Caradec. Fortunately, Pierre had not got as far as Saint-Marcel before the battle. Jeanne had managed to put him in touch with the commanding officers. "Go back to Captain Deplante near Pontivy," they said. So he had.

Thierry ranked a grade higher than Pierre, and Major Smith had a high opinion of him. He was certainly a good-looking young man, very charming, intellectually sharp and tremendously diplomatic: all strong qualities. Smith had decided to carry on northwards with Thierry in order to arm the regions up there (as far as I was concerned, anywhere further north was "up there").

As there was no immediate danger, Deplante had left Metz, who was still not completely recovered, at Coët-Bigot, ordering him to remove all traces of our presence and oversee everyone's departure in their various directions. Deplante wanted to know what the situation was and to retrieve the parachuted maps that had been left at the farm. I was therefore to go there that afternoon.

Metz, now on form, carefully chose the maps Deplante wanted and made a bulky parcel out of them. Showing that to the German patrols that were beginning to infest the countryside was not an appealing prospect. To wrap them I resorted to the crêpes on the table, and the farmer's family, overcoming their misgivings, willingly gave me a few. I stuffed the whole lot into one of my saddlebags. The weapons distribution wasn't quite complete, but Metz thought he'd be able to leave in a day or two.

The rain was torrential again. That morning, Antoinette had borrowed my raincoat: Deplante had sent her to the Guern region, where he hoped to set up camp soon. She was preparing for our arrival, as she knew some people there. I turned up my collar, reflecting glumly that there was no hope now of looking chic in this jacket from the suit that had been made for me in the spring. On which note I spared a thought for my kind dressmaker, with whom I'd missed a fitting for a summer frock on the 20th.

I could just see far enough ahead to make out the path, which was fast becoming a torrent. The seething, yellowish water rose right up to my bicycle chain. It sprayed up under my mudguard, spattering my legs, my body and even my face, while my feet plunged deep into the sludge. The path was actually just a succession of more or less flat rocks and I lurched into one pothole after another, but never coming off, because with practice I had developed a remarkable sense of balance. I pedalled fast, fearing that at any moment armed Germans might loom up in front of me, and the desolate landscape only deepened my anxiety. My bicycle was responsive and alive as an animal, supple, obedient, quivering as if intoxicated by this thrilling steeplechase. We were as one, intimately connected.

Suddenly I heard the sound of groups of men speaking in guttural voices. As usual, I made up a story to avoid being searched. I took the path at a furious pace; for once the Germans were combing the fields; I saw no one; no one saw me.

When I reached Saint-Nouay, dinner was over and everyone had retired to their own corner. I was so exhausted and drenched when I arrived in the courtyard that I thought I was going to pass out. I handed over the crêpes and the maps to Deplante and told him I was going up to my attic. But on the way I realised I was hungry: the dying embers of a fire were glowing in the parachutists' kitchen and I went to see if there might be something left that I could scrounge.

A strapping great parachutist was still busy in there: a strange character whom I had noticed several times, and one of the men of whom I was most frightened. Tall and lean, with hollow cheeks, an aquiline nose and very deep-set eyes, he always had the air of a Sioux on the warpath, silent and supple. He rode the farm horses bareback and his skill at throwing knives was unrivalled: he could hit a tree neatly at ten metres. With his black beret pulled down over one ear, he looked like a condottiere, or something out of the Wild West.

He looked me straight in the eye "You, child of my heart, you need your friend Tancer. Sit down here and watch." He pushed a wooden chopping board towards me, took some eggs from a salad basket hanging from a nail, and with an adroit flick of the wrist and fingers broke five of them into a large bowl. His fingers were long and thin. "He must be Basque or Spanish," I thought.

"You will see what you will see, my poor little wet hen," he said. He was whisking the eggs with ferocious energy, and once the butter had melted he poured the contents of the bowl into the frying pan. I felt good near the revived fire, and a warm steam rose from my clothes. Little flames danced in Tancer's dark eyes. What sort of life had he had? I would have liked to know more about him, but I didn't dare ask questions. His familiarity didn't bother me at all, though: it was comforting, more like being with a caring brother. He added some bacon bits to the omelette before folding it over, then slid it on to the plate that he'd put on my lap. He was pleased when I did justice to his cooking. "Now, off to bed with you, quickly," he said when I'd finished.

I didn't see much of the radio operators, as they were working all day, starting at dawn and often going on late into the evening. Deplante's messages were concise, but the same couldn't be said for Major Smith, who would bring entire pages to be encoded. Our group had two teams, which if not complete were at least enough to do shifts: Le Cudennec and Renaud on one, Geo and Bailly on the other. Exchanges with London came and went at a rapid pace, slipping between English and French without distinction, and I would see the men bending over the pad and the silk code chart for hours on end.

I would have loved to help them, as I loathed the inevitable hours of inactivity between missions, but it was "secret" work. To add to the complications, London struggled to hear our transmissions, and each side got annoyed with the other. When the radio operators thought they had earned a few hours' sleep, the Major would suddenly appear with a lengthy message to be put through "urgently". Occasionally he would indulge them by letting them wait until four or five in the morning before transmitting. The shifts allotted to each Pierre were no longer enough, and they had to resort to the emergency long wave frequency.

Relaxation was needed. Le Cudennec put on a theatrical performance in the attic. In shorts and shirt, the arm that had been dislocated by the static line when he jumped still in a sling, he stood in front of an audience who were struck dumb with wonder and with consummate artistry delivered his extensive comedian's repertoire. I can still hear him declaiming *"L'enfant grec"*. His public were reduced to tears of laughter. Geo told me that he wasn't just an actor but also an excellent artist, who had held exhibitions in Tananarive.

I was improving my acquaintance alternately with the parachutists and with our old bear of a host, Monsieur de la Roncière, who was still living obstinately in the Great War, and never tired of telling us about the exploits of the 4th Chasseurs. His handlebar moustache would bristle with pleasure, and his naturally florid complexion would deepen yet further. This illustrious assembly of officers around him delighted him. But he worried about the antenna of the radio sets that crossed his courtyard: "far too visible," he would say, and had we thought about the defence of his property in case of attack? He doubted it. Innocent soul that he was, his fears did not deter him from telling everyone in the village that he wasn't afraid of anything because the parachutists were at his house! Dangerous pride! Disastrous desire to have their hour of glory! How many people across France had died because of it?

Finally, one night I saw Geo encoding this message: "88 0 300: Smith leaving today with Resistance leaders and radio Pierre 4 to organise arming Côtes-du-Nord RNS, stop, Deplante remaining Morbihan with radio Pierre 5, stop, both anticipate need rapid radio facilities to and from the eleven BNS to coordinate convoy attacks, stop, what suggestions?" I was puzzled, and worried.

Deplante took me aside to warn me of this departure. The Major was going to go up towards Ile-et-Vilaine, via the Côtes-du-

Nord, with Thierry and the two radio operators Le Cudennec and Renaud, who could not be separated. He himself would go down in the direction of Guern the next day, and he planned to stay in that area. He would take Geo and Bailly, and Antoinette would go with him. Deplante was quiet for a moment. He hesitated before going on: "Major Smith would like you to go with him to do liaison work, and I must tell you honestly, for reasons I will explain, that I should like you to go with him." And he told me all his thoughts about the problem of the Brittany barricade. Yes, he would be pleased if I went on with the Major.

It felt as though the sky had darkened. He went on: "You must do as you wish. Come with us if you prefer."

I had found a big family, friendships that were growing stronger. I had found Geo. Yes, his friendship mattered. I would have to push myself even further into the unknown. I liked the Major, but I didn't have that direct connection that I now felt with Deplante.

Under the curious gaze of the FTP liaison agents, I stood motionless in the muddy courtyard. Finally, I went to tell Smith that I would follow him.

Geo said nothing, nor did anyone else.

It was still light when I left Saint-Nouay to make preparations for the group's overnight stop in the Glomel area. I shook Geo by the hand: "Goodbye," was all I said.

"Take great care, Marie-Claire."

"I shall never see him again." I thought. "We mustn't get attached to each other. *C'est la guerre.*"

CHAPTER 8

Chez Fauquet

We were trudging laboriously through marshes and peat bogs and I was jumping from one mound to another, dragging my wayward mount. Reeds stretched motionless as far as the eye could see; a stretch of water reflected the last glow of twilight. I was bringing up the rear and I stopped to listen to the sounds of the night: frogs croaking, toads calling, birds twittering when disturbed in their sleep, and now and then, rising over these muted background notes, the mournful hooting of an owl. The melancholy of the hour and the place was a perfect reflection of my state of mind, which had not changed since the moment I'd left Geo the day before. I was fed up with myself for being so stubbornly emotional by nature. Heaven knew how much I had already suffered at seeing all my friends disappear one after the another! What was the point of making new ones?

We were reaching the Nantes-Brest Canal, which we would follow all the way to distant Plélauff. Counselling extreme caution, the Major initially decided to walk along the bank without a towpath; it was nothing but dense thickets climbing a steep slope, a tangle of ferns, thorny brambles, bushy oak trees and shrubby growth of all descriptions. I thought I was going to get stuck there with my bicycle and regretted not having gone on the road.

"You can't possibly bring that bicycle with you!" Smith grumbled. "Leave it here."

"Never!" I replied. "Without a bike I'm no use to anyone."

He grumbled on and I dug my heels in.

I dragged myself along on my knees, I crawled, pulling my bicycle by one wheel, or pushing it along, flat; I bled, I wept, I couldn't take any more, and my foot slipped in the clay. I was about to fall in the canal with a great splash when hands held on to me and grabbed the contraption: Renaud and Le Cudennec had come to my rescue, even though they were well and truly laden down with their own very heavy bags and their weapons. We were level with a little bridge. Was it guarded? Were the Germans patrolling the towpath? It looked so tempting, that charming little path. We looked down on it from above, still catching our breath from our exertions. Two scouts went ahead to inspect the surrounding area: no one. "Let's take it," declared the Major. I examined my bicycle anxiously, but I needn't have worried: no flat tyre, just bent mudguards and a lopsided luggage rack.

A proper path has its advantages, even if it does turn out to be more puddle than terra firma. Our clothes were nothing but sodden rags and my feet were sliding about in my waterlogged shoes, but the sky was clearing and the moon made a few brief appearances between the ragged clouds: it was almost full, but it seemed to me to be getting fuller and fuller. Weren't the landings supposed to take place at the July full moon? And would they really happen? Doubts were beginning to stir.

I thought I'd overcome the worst obstacle with that wretched thicket, and now I was walking at a steady pace at the head of the line. An hour, two hours, three hours ... how long had we been walking? I had no idea anymore. I'd never walked for so long. Fatigue was catching up with me. Was the Major's stride still as regular? His little beret perched on top of his elongated silhouette seemed to be wobbling in a rather peculiar fashion.

Quite deliberately, Emile had put his bag on top of mine on my luggage rack. True, he was heavily laden. "We had just left Saint-Nouay," he told me, "and we had already gone some way when the Major slapped his forehead and exclaimed: 'Oh Emile! We've forgotten our little snack!' and I had to go back and collect this bag, an ammunition pouch. Believe me, rice pudding and marmalade can weigh as much as bullets and grenades!"

Earlier on we had exchanged a few remarks between us, but now no one said a word. The moon circled and dropped in the sky, and still we walked. I applied myself to detaching my mind from my body, so as not to feel it anymore, keeping just one thought in my head: I have to keep walking. Suddenly I found I was alone with the Major.

"I'm going back," I said. We had just passed a lock and the keeper had welcomed the others into his nice warm house. He had opened a bottle of wine, which he was handing around. I had gone to reassure Major Smith, who was sitting on the grassy verge, his body slumped forward, his head lowered. "You go on, Marie-Claire, you go on, I'll stay here." I didn't insist since he looked absolutely exhausted. "He's too old." I thought. "Let's hope we reach Plélauff before daybreak!"

Sitting on a bench beside the parachutists, I swallowed the Benzedrine tablet that Le Cudennec offered me with a glass of wine. "It's wonderful, you'll see. Your fatigue will just vanish," he assured me. They had each been given a tube of them before leaving England, to pep them up in an emergency. It seemed incredible, but almost immediately I was sitting up again and managing to stay upright, my thoughts cleared and all my energies restored. The lock keeper had lit an oil lamp that he put on the table, and I thought we made an extraordinary sight. I had initially seen it through a haze of exhaustion and sleeplessness, but now it was in brilliant, sharp relief. My cheeks were burning. I couldn't wait for the cool of the night and to be off again! But the Major would happily have dozed on until dawn. Day was breaking as we reached Plélauff.

The shutters of the houses were closed, and we slipped past like shadows. On a farm we found the FTP liaison agents Chantal and Maryse, but we had to go on to Ker-Lapin, where Metz had taken me one evening. After the customary introductions between the parachutists and the patriots in the house, we felt entitled to get some sleep, in a tiny loft, on a sparse layer of hay. I ended up squeezing in between the Major and Maryse. My neighbour had barely stretched out before he was fast asleep, but I couldn't follow suit. The oppressively low ceiling, the lack of fresh air because the skylight was closed and the smells of damp leather, sweat, mud and dirt made me feel sick. I ached all over but didn't dare move. Stretched out full length on his back, Major Smith looked like Don Quixote on his deathbed. But his breathing was strong, regular and calm. At about ten o'clock I couldn't stand it any longer and escaped, going to have a wash in a stream running through the meadow, dipping my feet in the icy water with delight. I wished I had a good book to read right there, sitting on the stone bridge, warmed by the sun.

We were told that Lieutenant Fauquet[35] would join us in the afternoon. I watched him arrive by the hill path, a blade of grass in his mouth, his black beret at a jaunty angle and adorned with two cockerel feathers. With his swaggering walk and his keen and lively expression, smiling, friendly and happy to be alive, he was a magnificent Robin Hood figure. He was in his early twenties, with a gift for leadership, a passion for combat and an indomitable need to fight for a just cause. Ever faithful to his native department of Côtes-du-Nord, where he had been dropped at Le Saint-Esprit-en-Plédéliac, nothing suited him better than the daring and varied missions of the SAS, and he deployed his skills in many different fields, including

---

35. Many times decorated, Philippe Fauquet was an intrepid soldier and saboteur. He died in a jeep accident in Rouen, on October 1944, aged twenty four.

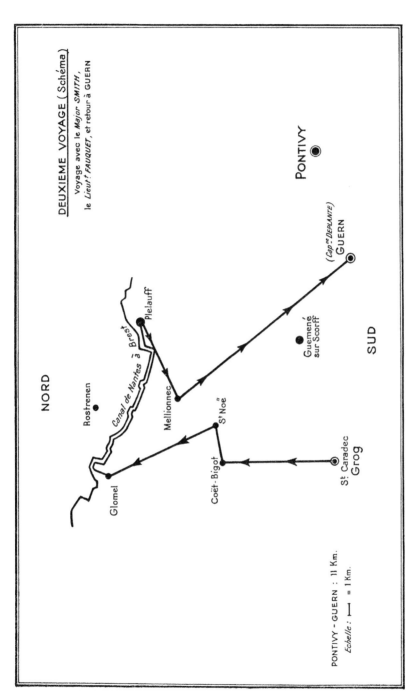

removing bolts and rivets from railway tracks, cutting electricity lines, training Maquis groups and organising parachute drops. Tired of losing valuable time by travelling on foot, he now drove around in a Citroën Traction Avant and invited us to follow him by car to the CP at farm of Le Rest in Mellionnec.

The Major was not enthusiastic, despite efforts to convince him by Fauquet, known to everyone as "Philippe". We finally settled on a rendezvous near Plélauff and I went to collect my bike from the farm where I'd left it. We were spoiled for choice; there was not just one Traction, but two. I'd had my fill of walking and the idea of a car ride was far from unattractive. Once again, my bike was tied to the bonnet. I got in the back, and we took off at top speed. The Major meanwhile had opted for the more prudent means of travel, under the cover of the local thickets.

The situation was not without its picaresque side, and threatened to become even more so. The dashing Philippe drove with one arm casually draped over the door, in parachutist's uniform, naturally. Sitting on his right was Pascal Fadda, his inseparable sergeant who never stirred from his side and who was devoted to him even unto death, a small man as tanned as a Berber, with shiny, very curly hair as black as a raven's wing and flashing eyes set in a long, thin face. He never stopped laughing and talking, making a big thing of rolling his "R"s and regaling us with a fund of random tales of the hoaxes he and his lieutenant had played on the Germans. The car windows had gone, either stolen or broken, and Fadda supported his machine gun firmly on the door, ready to fire at the first obstacle that presented itself. My neighbour on the back seat did the same. The belts of these gentlemen were well-accessorised with grenades, and I could just imagine the scene if we were to come across any enemy vehicles. But we were going so fast and cutting corners – would they even see us? I spotted Smith and Emile walking in Indian file along the ditch, lit up by a flash of lightning, and it did occur to me that going on foot might have something to recommend it. But the parachutists' motto, "Who dares wins", seemed to have been coined with Fauquet in mind. "And all those who go with him," I added silently.

The road to the camp was blocked by a zigzag line of piles of wood, from each of which the muzzle of a machine gun was pointing at us. The boys on guard duty set about clearing a way through for us. Raising clouds of dust, we drove on another hundred metres before stopping outside the general headquarters, a large farm.

There was a good deal of hustle and bustle going on, which intensified with the arrival of Pierre and Thierry. People were coming for orders and guidance and to report back on what they had done. I was having dinner when a very young, very pale young man turned up, cradling one hand in the other. He had just been shot in a skirmish. Straight away a nurse cleaned the wound and bandaged it with care, then took the wounded man up to the loft, which they called the "hospital". Major Smith had still not arrived, which didn't exactly set our minds at rest. Then Philippe Fauquet took me off to one of the farm outbuildings, where he hoped to find me somewhere to sleep. "I'd like you to come with me," I said to Maryse. I liked this very reserved liaison agent, and we'd already had several chats together.

The twilight was lingering on. Seated around a table, we all started telling stories. Fadda fished in his pocket for his most recent letter from his father, and we pictured the older man concentrating hard as he wrote down the local news and words of advice for his son. "He's quite a character, my father!" said Fadda. "You should have seen him when I left Bastia! 'Pascal Fadda, we are proud of you,' he said, 'and we count on you to bring honour to your family and to our city.'" The young Corsican stopped laughing and was suddenly thoughtful.[36] Philippe took us even further afield, into the

36. Pascal Fadda had served in the Corsican navy but was Sardinian by birth. He was executed by the Germans in the forest of Lorges in July 1944.

scorching deserts of Libya, where he had fought under the command of Colonel Stirling, a time he looked back on with nostalgia. He ended by reciting a poem written by Aspirant André Zirnheld,[37] whose death he had witnessed out there.

I turn to you, O Lord,
For you give
What we can only find in ourselves.

Give me, O Lord, what you have left over,
Give me what no one ever asks of you.

I do not ask you for rest,
Nor for tranquillity
Either of the soul or of the body.
I do not ask you for wealth
Nor for success, nor even for health.

All this, O Lord, people ask for so often,
That there can be none left.
Give me, O Lord, what is left over,
Give me the things that others refuse.

I want insecurity and anxiety,
I want turmoil and struggle,
Give me these things, O Lord,

---

37. A professor of philosophy in peacetime, André Zernheld was killed during the SAS raid on Sidi Haneish Airfield in June 1942, so becoming the first French paratrooper officer to be killed in action. The poem that became known as *La Prière du Para* ("The Paratrooper's Prayer") was found on his body. It has since been adopted by all French paratrooper regiments.

Forever.

Let me be sure of having them always
For I will not always have the courage
To ask them of you.
Give me, O Lord, what is left over,
Give me what others do not want.
But give me courage too
And strength and faith.

For only you can give
What we can only expect from ourselves.

• • •

Major Smith arrived so late that night and was so weary that he finally decided to take advantage of the cars. The next day, he, Fauquet and I drew up some plans. The Major would make his way to Moncontour in stages. I would go by bike to Peumerit-Quintin, where I would join him at the schoolmaster's house. A car would have dropped him there with Thierry. Fauquet gave us a long account of the situation in the region. Some names emerged. Abbé Fleury at Saint-Brieuc, the priest I was supposed to see on behalf of Marie-Hélène Lefaucheux, whose arrest Fauquet had only just heard about. Raoul, his second-in-command, who would certainly join them and take on a leading role if he had managed to elude the Gestapo. Sergeant Robert, a parachutist who had set up a veritable military camp near L'Etang-Neuf, with tents and a punctilious timetable like an army barracks. And Félix, Moncontour, Stéphan, Captain Lechat and a number of other parachutists from the Duault base who had not been able to reach Saint-Marcel, and who had set up camp in various sectors where they had taken command of the Maquis and were training them. Liaison had been established between them all, but there was less unity, I felt, than in the Morbihan. I couldn't see where overall authority lay. There were certainly a lot of active groups who wanted to work together to mount actions on D-Day in Brittany. But would they manage it?

I was tying my bag to the luggage rack on my bike when Fauquet asked for my Michelin map. "I'll give it back to you at Moncontour," he said. "See you soon and have a good journey."

The farmyard was full of a large crowd of people, and he strode from one group to another, the two cockerel feathers in his beret bouncing jauntily. I entrusted my squares of parachute silk and my sketches to Renaud, who had come over with Le Cudennec to check on the state of my bicycle. Suddenly Smith came over: "Right, Marie-Claire, you will be rejoining Captain Deplante with Jérome, who is also going to Guern. He will tell you where Commandant Bourgoin is, and you will go and see him straight away. You will ask him where he would like me to continue my operation. You will then meet me at Peumerit-Quintin. If I am no longer there, they will tell you where to find me."

Head south. No order could have given me more pleasure! I was delighted with the world, and I chatted away to my companion (Jérome not being terribly inspiring), an FTP liaison agent called Christiane, rosy-cheeked, blonde, fresh and pretty. She cycled all day by my side without a shadow of tiredness ever crossing her round face. Something in her held all the promise of spring.

CHAPTER 9

Halt at Guern

Doors were opening into the clandestine world of the Maquis: more often than not via a café where you could ask those in the know for the key, in other words the guide. The Querriec camp had its "door" at Saint-Salomon, from where I was able to rejoin my friends, led to them by a stranger. At the Kerivouallan farm, the Deplante group were as warm in their welcome as the Mellionnec group had been with their farewells: "See you soon."

Antoinette, Billy the American and Geo were sitting on a patch of grass, absorbed in their radio work. They were decoding a message. Geo would say a letter from the pad that corresponded to the one in the message below, and Antoinette would check them against the silk square to give a third letter, the correct one, for the decoded version.

"Where's Bailly?" I asked in surprise.

"He's picked up a throat infection too, so we left him to be looked after at a farm," Antoinette replied. "Since Geo couldn't do the work on his own, Billy and I have learned to encode and decode. It's a bit irregular, but needs must ..."

"Well, you'll have to teach me," I laughed, thrilled to have this opportunity. I had just told Deplante about the mission that Major

Smith had given me, as well as everything that I'd found out about the Côtes-du-Nord. Since he couldn't tell me the precise whereabouts of Commandant Bourgoin, he had advised me to stay with them while they sent a message to the Commandant's radio operators and waited for a reply.

Yet again I'd arrived after supper was over, so I was treated to an omelette, as at Saint-Nouay. This time it wasn't Tancer who made it but Geo, with great skill and care, and without a word.

The parachutists had set up camp about two kilometres from the FFI camp, which was commanded by Duboc, an energetic and loyal man of a certain age. Having had occasion to go to the headquarters of the FTP leader, Armand, I noted, with some amusement, the differences between them. The FTP leaders were younger on the whole than the FFI chiefs, and hardly any of them were career army officers or reservists as in the FFI. They commanded groups, all of which were made up of eight young men. Group leaders were regarded as sergeants. Detachment leaders, or lieutenants, commanded three groups, and four detachments made up a company under the command of a captain. The FFI tried as far as possible to maintain the traditional divisions of the army as well as its spirit, and they sought to develop ideas as a group and fostered concerted action, in preparation for rapid integration into a regular army. The FTP waged war like Spanish guerrilla fighters, and their solidarity gave rise to difficulties that often exasperated the parachutists.

The Deplante group had taken on its definitive shape. As well as Deplante, Metz, Billy, Bailly, Geo, Antoinette and me, there were also Adjutant Robineau, Sergeant Andrieu, Henri and young Bachet; the rest, like Tancer, only appeared from time to time.

Robineau was lively, very fair, with blue eyes that could be teasing or tender, passionate, quarrelsome or paternal, stormy or suddenly serene. He was from New Caledonia on the other side of the world, where he had left his wife, his two little boys and his air transport business, which served the Pacific islands with "an old crate": "You had to sit beside the pilot to give him confidence," he used to say.

Andrieu's accent brought with it the sunny climes of Avignon. You could depend on him utterly, and he was serious, calm and relaxing company. Henri from Lorraine was a tougher character altogether. He nursed a deep hatred of the ancestral enemy of his people, which lent a hard edge to the expression in his dark eyes. He said little, but saw things for what they were and knew the right thing to say at the right time. He was responsible for the group's Bren gun and looked after it lovingly, which gave me an intense feeling of security.

And finally there was Bachet, known as Tony, very shy, very reserved, very gentle and with beautiful manners. He seemed younger than the others. And mysterious. We used to wonder where he came from. Though delicate in appearance, he was a true Resistance fighter. He accepted with great equanimity the lowliest of tasks, such as doing the cooking, peeling the vegetables, making the fires or organising supplies, even though, like the others, he dreamed only of sabotage and raids on the enemy. Deplante would organise these on a regular basis. In lowering the morale of the enemy, they simultaneously raised the morale of the parachutists.

• • •

Since Bailly's illness lingered on and Commandant Bourgoin's answer didn't come, Antoinette initiated me properly into the mysteries of the conversations with London. These conversations should only have taken place during shift hours and on the special frequency of the wireless set, but they often spilled over onto the emergency long-wave frequency. Geo kept a quartz crystal in his pocket for each frequency band, little crystal rectangles enveloped in a moulded material, and very heavy. Depending on the time of day, he would plug one or other into the transmitter, and when the work of the day and sometimes the night was done he would push both of them down to the bottom of one of his trouser pockets, which were lined with thick chamois leather. "Now I can relax," he would say. "No one can use the wireless set." His set didn't work terribly well. One day, the quartz crystal for the emergency wavelength stopped working altogether. They asked London for a new quartz crystal, they asked London for a new wireless set, and a flurry of messages went back and forth on the matter. The quartz crystal appeared in the end, but the wireless set, patched up by Geo and Bailly, had to carry on transmitting its piles of messages for better or worse right up to the Liberation.

Most of the messages were about parachute drops, for us and all the FFI and FTP battalions. And most of these were requests for arms, but also for supplies and kit. There was one message that amused me greatly when I encoded it:

"303 – naked as the day born, stop, request send to DZ 935 540 mark P5 containers with: 10 torches, 30 batteries, 5 litres petrol, 8 rucksacks and sleeping bags and boot liners 7 and a half plus puttees, stop, coffee, cigarettes, stop, 20 boxes of 20 kg sugar rations, stop, 30 pairs socks, stop, 5 sets maps Pontivy and 8 surrounding regions, bar Lorient." In the confusion of sudden and rapid departures, many of the men had lost bits of kit, though not of course their weapons and the wireless sets and generators. The splendid and all-encompassing kit they'd arrived with had melted away. All Geo had left were his escape jacket, one shirt, one pair of trousers, his camouflage jacket and a single pair of shoes, and he didn't have either a sleeping bag or a blanket.

These curious exchanges, in either English or French or a mixture of the two, would send Antoinette and me off to take letters to the battalions who were involved in that night's parachute drops. We would come back to the camp at a more leisurely pace, only to be told, sometimes after curfew: "We've just got a message cancelling tonight's operation. Run off and tell them." Or, "Right, there's a parachute-drop on the same DZ. The letter is P. Take it to them, no time to lose." And we would set off again with empty stomachs, or hastily shoving a hunk of bread into our mouths.

To put a stop to all this frantic racing around, and also because at one point we feared the Germans were going to ban bicycles, one day Deplante sent the following message: "Liaisons exhausted by daily transmission call signs, stop, understand cars and bicycles forbidden, stop, suggest give each DZ animal name, stop, BBC to send messages like this via French Service, stop, Paul will see the wild boar and four piglets tonight, stop, initial letter of first name designates day, stop, request your agreement, stop, will send code names for Deplante DZs." In the event, this system was only used in certain cases, for groups in remote locations who, on hearing their message broadcast by the BBC, would know that they should go and wait for the aircraft that night. There was also agreement on a code word to indicate that that night's operation had been cancelled: every time we decoded the famous MILTON it was with the same furious disappointment.

Delays and postponements meant that the number of requests increased, particularly for money. Which was certainly needed! As Deplante told London: "Impossible to continue without money, stop, each BTN needs: 250 000 support for patriot families and 550 000 for food, stop, need advance of 6 million for twelve battalions, stop, would like to receive 935 540 in W, each BTN to keep accounts of expenses." Setting up a financial organisation on such a scale was not the least of the parachutists' worries.

Even more fascinating were messages to do with the arrival and deployment of the Jedburgh teams, and messages intended for other parachutist groups in Brittany who had a wireless set. The Jedburgh teams, known as "Jeds", were made up of one French, one British and one American serviceman: two officers and a radio operator with a transmitter and a receiver.

One of these teams was supposed to go to the Finistère area to speed up the distribution of arms there, which delighted me. I often talked to Deplante about my region, which was still sadly overlooked.

I would forget about the tedium of encoding and decoding as I watched the gradual formation of the army that would go into action on Brittany's D-Day. It was already active, moreover, and Deplante would periodically report back on operations against the enemy undertaken by the men under his command. The final item in this intense radio activity was the precious military intelligence that arrived daily, and which we immediately re-transmitted, most of which led to aerial bombardments by the RAF.

Deplante was forever dictating new messages. The Germans would jam the transmissions, forcing the operator to repeat messages or ask for them to be repeated. Headphones clamped to his ears, teeth clenched, Geo would repeat: "QSA1, QSA2, QSA3, that's it, got it..." At QSA5 he was jubilant, he could hear London as clearly as if he were there. The Germans would use their radio direction-finding system to attempt to locate these transmitters with all their intolerable activities, installing it on cars that would then drive around slowly and surreptitiously. The only defence was to move on, which we did more and more. The women who worked in England had such keen ears and were so well trained that they could recognise the operator who was sending a message purely by the way they tapped their Morse code. When in doubt, they could always ask the operator for their secret name. Geo's was Hélène.

Naturally we were glued to the BBC bulletins, as our operation and its duration depended directly on how the campaign in Normandy was going. The storm of 19 June had already set the intended schedule back by a week, and the persistent bad weather wasn't helping the situation. Would the pessimistic prophecies about

"Overlord" be proved right?[38] Eisenhower was increasingly opposed to the Quiberon plan, but all we knew was that the landings had been put on hold and that no one could say how long we would have to stick it out in the Breton heathland, whether days, weeks or months.

The desperate state of our bicycle tyres[39] took us off to Pontivy for an entire day, Antoinette and me, without anything to show for it except that we managed to order haversacks to fit us from a saddler. A notice on the town hall declared that all correspondence to and from the *zone interdite* along the coast was now forbidden. So I could no longer put a note in the post to reassure my parents. Deplante gave me permission to take a letter to Le Faouët. I hoped that someone would take it on to Concarneau, as I could imagine only too well the tales that might be doing the rounds about the horrors of the German repression of the Maquis.

But my sister Françoise sensed that my mother was so desperately worried about me that she decided to go and see the Fravals in Le Faouët herself. Arthur worked out a careful route for her and she set off. The Fravals gave her my letters, reassured her that they had seen me and that I was well, and told her whereabouts I was. On a map of Brittany, my family drew pencilled circles round the towns they mentioned. My mother would often look at them.

How far away my family seemed, and how strange the world around me was! Sometimes I became aware of things that triggered episodes of deep reflection, as I struggled to balance the realities of life against what I had been taught. How was it possible to ignore such realities? Wasn't it better to try to understand them? Which is what I had to do one night.

---

38. "Therefore, the particular spot we had decided upon as most useful for supply and maintenance purposes in Brittany was Quiberon Bay, a large, well-sheltered but undeveloped harbour on the southern flank of the peninsula's base. As June faded into July, we closely watched the situation to determine whether or not a second landing would be profitable to us. More and more I turned against it." *Crusade in Europe*, Eisenhower.

39. We had asked the British for tyres, but when they came they were embossed with the words "Made in England".

It was well after nightfall and I was exhausted. I was so looking forward to the mattress I'd laid out that morning, made from some wool I'd found in a chest. The moon lit up the yard and I had no trouble finding the ladder that led up to the loft where most of us slept. The floor beside the chest and my bag was bare: both wool and blanket had vanished. I could hear only the regular breathing of the sleeping forms who were silhouetted against the end wall in the pale light. I recognized my blanket draped over Morgane, who was sleeping soundly at the side of a patriot from the group, with my wool spread out underneath her. She was a liaison agent who was often with us. She must have found her troubling name in a book of legends: it suited her perfectly.

I lay down and tried to sleep, but it was no good. Eventually I stood up again, stiff with fatigue and resentment.

At the far end of the loft Morgane's fair face, her complexion pink and clear and her thick mane of golden hair spread around it, glowed in the half-light. She lay in a deep and satisfied sleep, her lips slightly parted and still plump from the pleasure she had just been given. She was unbelievably beautiful. I gazed at her; I gazed at this man and this woman, both of them so young and so beautiful. All my anger and resentment vanished: my only thought was that it would be a crime against creation to spoil or kill such beauty. Who was I to judge Morgane? Who was I to judge anyone? We never truly know other people. Morgane possessed within her a great warmth of genuine love, I knew, which went far beyond any passing pleasure; also we had been brought up differently.

But I was freezing cold and wondered where I could find a warm spot, I didn't care where, anywhere that was warm. I remembered there was another small loft, full of freshly cut hay, just above the cowshed. Moving carefully so as not to wake anybody up, I climbed up there and burrowed down into the hay, curling up like a cat, my knees under my chin, to preserve any warmth left in me. But I was still dreadfully cold. I could hear the cows shifting about and slapping their tails against their flanks. Their breath, accompanied by a pungent aroma, rose through the wide gaps between the floorboards. I dozed off into frozen slumbers. I was travelling over white steppes and shivering with cold, when a thick, sweet liquid, milk fresh from the cow, poured down my throat and over my chin. A gentle warmth spread right through me. I felt wonderful, and even better when someone put a warm blanket over me. Who? I could guess! I sank into a deep and restorative sleep at last.

The bonds between Geo and me were growing stronger, whatever we did. I fought against these ties that we would have to break, of that I was certain. Outside our shared work, we avoided being alone together and mixed with the group, hoping to drown our special feelings amid the general camaraderie.

• • •

Following a close shave, we regrouped in a hollowed-out haystack belonging to a farmer at Malneven, a hiding place he was happy to offer us, but that he'd only intended to "keep a few things safe".

I still didn't know where to find Commandant Bourgoin, who was being hunted by the Germans; so I decided to keep my rendezvous with Major Smith without seeing him. Since my bicycle was completely out of commission, Duboc, the chief, sent me to a café in Guémené to collect another one that he'd requisitioned. I abandoned my trusty steed at Malneven.

Another round of farewells to the Deplante group.

• • •

No Major Smith at Peumerit, just an irritable schoolmaster who eventually admitted, after lengthy negotiations, that he had seen the Major; he had gone and he didn't know where to. Somewhere over

Lamballe way, or possibly in the Finistère direction. Before slamming the door in my face, he told me loftily to come back in the afternoon; he would take me to Captain Aguirec,[40] one of a Jedburgh team. He could probably give me some information. Which is what I would have done, had it not been for the café and Yves: and then I would have found my Major Smith again and stayed in the Côtes-du-Nord until the Liberation, without seeing Geo again!

I was waiting for some lunch in the grocer's-cum-stationer's-cum-café, when a group of young men came in with "patriots" written all over them. I kept my ears open, hoping to sniff out a trail that would be quicker than the schoolmaster's. They were talking about the Bourbriac attack and a girl who had been throwing grenades: "A lioness, I'm telling you!" At that point a mere youth came in, very pale and with his head bandaged. The woman in the café told me the Germans had left him for dead in a ditch; one of them even finished him off, or so he thought, with a bullet in the head. But he was still breathing, and they had hidden him and nursed him; it was a miracle to see him there, alive. Hard on his heels came Roger, and I could tell he was their leader.

"Do you know of any parachutists in this area?" I asked straight off. "Did you see a British officer a few days ago?"

"You must have a sixth sense," he said. "I happen to be a parachutist sergeant reporting to Captain Botella. I'll take you to him." I was rather amazed that he was so quick to trust me, but delighted that he had! So, I was about to meet Geo's stick leader.

The sergeant led me to a hovel on a wild hillside where the three badly wounded men from the battle of Duault were quartered.[41] They were lying on some rather wretched-looking iron bedsteads, and looked at me in astonishment. The sergeant introduced me to

---

40. Code name of Paul Bloch-Auroch, of Jedburgh team "Frederick".
41. Captain Botella, Lieutenant Lassere, and Corporal Faucheux.

Captain Botella and went out. "Have a seat," said the Captain, "you must be tired," and he pointed to the foot of his bed.

While I explained what I was doing in his area, I took in the abject poverty of the place. I could only imagine the life that the three wounded men must have been living there for the past month. "The doctor comes once a week, and a nurse," the sergeant had told me. "A young boy does their errands and I go every day to take orders from the Captain; our organisation here isn't too shabby, believe me."

Botella was bearing up well, but I imagined the endless days and the interminable nights, with the winds whistling around the building and rattling the ramshackle door, and the ever-present fear of being discovered or betrayed, without any means of defence and with those wounds that were taking so long to heal.

They were pleased when I told them about Captain Deplante, and Botella asked me a lot of questions. I told them what had happened at Saint-Marcel, and I also told them how the clandestine army was taking shape and was being armed, structured and organised by the parachutists, from south to north, following a line that cut through Brittany.

Captain Botella couldn't give me any information about the Major, but I hadn't given up hope of finding him again. "Afterwards", I added, "I'll go back to Commandant Bourgoin."

"In that case, you can take him a message from me," said Botella, and he took out paper and pencil and wrote down all the information about his sector and his requests.

I folded the piece of paper and, as I had before with the one Deplante had given me, inserted it in my turban. I would have liked to say more but felt too intimidated, so I stood up and shook their hands. "Goodbye, mademoiselle," they said. "And good luck. It's been a pleasure to meet you." I went out into the sunshine, moved to tears.

The sergeant returned and took me back to Peumerit. There I found Yves Lagardère,[42] head of the Châteauneuf-du-Faou Maquis, who had been waiting for Major Smith for several days. He was so much more positive and precise than the schoolmaster that I immediately believed him, and like him was worried that something might have happened to the group. "Come and stay the night with the Boby Maquis", said Yves, "and tomorrow you can go to Plourac'h with Alain, my second-in-command. The Major may already be with our Maquis. I'll carry on looking around here for another day or two."

And then I got lost in the Monts d'Arrée, in the west, when I should have been pedalling to the east, where the Major was getting worried about me!

Lagardère's Maquis had set up camp in the hollow of a ravine. No one there had heard tell of the Major, but they had caught a member of the local Milice[43] who had some dark deeds on his conscience, and they were determined to make him confess to more.

"Come and see," said the patriots. "He'll talk in the end. He hasn't opened his mouth yet, though we haven't been gentle with him. And there's worse to come. He's brave, in a way," and they nodded their heads. The prisoner was in a ruined house, from which there came a smell of burning flesh.

"Kill him now," I said. "Don't torture him. It's horrible."

"You don't know all the things he's done, and how many people have died because of him, our comrades."

I couldn't wait to get away. "Weakling," muttered one of the men, shrugging his shoulders. Well, in that case I was glad to be weakling, I wanted to be horrified by such things, until my dying day. There was nothing more for me there; the race to find Major Smith was

---

42. Code name of Yves le Gall, killed in action on 7 August 1944.

43. A far-right paramilitary organisation set up by Vichy in 1943 to combat the Resistance, the Milice was extreme in its methods and – since its members were French – feared by the Resistance for its local knowledge.

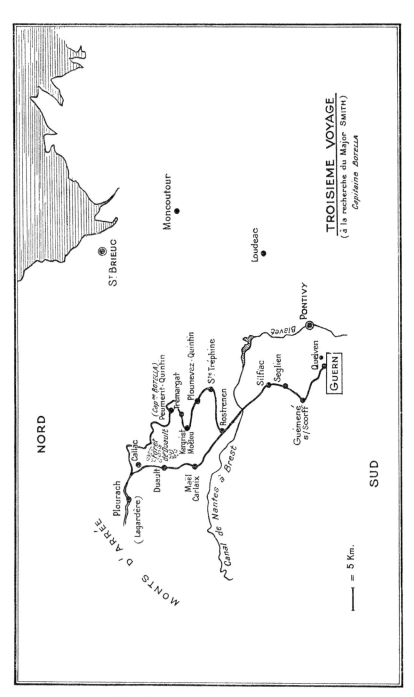

Third Trip: Looking for Major Smith

becoming ridiculous. Either I was on the wrong track, or he had disappeared. I would go back to Guern.

Yves appeared at the top of the hill, and I was glad that he had arrived to put a stop to the unbearable interrogation. His search had been as fruitless as mine, and instantly he asked me to pass on to Deplante a request for parachute drops for his Maquis. Yes, I would ask, as these men were well led and were neither better nor worse than the rest. I went on my way, pedalling furiously, pursued by images of the suffering and the horrors that I had seen and heard over those two days.

I went via Duault and spent a long while sitting on a bank and gazing at the forest on the other side of the valley. A week after the battle, the Germans had torched it with flame-throwers. I could clearly see the blackened tree trunks and bare branches, and I thought: "This was a beautiful forest when Geo was dropped on 5 June, and one day it will be a beautiful forest again. The violence of men will fade away."

CHAPTER 10

Interlude

Gisèle put some bread and smoked sausage beside the butter on the round garden table. Her husband was opening a bottle of beer. It was cool in the shade of the house and I was feeling relaxed with my new friends the Le Mennecs, Antoinette's cousins. After that gruelling trip in the Côtes-du-Nord, which hadn't been entirely pointless but hadn't achieved its real goal either, this warm welcome was like a gift from the gods. I felt I had found a second home. Alongside Kerancalvez, which was still the most important one of all, I'd already had a long list of other homes, none of which I would ever forget. I pictured myself again in Elisabeth's apartment, so close to her, reading and working in the evening, and worrying about Paul, or having tea with the Faussemagnes and Jean-Marie, or with Charles Verny's parents between two trips across Paris, or turning up unannounced at my Aunt Guite's in Quimper, or at the Fravals in Le Faouët. Now I would also have my friends in Guern.

It was a quiet village, its houses clustered around the church. Everyone knew everyone else. The few unreliable elements were held at a safe distance from the dangerous secrets of the Resistance. All the same, the only people who really knew about the comings and goings of the Deplante group were Antoinette's cousins, the Le Doze family – both parents and children – who we would see a lot of from now on, our guide Le Pen, and the secretary at the town hall, Jo Pérez, known as Jopé.

Monsieur Le Doze had come to sit with us in the garden. Suddenly he said: "Marie-Claire, if you want to be at Coët-Niel this evening we should leave now," and I followed him. Deplante was astonished to see me again but was interested in what I told him about Botella. He had just had a message from Smith, who was roaming around to the far north-east of Trémargat, in the opposite direction from Plourac'h. My mistake. There was nothing for it but to ask him for a precise rendezvous and set off again.

What good people the Le Trouher family of Coët-Niel were, so proud to have seen the parachutists arrive and so anxious to take care of their every need! But at Kerriec, the farms we had passed had been burned down, and the Germans were arresting and killing people on the slightest suspicion of aiding the parachutists or the patriots. Deplante decided that night that we should no longer sleep on farms: we would sleep under the stars.

For our dormitory he chose a hillside, half gorse, half grass, about three hundred metres from the farm. A little stream ran along the foot of the slope. Luckily it was a fine evening. Our Captain had a bright yellow cotton parachute for a sheet and gave me a good piece of it, ripping the material in one go. He also gave me the waterproof cover of his sleeping bag. I'd had my own blanket since Coët-Bigot. Carefully making my bed at the edge of the heath, I lay down and watched the day fade away, and the stars shine ever more brightly until the moment when the moon appeared behind the trees. Creatures by the thousand were flying and creeping about, calling to each other with weird cries. Would a snake or a toad crawl into my bed? I wrapped the yellow parachute so tightly around my neck that I nearly throttled myself. Bats were swooping in great circles at ground level, but I didn't have to worry about them getting caught in my hair as I never took off my turban now. My big leather bag covered in a square of parachute silk served as a pillow; I was glad I'd kept it. We could never have imagined it would be used like this. Sylvie, Nicole and me. What had become of the other two?[44] None of us might ever know what had become of the others.

I didn't sleep that first night, but I slept for a little the second night, and for a very long time on the third. It's not good to sleep in houses: the earth has qualities that she transmits to us. I should perhaps have fallen ill in those cold, clear nights and later in the rain, but I felt on top form and different, better.

Waking up on those soft, luminous summer mornings, I felt such fulfilment in all my being that I would suddenly be filled with anguished thoughts: "Take care, little Mic, you're going to lose the best of life. Is war really your affair? You're going to lose the coolness of the dawn, the dew on fresh grass, the first rays of the sun on your still unlined face. Take care! You'll lose your life, the only one you have, for notions of liberty and justice, ideas instilled in you from childhood. And who's to say that dying for them will serve any purpose?"

I fought against these doubts, telling myself: "Come now, for generations your people have known that these ideals are necessary, your reason knows it, your heart knows it too, and you must fight for them. Is life worth living without certain values? You can't argue against it. Don't even try. There's no point." I disliked these thoughts that often went round in my head as I went to sleep and woke up. Was I nothing more than a thinking machine, always reasoning? Did the fine minds of my ancestors weigh so heavily on me? I just wanted to be bursting with life and not have to analyse a thing, to just follow my heart wherever it led me.

---

44. Sylvie was horribly tortured in Paris before being sent to Buchenwald. She was rescued in extremis in 1945, and survived thanks to the kindness and care of the Swedes.

And I would have loved to discuss these problems with Geo, but they had parachuted in a new radio operator from England, called Fraysse, and I didn't have to do any coding or decoding anymore. We had deliberately taken advantage of this, Geo and I, to meet less frequently and to try to be no more to each other than just friends among a group of others.

I often joined in with Antoinette and Deplante's conversations. The Captain would explain the situation to us and how he probably saw it developing. He talked like my father, taking an overview. I was reminded as I listened to him of my time in the Resistance in Paris and Brittany, and I thought that it all held together from the beginning. The plans for D-day had turned out as Charles and Richard had hoped, and Deplante's ideas about how to lead this clandestine war were so closely akin to theirs that I was sorry that they couldn't be as happy as I was about it. Week after week, order was becoming established. Contact had been made with Captain de Mauduit, who had not been able to get to Saint-Marcel and had set up camp in a sector between Scaër, Rostrenen, Mur-de-Bretagne and Plouray, while Captain Deschamps was in another sector. As well as putting units in place, Deplante was also actively involved in officer training. Yes, we needed more officers. Young people were flooding in from all sides and there were very few trained and capable people to command them. Some were too young, while others were too old.

He talked about it with great bitterness, even rage. "Where are the men in their forties who have gone to war and know how to command?" We said nothing. There was nothing to be said against those who were waiting in German camps or rotting as political prisoners. But what about those prudent individuals who were fighting the war in the comfort of their homes, using a map pinned to the wall to offer a commentary on operations? There were only a handful of us. It was the natural order of things, after all. History is only written by the few.

For the moment, requests were being sent to London for more SAS reinforcements, and the zone where the battalion was to take action to stop the Germans getting through and reduce their numbers was being accurately demarcated. Contact was also being made with Morlaix.

Why Morlaix, a port so far from us on the coast of Finistère? The reason became clear after a visit from Major Cary-Elwes, whom Antoinette and I went to fetch the day after my return. The British "team", the Major and his batman Corporal Mills, had extraordinary style. The Major walked with long relaxed strides, his rifle balanced on his shoulder like a true huntsman. The figure who appeared before us round a bend in the road was tall and very slim, bright-eyed and fresh complexioned, with a dazzling smile, a handlebar moustache, and an evident joy in being alive. Parachuted into the south shortly after the battle of Saint-Marcel, his mission was to assess the state of the Resistance. After he had seen Deplante, he persuaded the Allied High Command to continue with parachute drops in Brittany. Together Deplante and Cary-Elwes carried out an intensive arming of the Morlaix region, because there was now talk of a potential landing in region. We didn't want to worry about the moon any longer: it was already on the wane and nothing had happened. The Allies must have a lot of plans up their sleeves and would focus on one or other of them according to circumstances. They would probably warn us only at the last moment. Major Cary-Elwes, his mission accomplished, was to return by the "direct" route to London, in a pocket submarine that would pick him and Mills up near Plouha on the north coast of Brittany.

The evening we all spent in the large hall at Coët-Niel, by the light of a paraffin lamp, was very convivial. Cary-Elwes and Deplante were delighted to see each other again. Cider and Calvados were brought out as they reminisced about the good old days in Scotland, spent in a gloomy, romantic castle, the headquarters of the demi-brigade of French parachutists for whom Major Cary-Elwes was the liaison officer.

I was particularly interested in the business about Morlaix that was being discussed around the table, and I thought of Yves Lagardère and his muscular Maquis, who would need to be put on the alert. I was keeping my promise. Finistère would no longer be overlooked! I gave the information I'd been able to gather to Antoinette, who was about to go there with Major Cary-Elwes.[45] As for me, at last I was going to find Commandant Bourgouin: we had just heard that he was now at the Moulin de Guillac, and Deplante had sent a message to Major Smith to ensure that I could join him immediately afterwards: "Marie-Claire to Smith, stop, I can't find you. Please give your position." As soon as the answer came I would be off.

• • •

Once again Bailly gave us his racy songs and funny stories, all in his inimitable Parisian accent, but Mills put him in the shade during his time with us. He would tremble and turn pale at the thought of the parachute jump he had had to make to follow his officer into Brittany. When he unrolled a spanking new British sleeping bag in the meadow, Paul Robineau, Andrieu, Henri and the others gathered round to admire it. "Well!" said Robineau, "you're a lucky devil to be tucked up in that neat little sleeping bag. Stay for a few days and your fleabag will fall into the clutches of the Krauts like ours." Mills wasn't keen to hang around in the region for too long! Bailly came up and said, also in English: "By the way Mills, how long have you been your Major's batman? He's a great guy, brave, certainly no 'Buckingham', one might say."

"For a long, long time," answered Mills. "I saw him for the first time at the baptismal font, or virtually. It's a tradition in our army

---

45. A Jedburgh team was able to set up in Finistère soon afterwards.

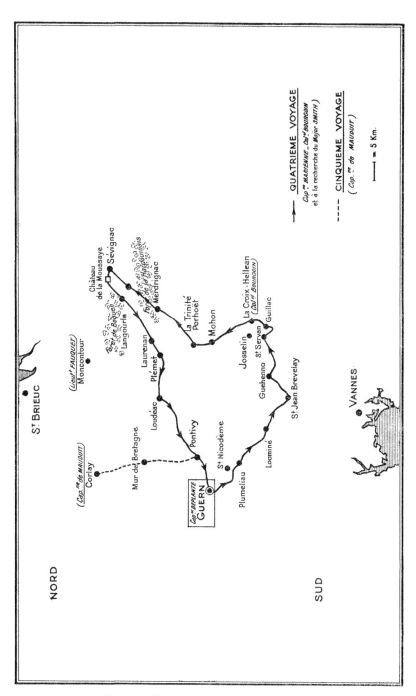

Fourth and fifth trips: Captain Marienne, Commandant Bourgoin

that an officer can choose his batman and keep him with him come what may. We met and we liked each other! I was at his wedding. Since then we haven't been apart. I was with him in Libya and here I am in Brittany. I follow him like his shadow, on land and in the air! I'm telling you, when I jump, I follow him so closely that last time, he even said to me: 'Old boy, for goodness' sake keep your distance, or you'll be sitting in my parachute when we land!'" The SAS had loved Scotland, and here they were at twilight on this heather-covered moorland remembering it with nostalgia.

"Come on," said Andrieu, "you were there a week ago, tell us the latest."

"Nothing changes in my country, nothing, as you well know," answered Mills.

"Ah! Mills," said another, "how I would like to see our little Scottish village of Sorn again! It's Saturday night and there will be a dance in the village hall. I would find my beautiful redhead Maureen again and we would dance the 'riots' with our friends shouting 'whoop, whoop!' under the benevolent and amused gaze of the old people in the village. Then we'd go and drink a few lagers at the pub, until we were thrown out at eleven o'clock: 'Time, gentlemen!' But then came the hardest part, Mills, which was to get back to the SAS brigade's castle in good order without the Captain noticing. When he did catch us, drunk as lords, he never missed a trick. He would invite us for a 'little night-time stroll' and then at nightfall take us in his big Humber and drop us out in the wilds, twenty, twenty-five kilometres from our billet. With a smile, very calmly, he would hand us a compass and a map on which he would point to what he called 'the drop spot' and then he would wish us good night, and he and the car would disappear into the distance. All that was left for us to do was to get on with it and find our way across the moors. In the end I have happy memories of those moonless treks back to the castle over the soft loamy soil, or staggering through peat bogs. At least you didn't get stabbed by blasted gorse bushes there! No, it's not a bed of roses here. Not to mention what we've been eating for weeks on end: crêpes and bacon, washed down with cider that often tastes more like vinegar. Give me "a nice cup of tea"! And a proper breakfast tomorrow morning: porridge or haddock, eggs and bacon, and then cocoa at ten o'clock, and a whisky before lunch!"

Our group grew for a little while, as we were joined by Captain Fay and his batman Lieutenant Patrick, who after Saint-Marcel had gone to Marienne's camp and then to Deschamps'. The British contingent installed itself comfortably on the other side of the bank, well hidden among the clearings on the heath. Sergeant Capelin, who had just been parachuted in with the many millions that had been requested (London had decided to only send the money if it was accompanied), had made himself comfortable too. He had all the field rations that the others had told me about, but that I'd never admired in their full glory: meat cubes, sachets of tea with milk, chewing gum for long marches, a portable stove with its little disks of solidified alcohol, and sweets, chocolate and biscuits galore. He gave me some together with some beautiful bars of soap decorated with His Majesty's crown.

There was a tremendously lively atmosphere. Endless discussions were held in the shade of an oak tree. Deplante, in a pair of shorts and red socks that he had unearthed from who knows where, acted as arbiter, like Saint Louis, between the many different opinions. The radio operators would come and go, holding messages. Billy the American major had got his smile back: Major Cary-Elwes was to take him with him on the "direct" route back. He was already picturing himself at the controls of a new aircraft.

On the morning of 12 July, a furious Bailly came to find me: "Last night we had the devil's own job of decoding a message that London absolutely insisted on sending us. The jamming was hellish. And what did we decode, Geo and me? 'Smith to Marie-Claire…' So now you're getting your own little messages! Well, well, well. And we haven't finished yet …"

Smith said: "Meet me 12.00 hours, 13 July, Château de la Moussaye, 3 km west Sévignac, 8 km east Gouray, stop. Ask for owner de la Motte." It was nine o'clock on the 12th, and I had to see Commandant Bourgouin first. I couldn't make the rendezvous. My answer went back via same route: "Marie-Claire to Smith, stop, impossible to make rendezvous, stop, will be there as soon as possible."

When I went to see Deplante to find out what message he wanted me to take to Le Manchot, I found him contemplating a pigeon that had been brought to him in a wicker cage, to which was attached a small parachute. The bird had a small tube attached to a ring on one leg, in which was a piece of paper marked "On His Majesty's Service". The Captain had unfolded it and read an astonishing questionnaire: in faultless English, it asked for particulars on the enemy positions around us and invited us by the same token to supply our bearings. A farmer had found the basket in a field of rye, and since there were no traces on the ground he thought that it really had been parachuted in. Captain Fay sniffed it and thought it smelt right. But Deplante decided to consult London, who responded: "Pigeon likely dropped by enemy, stop, suggest make a pigeon pie!" Which we did.[46]

After the farmer came a liaison agent. As he spoke, Deplante's expression became sombre, and I could see that he was suddenly far away from us. "Our great Sloughi is no more," he said. He had just learned of the death of his friend Roger de la Grandière.[47]

"It's not going well in the south, far worse than here. Go and see Captain Marienne first," concluded Deplante. "Captain Fay will give you directions to find him, and he will tell you if it's possible to reach

46. British, American and German intelligence all made extensive use of carrier pigeons, and the risk of deception was real. MI5 had a "counter-pigeon team" and trained peregrine falcons to kill German pigeons.

47. Lieutenant Roger de la Grandière was parachuted into Saint-Marcel with the jeeps on 17 June 1944. After fighting at Saint-Marcel, he was killed near Pontivy on 20 June, on his way to rejoin Deplante. He was twenty-seven.

Commandant Bourgoin. I'll send a message to tell him you're on the way. You can go now and you'll be there tonight."

Go now. Yes, I could. It was beautiful westerly weather, with a delicate blue sky and fluffy cumulus clouds swelling and dissolving on the horizon. Yes, I had time to get to the Alexandre farm at Quénelé. Captain Fay had given me copious reference points. "Mention my name," he said, "we fought together at Albert, in 1940," adding, "If you have any trouble, go and find the butcher in Guehenno or the hotel owner at Saint-Jean Brévelay, on the way." It was all clear and precise, with no grey areas or pitfalls. But I said: "I don't want to go." Deplante looked at me, amazed. "But if you order me to, I will."

"I can't make you go, you must do as you wish!"

"I'll give you my answer in an hour," I said. I couldn't explain it. A strange force was holding me back, exactly like the feeling I'd had at the bottom of Madame Jullien's steps on Rue Alasseur.

An hour later I went back to Deplante. Swallowing my misgivings, I said: "I'll go tomorrow, for certain."

CHAPTER 11

Terror

The next day, Thursday, I said goodbye to them all. I didn't want to disturb Geo, who was inundated with work, and it was better if we didn't see each other again.

It was very early in the afternoon, I had time, and with my new bicycle I could go fast without getting tired: it was a thoroughbred, whereas my old mount was a wheezy old nag in comparison! So I allowed myself the luxury of a visit to the church of Saint-Nicodème, whose decorative openwork bell tower soared above the countryside. The Bretons had studded their land with wayside shrines and chapels in the most remote and wild places, as well as in the pretty valleys and verdant woods. Whenever I saw one of these sanctuaries, I would go in to pray and to admire the touching wooden Christ figures, the naive statues of Celtic saints, and the lacy carving of the rood screens. Afterwards I went to the neighbouring farm, where with great kindness they gave me a glass of water, as I was parched with thirst. I was admiring the black cherries that were weighing down the branches of a tree in the yard, when they fetched me a ladder and told me to help myself, which I did, my forebodings forgotten.

But when I saw the church at Pluméliau, burnt out and still smouldering, it brought back all the inexplicable feelings of unease that I'd been unable to shake off the day before. To the point that I stopped on a hill, thinking about the bag of British sweets that I'd brought with me and the crown on the soap. Leaning against the bank, I started to work my way through the sweets, one by one, and then I carefully scratched off the imperial crown.

I was nearing Saint-Jean Brévelay; soon I would be at Marienne's camp.

Just then, Deplante received two messages one after the other. One was from the broadcast:, "Le Manchot camp attacked." And the other from Bourgoin himself: "Have withdrawn by miracle through Germans and Milice. Manceau and four others arrested, stop, Deplante to delay making contact until further notice, stop, am near radio position, Milice in the area, Le Manchot."

And Geo, crouched over the radio transmitter, immediately sent a message to Marienne, via London. "Deplante to Marienne: warn Marie-Claire dangerous to contact Le Manchot." He was worried: "What if she's already left Quénelé?"

• • •

Lieutenant Skinner[48] and the stick he had formed at Callac had left their self-appointed theatre of operations to go to the rendezvous arranged by Captain Marienne, and were approaching the liaison point at Pont de Lézourdan. Skinner, who at twenty-eight was much older than the others, was a doctor from Paris, the son of the journalist Henri de Kerillis. He had already fought bravely in 1940.

Pams, Serra and Croënne were all nineteen, while Harbinson was barely eighteen. They had just carried out some successful operations around Vannes, and they were reluctant to leave that area. But

---

48. Code name for Alain Calloc'h de Kerillis, executed on 20 July 1944.

Marienne had made meticulous preparations for future operations, and the parachutists needed to regroup before the anticipated landings.

The farmhouse at Kérihuel echoed that night with the happy chatter of a large crowd who had gathered to celebrate the arrival of Skinner and his young men. At about eleven, Marienne suddenly looked around him and said: "Put some distance between us tonight. There are too many of us here. We'll see each other again tomorrow." A guide took Skinner and his party to La Roche de Milgourdy.[49]

It was very late and Captain Marienne and his second-in-command, Lieutenant Martin, were still working, while the radio operators sent message after message. Men had been stationed to keep watch. From the outset, Marienne had insisted that his men should stand guard in shifts, to avoid any surprises.

When the parachutist Coffin arrived at about three in the morning with Captain Mackay, an American fighter pilot shot down locally, the FFI guard on duty told them that the Captain and his men were asleep and that he would take them to a barn about fifty metres from the farm, where they could spend the night. In a lean-to attached to the barn were a group of FFI men with Captain Morizur. "You have nothing to fear," said the lad, "we've only been here for two days and the Germans certainly won't have managed to locate us yet." More parachutists under the command of a sergeant arrived a little later and settled down near them.

• • •

"Here we are," said the guide to Skinner. It had been an arduous trek across the high moorland, and they were glad to arrive at last. "It's a fine dolmen," the guide went on. "Beneath it you won't need to worry about the rain, and no one will see you. You won't be the first

49. A large dolmen in a cairn (now privately owned) in Plumelec.

to sleep here and you won't be the last either. You are in the valley of the River Claie," added the boy. "It's a valley that's easy for aircraft to spot. That's why the La Baleine drop zone was so good. The people in the valley are all for you, you know. They'll help you now and in the future, whenever it's needed." The windmill at Plumelec looked very close. They crouched down among the ferns and asphodels, afraid of being spotted by the Germans, who were still there in spite of a wave of RAF bombardments.

• • •

The man had made a sudden entrance: the patriots who were drinking a glass of cider sat motionless for a moment, looking at him. He opened his raincoat to show his parachutist's uniform. The men got to their feet, concerned. There was starting to be a lot of talk about bogus parachutists. Seeing their hesitation, Munoz pulled out an identity card. "You can see now I am one of yours," he said. The identity card of Lieutenant Gray[50] was passed from hand to hand. How could they have guessed that the lieutenant had just been arrested with Jégo? The card was genuine, there was no doubt about that. François Munoz[51] sat down with them and they had another drink. He was shrewd in his conversation, talking of things that only genuine parachutists could have known, and they believed him. He asked them where Mahieux the butcher was. "He is the one," he confided, "who will take me to Captain Marienne." Why send for Mahieux? The lads could tell him where to go. "Ask the wheelwright at Cadoudal, near Kérihuel," they told him finally.

• • •

50. "Jean Gray", code name for Jean Pessis, had already been imprisoned at Pontivy. A medical student, he was executed on 18 July 1944, aged twenty-three.
51. François Munoz, a French collaborator along with Maurice Zeller and Alfred Gross.

It was nearly dawn. The young guard had dozed off. A cock had crowed. In the thickets where they had made their new camp, they were still in a deep sleep.

Three cars had already left Locminé, with twelve men on board armed with revolvers and a submachine gun. This time, Munoz was accompanied by Maurice Zeller, Alfred Gross, Luiz Deniz, Herr and Fisher. Zeller wanted to be there for the capture of Marienne, for he envied this man whom everyone admired; he hated all these men. He could have been like them. Perhaps there simmered, deep in his innermost being, a regret that he could never be their equal. His actions had singled him out like a leper: there was that drugs business when he was a young and brilliant officer in the Navy. Everything might have been different if he hadn't been cashiered from the Navy. And all might not have been lost if they had taken him back in 1940, or even if it had been with the French who had saved him when he nearly drowned off the Breton coast, rather than the Germans. They had become his friends, and he was so impressed by them that he had gone off with them as a captain – a German captain, on the Russian front, at Smolensk. Invalided out, he had gone back to Saint-Brieuc where he had joined Doriot's Parti Populaire Français.[52] For four thousand francs, he had then become a recruiter for the Légion Volontaire Française. But four thousand francs wasn't enough, and the Germans caught him with his hand in the till. They knew then that Zeller would do anything they wanted. So yes, he hated all those men and he would kill them. He had missed Deplante, he had missed Le Manchot the day before, at the Moulin de Guillac, but he was not going to miss Marienne that day.

Munoz got out of the car just before the village of Cadoudal and went to see the wheelwright. "Go to the Danet farm, over there,"

52. Jacques Doriot was a prominent French fascist and collaborator who founded both the Parti Populaire and the Légion Volontaire Française, with which he fought in German uniform on the Eastern Front. He was killed by Allied aircraft fire in Germany in February 1945.

said the wheelwright. "Ask the people who are sleeping here," said the farmer in his turn when Munoz asked where he could find the Captain. Zeller, the Milice men and the Germans were following, lurking behind a slope. When Munoz gave the signal, they came out into the open and surrounded the lean-to where eight young men were asleep, their weapons piled up at the entrance. They bound the patriots and flung them into the farmyard. "Where is Marienne?" screamed Fisher. A soft light spread over the tranquil countryside and the sleeping camp. And at last the traitors found them, sound asleep in their tents in the woods.

Before they could think, Marienne and his companions were already overpowered. They were thrown against an old wall that ran alongside the thicket and tortured to make them talk. Marienne protested that this was an ignominious violation of the rules of war, but they just laughed. Zeller wasted no time in filching anything he fancied from the tents and the parachutists.

After a quarter of an hour of blows and insults had yielded nothing, they took the prisoners to Kérihuel farmyard. The young FFI men were still flat on the ground. "Where are the officers?" demanded the Germans. Marienne and Martin stepped forward. "Remember we are soldiers!" said Marienne again, but they made him and Martin lie down with the young men. They pushed the other parachutists up against a building with their hands in the air. Then they searched the ones who were dressed, since some of them, like Sergeant Judet, were in their underpants. In the first burst of gunfire, Judet's comrade fell beside him. As he looked at him, he also saw his own open hand against the grey stone, with a lifeline so long that it stretched right across his palm. He felt strangely reassured. A German soldier had just shown him a photograph of his wife that he had found in his wallet, saying: "Take a good look at your widow!" But he was wrong: before the second burst of gunfire, Judet had leapt like a young deer over a hedge that he would never normally have been able to clear.

They killed them all, the eight patriots, Danet the farmer, Morizur, another man from the hamlet and the seven parachutists, in front of a group of terrified women who were huddled in a corner of the farmyard. The traitors had their photographs taken in front of the dead men, lying face down in the dust. Zeller looked sombre, the others were laughing.

They torched the hamlet and threw some of their victims onto the flames.

• • •

The parachutists in the barn were violently shaken from sleep by the bursts of gunfire. They rushed outside and headed for the farm. Suddenly the sergeant collapsed. Coffin dragged him by his feet to the shelter of a wall. "He's dead," said another man behind him. Led by an FFI man, they ran to Marienne's camp, to find it wrecked and abandoned. Then they went to a hamlet they knew, where they found Sergeant Judet; by a miracle he had managed to escape the Germans, who were now hunting for him.[53]

• • •

Skinner sat up suddenly. He could hear fighting over towards Kérihuel. He came out from under the Milgourdy dolmen and looked over to the windmill and the road. Agitated Germans were jumping down from a lorry. A liaison agent suddenly emerged from the thickets shouting: "Marienne, Martin, they've all been caught. We've been betrayed!"

"We have to save the wounded," thought Skinner. He knew they had been sheltering in the woods at Trédion since the battle at Saint-Marcel. He gave orders to leave.

---

53. Gabriel René Judet was killed in action in the Netherlands on 9 April 1945.

• • •

There were no problems this time for my point of contact: I had been announced and they were waiting for me. Alexandre himself arrived, driving a cart along the road to Quénélé.

"I'm Marie-Claire," I said, thinking that Marienne would have mentioned me to him. "Don't know you," he replied in a surly tone. "What do you want?"

"To see Captain Marienne."

"Don't know him," he replied. "There's no Captain round here." I could feel things were going badly, not to say disastrously. How could I have known that owing to an error Alexandre was expecting a Marguerite, not a Marie-Claire? He thought I was from the Milice. I tried mentioning Captain Fay, the fighting at the Albert canal in 1940, the butcher and the hotel owner, but the farmer remained inscrutable and unhelpful. "Well then, if you know folk at Saint-Jean and Guéhenno you'd better go there, they'll know better than me, for sure." There was nothing for it, I'd have to go. Was it going to be like the Côtes-du-Nord all over again?

Back on the road, I hesitated. What had Fay said? The big butcher at Guéhenno, and the small hotel owner at Saint-Jean-Brévelay? Or the other way round? Why had Alexandre been so tight-lipped about the parachutists? What was behind it all? It was eight o'clock; curfew was at nine. I hadn't eaten. My lovely carefree feeling from Saint-Nicodème had evaporated.

I opted for the butcher at Saint-Jean-Brévelay, but there were two butchers' shops on the town square, both shut and with no butchers to be seen behind the metal grilles. I turned back towards a restaurant I'd glimpsed on the outskirts of town. Au Bon Accueil, the warm welcome, was well-named, for the house with its pink roughcast was charming. I went in and asked for the owner.

"He isn't here," answered the owner's wife, looking worried. "What do you want him for?"

"To speak to him personally."

"Come back in a quarter of an hour," she said.

My memory, usually so good, was letting me down. Which was the right hotel owner? The church, where a lot of women were saying their rosary, offered me a refuge. How they prayed, those women, for their husbands and sons! The Germans had rounded up their men one Sunday after Mass, and were still taking them every day from their houses in the town and the farms around. The prisons in the little towns of the area were full to bursting, as was Fort Penthièvre in Quiberon. There were atrocious accounts of tortures and massacres.

After saying the rosary, the women recited a prayer that had been distributed throughout France:

> *Holy Mary, Queen of Heaven and Queen of France!*
> *Lift France up, give her back her strength and independence:*
> *For this, give each one of us trust in our own personal effort.*
> *Unite our hearts and renew our faith in God.*
> *Holy Mary, Queen of France!*
> *Deliver our country from the foreigner's yoke.*

Feeling a close affinity with those women sitting around me, I was soothed by their presence.

When I returned to the "Au Bon Accueil" there was still no owner, and his wife was still hesitant. Then she called me into her kitchen, separated from the main room by a half-height partition. "Why do you want to see my husband? Perhaps I can give you some information instead."

It was my turn to hesitate. "Well," I said at last, "I'm looking for the patriots."

"What!" she said. "Don't you know?"

"Know what?"

"The Germans captured a big group of them this morning and shot them all. And they've arrested a lot of people in the area. My husband had to leave, and I don't expect him back any time soon." I was afraid for Marienne, but she had no further details: "At Guéhenno you'll get more information at the butcher's," she assured me. "He's in it." She had given me an omelette and some green beans. I'd finished eating and I got up. I would go to Guéhenno straight away.

Caution made me go into an impoverished-looking house on the outskirts of the village. A weeping woman said, "So, you want to see the butcher? This morning he was taken by the Gestapo, heaven knows where, and they arrested my husband, and Monsieur Gillet from the cafe, and others as well. What will they do to them? If you only knew what they've done to our people before killing them!" What could I say to her? She was probably a widow.

When I tried to get some more information at the hotel, they more or less showed me the door. The owner was away for a long time, they told me. The few men who still lingered at the tables gave me hostile stares. I took one of the girls working there aside: "Tell me where I can stay the night." Then I insisted. "Help me out. It might save some people; I have to find the patriots." Eventually she gave me the name of a farm where they would probably put me up for the night, and told me about a café called "Au Rendez-vous des Garçons" where the Maquis often met up.

There they would tell me something. But I was beginning to be filled with doubt. What had happened that was so terrible? Why were they all quaking with fear?

• • •

They wanted nothing to do with me at the farm of Le Calvaire. A little old lady at the Maquis café shook her head and said again and again that they'd never been there, ever. I was too exhausted to insist.

Now all I wanted was to be on my own and not feel the weight of suspicion pressing down on me. I would pick some remote wood, make a hollow in the undergrowth and sleep there. Where was the gentle meadow of Coët-Niel?

It was long past curfew time. Wisps of orange and green trailed across the sky, which was clouding over with great purple clouds. On all sides were large, mysterious expanses echoing with strange calls. Was Marienne over here, or over there? Where was he? I had been so happy to have the opportunity of getting to know him properly, and I had so many messages to give him from Deplante. The menacing clouds were closing in on me, and deep down I knew I wouldn't find Marienne. Tomorrow I would go in search of Bourgoin.

A man with a scythe over his shoulder was heading home. "Do you know a farm where I can spend the night?" I asked. He stared at me. It was heartless. I was so fed up with being stared at.

"Go and see over there," he said to me, pointing to a wisp of smoke rising from behind a hill. But I knew what they'd say, so I walked along beside him. "Monsieur, you must have a barn where I can sleep, it's coming on to rain."

"Mademoiselle you can't sleep in the straw, and I don't have an extra bed, I'm not rich, and then there are the Germans…" I went anyway and followed him into a small house where his wife and young children were waiting for him.

"What danger can I pose for you? I've come from Rennes and I'm on my way to join my parents in Finistère." But he wasn't taken in. He explained to me that as of that day it was obligatory to display a notice on the front door of every dwelling stating the number of people living there. If someone extra came, they had to be declared at the Kommandantur. The order had been posted at the town hall in Guéhenno the night before, and he showed me the piece of paper pinned to the door. So, if I was seen at his house, what would happen? They would be taken away and put in prison. As if there weren't enough people in prison already!

Even so, in the end he relented, telling me to follow him behind the house where he put a ladder up against a dormer window. It was in a loft three-quarters full of hay that I laid my head down: there was just a tiny window opening and the stench was appalling. I turned to say goodnight to the man, but he'd gone, taking the ladder with him. I felt like a rat in a trap. But I didn't care about the trap, I didn't care about the fleas, I didn't care about the unbearable stench. I slept.

I slept in the warm and prickly hay. My host didn't sleep, as he was too worried about my being there. But no, he didn't go and denounce me at the town hall.

At dawn, the ladder was back in place.

• • •

Dawn on 14 July. "A bad day for me. You should go," said Skinner to his companions, who laughed at him. They had found the wounded in the woods at Trédion after a tragic journey.

On the morning of 12 July, Lieutenant Skinner had left La Roche de Milgourdy with his stick and had joined up with the sticks of Lieutenants Tisné and Fleuriot. That same night they all left together, with barely ten kilometres to cover. Before arriving at Trédion village, which a local man had assured them was quiet and "free of vermin", they took cover, as a precaution, near the "Le Bois-Sabot" café. But at the corner of the street a German was waiting for them. A round of gunfire killed Lieutenant Tisné and a Polish lieutenant, Jaciensky, and a bullet went clean through Lieutenant Skinner's arm. They turned on their heels and took off across the fields.

All of a sudden, Lieutenant Fleuriot vanished behind a hedge, having failed to spot a deep sunken lane, and knocked himself out on some rocks as he fell. Skinner rushed forward to lift him up; he seemed to be in terrible pain and said in a strange voice: "It's nothing, just the bells of Cambridge." They stopped for a moment. There was nothing but the sounds of the countryside. Skinner's arm was badly injured, and he made himself an improvised bandage. Then Fleuriot asked for his glasses and his rifle and assured them he could go on. A little further on, exhausted, he fell again. Skinner examined him carefully, with all his medical knowledge as a doctor. His face showed nothing, but he feared a ruptured liver. He encouraged his friend, and once again Fleuriot went on, leaning on the shoulders of the other two, only to collapse again a little further on. "You go on ahead; leave me," he begged them. At the nearby Beauvais farm, they agreed to look after him. They laid him down in a field of buckwheat and the young radio operator Perrin stayed at his side, while the others went on towards Kerlanvaux farm, near to where the wounded men were in hiding.

They made a new dressing for Skinner, who was in great pain, and then the farmer took them to a pinewood opposite the farm. In the centre of the wood, a dense thicket had offered an ideal hiding place for the parachutists. A host of birds sang among the hazels, dwarf oaks and young beeches. The wounded men were able to walk, and Skinner would have liked to leave that night, 12 July. But there was absolutely no question of abandoning Fleuriot, and they went to collect him, carrying him on an improvised stretcher. Although he was pale, he seemed a little better.

The night was over, however, and they had to wait for the following one. The men felt relaxed in this thicket. A sentry was on watch at the start of the side road at the edge of the wood. They played the card game *belote* and chatted. Soon they would hear the welcome clink of the cider bottles in the farmer's bucket as he brought them lunch. They watched the insects scurrying in the moss and the birds flitting from tree to tree.

Surely that was the familiar chink of dishes and bottles? The sentry hadn't fired a shot, which was the agreed warning. They were hungry, they got to their feet. Then someone shouted, "They're here!" and someone pulled the branches apart. Simultaneously, machine guns opened fire. It was the Germans. Freddie Harbinson was directly in front of them. As they fired he fell forward, clutching his hands to his chest. Men were falling all around him, while others fled or tried to flee, pursued by the Milice and the Germans, who were firing their machine guns indiscriminately. Galliou and Collobert, mortally wounded, dragged themselves to the densest part of the woods, where they were to die for lack of food and medical care. Some local people found them a few days later.

Coralled around the stretcher on which they had laid young Freddie, the captured parachutists were taken to Kerlanvaux farm. Earlier, a man had brought Zeller and his gang there. For Zeller was not a man who wasted time. He wanted to catch them all quickly; he wanted to thwart all the counter moves of the alerted liaison agents, who would be running in all directions to save the parachutists.

Zeller threatened to kill the farmer in order to panic his wife into telling him where the terrorists were. But she refused, and he was machine-gunned in front of the farmhouse. One of the Germans, more humane than the rest, bent over the farmer's wife in her agony of grief, saying: "Oh! Madame, much unhappiness for you."

The parachutists were thoroughly searched and stripped of everything, while anything of any value was taken from the farmhouse. Skinner, who now had a fresh wound to his abdomen, made furious protests in German against this mistreatment: "We are soldiers!" In the end, the Germans put the two officers to one side, pumped bullets into the others, Decrept, Harbinson, Miot, and Perrin, tossed them with the farmer onto the dung heap in the stable yard, then doused all the buildings with petrol and set light to the farm, which was consumed by flames.

The Milice poured any alcohol they could find down their throats. Zeller heated a poker in the flames until it was red hot and amused himself by searing the farmer's wife and her daughter with deep burns. Those depraved creatures were possessed by a crazed hatred, an infernal jubilation that prompted howls of hideous laughter. The flames roared, beams fell to the ground with terrifying crashes, the stable roof collapsed in a shower of sparks.

• • •

The following day, the Mayor of Trédion, Monsieur de Charette, went to Kerlanvaux with a nun. The embers were still glowing. They took the human remains to the town hall. The Gestapo had forbidden them from placing the coffins in the church.

• • •

The Germans threw the two wounded officers into the cells in the prison at Pontivy,[54] with no medical treatment. Despite his wounds, Skinner was tortured for days on end, but said nothing. Neither did Anne-Marie, Marienne's secretary, who had also been arrested on the road, along with Madeleine Rolland, Le Touzic, Le Berre and many others.

On 18 July, the two men and twelve other detainees from the prison were loaded into a new lorry. A car followed behind, carrying Zeller, Munoz and Gross in enemy uniform, and some Germans.

The prisoners' lorry and the executioners' car stopped at Bieuzy-les-Eaux in Rimaison. There the Germans went to the lengths of simulating a gunfight, firing at point-blank range and summarily executing all fourteen men. A further execution at Pluméliau on 29 July killed Jean Jamet, the police lieutenant from Quimperlé whom I had met at Saint-Marcel, the architect Mathieu Donnart, director of Ozone at Brest, and the radio operator "Rolland" from Morlaix.

---

54. The prison at Pontivy was a girls' school (École primaire supérieure de jeunes filles de Pontivy), that had been requisitioned by the Germans.

Zeller and his henchmen would continue their work to the end, and there was no shortage of it. Despite their naturally suspicious natures, the country people let themselves be taken in by the fine words of the bogus parachutists: "It's dangerous," they would say. "You need to move the arms to new hiding places." And those brave people fell into their hands. In how many other places would the tragedies of Kérihuel and Kerlanvaux be repeated? This was terror.

• • •

A very ordinary café, spotlessly clean. The copper pots hanging on the wall gleamed. A young woman with a pale complexion and flaxen plaits was rocking a baby at the far end of the room.

"Could you tell me whether Captain Guimard or his liaison agents are due to come here?" She shot me a dull look:

"Dunno."

Two glasses of cider drunk in tiny sips and a glass of cassis drunk even more slowly: it was about time she told me something! She would come to serve me, then go back to her place beside the baby; when it wailed she would rock the cradle, and she would repeat the same refrain: "Dunno what you're talking about." I'd had enough of all these mulish, suspicious, pitiless people! All my host of the previous night had given me was a glass of cider as I was leaving. Gnawed by pangs of hunger and feeling as if I was about to pass out, I'd knocked on several doors. No one had given me anything, anywhere, not a crumb, not a morsel of bread, not a crêpe. I felt like a beggar. Yet they were good people, just terrified. Happily, Quinquis, Villard and the nurse had been more welcoming at the chateau of Saint-Servant. They had told me about this rendezvous spot by the bridge at Ploermel, beside the canal, since Le Manchot had very nearly fallen into the hands of the Germans (Zeller's gang again) at the Moulin de Guillac and had had to flee elsewhere.

Once I had proffered details about Guimard and the girls I'd known at Saint-Marcel, the nurse perked up a bit and said: "A liaison agent is coming later on, you just need to wait. But why haven't you got the password? It's not right, that."

Then a little later: "You can come, he's here." She took me into a small sitting room.

Emile Guimard, not a liaison agent, came towards me, his face gaunt and sallow, his beard unkempt.

He was sad, Emile, and bitter. "It's bad," he said, "They're going to be picked off, one by one, those parachutists. There won't be any left on the great day. The Allies should have landed at the end of June, then mid-July, on the Rhuys Peninsula. Saint-Marcel was perfectly placed for taking the Germans on the coast from the rear. We were moving down the Lanvaux moors, towards Vannes. I'd spent so much time planning Saint-Marcel, and now it's up the creek. The landings are up the creek. Too much wind, too much bad weather. We were constantly on alert for the moment to warn the people of Vannes. The British were even supposed to send leaflets telling them to evacuate. Marienne worked so hard to prepare for these operations that we were expecting again, any day.

"We had to find new drop zones: Tinchebraye was caught on 19 June, with the sites of the eighteen agreed zones in the Morbihan! Anyway, I think we were ready. But Marienne is dead. Now we have to wait for another moon. We'll have plenty of time for that. I still don't know how we managed to escape at the Moulin de Guillac! The Germans and the Milice only just missed us. They're tightening their grip with every day that passes."

He told me about Jeanne, and the others who were on the road like me, and about Anne-Marie, who had been arrested and was being tortured in the prison at Pontivy. Then he made me hide my bicycle in a field below the road. "Do you realise, Marie-Claire, they're searching the countryside with dogs. These are SS men armed to the teeth who'll shoot you as soon as they look at you. They space themselves out every five metres and advance like an irresistible tide across fields, woods and villages. Impossible to escape if you're in their area."

Major Morice was sitting on the grass a little further on, in civilian clothes like Guimard. He was even more bitter. "If you go up towards Guern you'll be safer," I told them. "Captain Deplante is very keen for Commandant Bourgoin to join him."

"Yes, that would be a good thing," they answered, then started talking about where to put me up for the night.

"It doesn't matter," I told them, "I'm used to sleeping outside." That amazed them. I left them to join Major Bourgoin's liaison officer, who had just arrived and was leaving again straight away.

• • •

"What! You're not dead, Marie-Claire? I thought …" It was odd the way all these men seemed to think I'd "passed over". Quite remarkable. "Oh! How happy I am to see you!" he said, shaking me by the hand and tweaking my ear. He towered over me from his great height and the wind ruffled his wayward curls. His big navy-blue jumper brought out the palest blue of his eyes.

He took me a little way off so we could talk. I passed on what Deplante had told me and gave him Botella's message. Liaison agents were able to explain so much more than laconic radio messages! We were walking side by side through the cloying mud on the edge of the fields. He showed me the hut in the hollow of a ditch where he hid during the day. "They'll be hard put to find me there," he said. "I'm 'worth' five million francs, it seems; they're arresting all the one-armed men in the entire region."

"They're really clever, the Milice," I replied.

"Yes, they killed Marienne," he muttered angrily.

• • •

Back at the farm, I sat at the big table with the five Moureau daughters to clean and trim the harvest of ceps they'd collected in the woods. The recent rains had made them pop up all over the place, even though the season was over. Bourgoin watched us with a fatherly eye. He asked how old I was. "The perfect age to marry one of my parachutists," he said.

A gentle atmosphere, clean and calm, reigned over the farm at La Croix-Helléan, a serene acceptance of whatever fate might bring. The bedroom to which the older ones of those lovely girls took me reflected an eye for harmony and beauty, with gleaming light walnut furniture, flowers on the round table, and beds covered with fringed bedspreads that were as white as the muslin curtains. They went to fetch me a towel and a kettle of hot water. I shared a bed with one of the Moureau girls; the sheets smelt of freshly picked lavender.

Bourgoin arrived at the farm for breakfast, and we studied one of those calendars brought by the postman to work out my route to find Major Smith – I no longer had my maps! – and then he helped me pile my things on my luggage rack. "This big leather bag will get you caught," he said, just as Richard used to say. And I saw myself again in Elisabeth's apartment on Rue de Lille. When? Years earlier? Just a few months …

"I'll send a message to Captain Deplante to tell him I'm coming. I might see you there. Don't go and get arrested."

When we reached a gate, he left me.

CHAPTER 12

Rendezvous with Major Smith

A hundred kilometres to Sévignac. The exhaustion was crushing after about twenty kilometres, as usual, which always slowed me down, but then by some curious phenomenon I would pick up speed again around thirty kilometres and keep up a steady pace for another thirty. After that, my only thought was to get there.

Summer seemed to be here to stay at last, and I savoured the cool shade of the noble forests of Lanouée and La Hardouinais, handsome survivors of the forest of Brocéliande, the haunt of Merlin the enchanter and Viviane, Lady of the Lake, in the time of King Arthur and Parsifal. My bicycle sped along so perfectly that I hardly dismounted on hills, and I didn't even yearn for a vehicle with an engine, which would have broken the wonderful silence that lets you hear the sounds of nature, just as a sailing boat lets you hear the sounds of the sea.

A crowd of people kept me company: my mother and father, Elisabeth and Françoise and all my family, friends in the Resistance and others such as Brite-Marie, the Swedish girl, all the people I loved. I would talk to them of the things I learned every day and imagine their responses. Distance didn't really matter; only death did, and it was all around. It was in the magnificent trees and the flowers in the fields, in the leaping hare and the lark that soared skywards from a field of corn. It lay within me and it was no respecter of either youth or beauty. Yet during this interminable war it had not shown its face to me. People around me were dying, Marienne and so many others, but I was never there. I loved the world with a fierce passion, people and animals, plants, the ever-changing seas and landscapes in their infinite variety, and I was outraged by the victory of death. I couldn't accept all that destruction.

And little by little, in spite of my outrage, the conviction grew in me that nothing was worthwhile in what we were doing and nothing should be done that we couldn't confess to as good at the moment of our death. I wanted this idea to take root inside me with such strength that it would shape the rest of my life.

Was the war teaching the same thing to my friends in concentration camps, to Elisabeth in her unbearable wait for Paul, to those who were fighting in the face of overwhelming adversity in Paris, Sylvie, Marie-Louise, Nicole, Claude and Frédéric? Was it teaching the same thing to my father in Concarneau, and to the women consumed with anguish for their children of whom they knew nothing, like my mother?

Once peace and order were restored, we should never forget this feeling of vulnerability. We should have to find ways of not forgetting it, for the sweetness of peace is so insidious. And the established order of things is so good. We so easily accommodate its injustices for the sake of ensuring our own safety. Everything would come to distract me from that thought. Where had I come closest to the truth? In the certainty and comfort of my childhood, or in the urgent danger of the war that I had been living for over a year?

A heavy silence weighed on the countryside, towns and villages I was cycling through. I arrived at the Château de la Moussaye at about three o'clock.

• • •

Once through the gates, I came to a halt in front of an imposing Louis XIII edifice in a courtyard overrun with weeds. The sun was shining, and the only sounds were of birds singing and crickets chirruping. Suddenly, from nowhere, there appeared a man of immense dignity. "May I speak to the Chevalier de la Motte." I asked.

"I am he."

"I am Marie-Claire. I have a rendezvous with Major Smith."

He studied me for a moment, then exclaimed, "Ah! So you're Marie-Claire... He waited for you until nightfall yesterday, and thought that some misfortune must have befallen you. He kept saying, 'I've been waiting for her for two days. What is she doing?'"

I heaved a deep sigh: "Has he left directions for me to find him?" "No," said the Chevalier. "He has left for Finistère, from where he will return to England."

"Yes," I thought. "He'll take the 'direct' route with Cary-Elwes and Billy, at Plouha." The situation was changing: there was no need to rush to Moncontour now; once again, the only thing was to go back to Guern. Not tonight though: I was too tired. The Chevalier saw this and invited me in.

He was the very epitome of the Breton country squire, with a sprightliness and elegance about him despite his broad shoulders. He wore heavy boots, stockings, jodhpurs and an old-fashioned jacket, with a magnificent and very wide leather belt with a buckle in chased silver. His brother, to whom he introduced me, looked like him. He had just finished dining with Captain Lechat, a fine and distinguished looking man who they told me later was also a surgeon in Rennes. They rang for the maid, who laid a place for me, and they gave me some dessert with a small glass of liqueur. When I mentioned the memories that the names of the villages of Plénée-Jugon and Broons, the Hundred Years' War and Bertrand Du Guesclin, stirred in me, the brothers told me that they were descended from him. I examined them more closely. No doubt about it: they looked like the portraits of the famous Constable of France!

Major Smith had spoken to them of me: Captain Lechat knew that I had just seen Commandant Bourgoin and Captain Deplante. As for him, he was head of the Resistance in the region, knew the situation in the Côtes-du-Nord well, and was working in liaison with the Jedburgh "Frederick" team of Captain Aguirec. He took me to the bedroom that he was using as his CP to update the report that I would take to Guern, since I was going back there and would also see Bourgoin and Deplante again. We crossed a vast hall, submerged in semi-darkness. A few shafts of light here and there fell on some impressive cobwebs that hung like curtains from the ceiling. The wall hangings were mildewed and torn. Suits of armour from the time of Du Guesclin himself stood guard, lances in hand. I followed the Captain for a long time down the dark, bare corridors.

Like the rest of the castle, the room had a certain grandeur in its austerity. In the middle of the wall was a four-poster bed and on the floor beside it a mattress covered with a blanket; adrift on a very beautiful parquet floor was a deal table, just big enough for the typewriter that stood on it; between the two tall windows was a sofa, on which a youth was fast asleep.

"Hey," said the Captain, "you still asleep?"

The sleeper sat up smartly, looked at me and immediately started apologising: "You see, mademoiselle, this is the fifth or sixth time we've spent a sleepless night waiting for a weapons drop, and all for nothing." Then he added crossly, "Next time, I'm not going!"

"Come now, Hervé, of course you are." And they told me the latest news of the Maquis. I heard once again the names of Fauquet, Raoul, the Frederick mission, Stéphan and Sergeant Jean Robert, head of the Plésidy Maquis at l'Etang-Neuf, and Saint-Connan, where well-trained, disciplined, well turned-out and enthusiastic young men were raising the colours, as at Saint-Servant. "A cracking Maquis" observed Hervé. Although the repression was not on the scale of the southern Morbihan, the SS threats were closing in. They had begun a major operation in the forest of Boquen, very close by. It would probably be best to leave the chateau without delay.

Lechat had uncovered his typewriter. "Let's type up the report for Commandant Bourgoin." I begged him to do nothing of the kind. What was the point of carrying such dangerous documents, when I could commit it all to memory? But he wasn't convinced, and took a sheet of flimsy paper on which he typed a tightly spaced report on his activities, the number of men available to him, their weapons, and so forth. I had no choice but to accept, or else I would have looked scared.

He was typing. Now and then he would stop and say: "You must stress that we don't have enough weapons. We need more operations like Captain Aguirec's. If we want to close the net around the Germans in Brittany, which is the plan, the northern part of the region needs to be as well armed as that of the south. Which it isn't yet. We have to unite our efforts." Tersely, he reeled these items off one after the other. Sitting on the sofa vacated by Hervé, I gazed at a painting of a shipwreck that filled a whole panel on one wall. A tumultuous, foaming, deep-green sea was hurling a stricken ship onto the rocks. I wondered if it was just the storm that had thrown it onto the rocks, or had it been lured by the deceptive lanterns of wreckers?

It was almost time for dinner, and the Captain showed me to the bedroom that the Chevaliers had prepared for me, the same one that Major Smith had occupied. Small but with a lofty ceiling, it had pale grey panelling and old rose wallpaper, a white marble fireplace, a Louis XV chest of drawers, a bergère chair that matched the wallpaper, a secretaire and, in an alcove, a stately tester bed. The dense silk draperies fell in heavy folds to the threadbare carpet. The gilding on the wood had tarnished over the years. It was a room full of presences, intimate, secret and welcoming. The casement window faced west and the sun came streaming in. In the distance, I could see only blue hills and rolling woods. At the foot of the wall below me was a wide and deep dry moat choked with brambles and nettles, crossed by a little bridge. In front stretched a terrace on which flowers must once have bloomed in formal parterres.

For centuries there, despite the depredations of the times, the essence of the place had been upheld, and the Chevaliers continued to uphold it, just as at the Moureau farm. We need to preserve these fortresses where the old values remain intact, standing as witnesses, so that in them we may rediscover the foundations of a civilisation that is being shaken by modern life and the war. There we shall find the materials to build a new country. In that ancient dwelling, you could breathe a reassuring sense of continuity. The length of our time on earth hardly mattered, after all, if we could pass down, if only on our last day, the best of our ancestors added to our own, different for each of us but infinitely precious and irreplaceable. I lingered a long time at the window, under a sky that the evening had turned to gold.

I had no smart dress in my bag, and I wished I had. At least I could change my blouse and make some attempts at giving myself a "coiffure".

The round table had been laid with care. The elder of the Chevaliers made me sit on his right, and a young girl served me fine cuisine with impeccable professionalism. The tablecloth was soft to the touch and the cutlery had a reassuring weight to it. And the vintage wine they served me was beyond compare! The four men treated me with exquisite courtesy and were dazzlingly witty and brilliant company. Captain Lechat regaled us with the tale of the escape of his friend Halna du Fretay, who had dismantled his aircraft and concealed the parts in order to hide it from the Germans, before putting it back together with Lechat's help and flying it to England at the beginning of the war.[55] He also had some anecdotes about Major Smith, with whom he had spent several days. Before arriving at La Moussaye, he had had to make him spend the night in an abandoned hovel at the foot of a rocky ravine. "Watch out for adders, the area's full of them," Captain Lechat had warned. At the time our Major said nothing. But soon after everyone had stretched out on the ground and started to drift off to sleep, the light of the moon that shone through the gaping doorway revealed to the Captain the sight of Smith sitting up on his derrière and tying bits of string tightly around the bottom of his camouflage jacket and the legs of his trousers.

"Is all well, *mon commandant?*" asked Lechat.

"Oh! Yes. It's just so that a little viper can't come and bite me." It still made Lechat roar with laughter.

We discussed the best route for getting back to Guern. The Chevaliers had an idea about this, since, as they told me, "When we were young we used sometimes to do the trip to Pontivy on minor roads. On horseback, we could only get there within the day if we left very early in the morning." They both spoke with that pungent turn of phrase that only those who live deep in the country and far from the towns have kept. The next day was a Sunday, and we decided that I should go to High Mass at Langourla at eleven o'clock: I wouldn't be long in the Boquen forest, which was a good thing. From there, I would go on to Laurenan, Plémet, Loudéac and Pontivy. After our liqueurs, we each took a Pigeon oil lamp from the hall and went up to bed.

I woke up still desperately tired from my journey of the day before, and a copious breakfast – it has to keep you going until Pontivy, they said – did nothing to dispel my weariness. Were my physical resources becoming exhausted? I couldn't believe that: I was too young. I followed one of the avenues through the park to get back

---

55. Maurice Halna du Fretay was shot down over Dieppe on 19 August 1942. His body was never recovered. He was twenty-two.

to the road to Langourla. The mist that enveloped me heralded a scorching hot day. Despite Captain Lechat's troubling intelligence, the Boquen forest echoed to no untoward sounds and I didn't meet a soul. I still resented him for more or less forcing me to carry a written report. After long reflection about the best hiding place (the turban no longer inspired me with any confidence at all), I had pushed it inside my bicycle pump, though fully aware that as an idea this wasn't really up to much. Taking bicycles apart on suspicion was just the sort of thing the Germans would do.

Langourla consisted of a cluster of low houses around a church, just at the edge of the woods. The service had already started, for the square was deserted. I went into the courtyard of one of the houses and asked the owner if I could prop my bicycle against his hedge while I went to Mass. He agreed, but shot me a strange look to which I didn't pay much attention. Although I slipped into the back of the church as discreetly as I could, a lot of heads turned to look. Who was this strange girl coming to High Mass in her clumpy shoes and blue cotton skirt?

An hour later, I was surprised to find some men standing around my bicycle. They were talking together. I greeted them politely and was about to grab the handlebars when one of them, a tall man with craggy features and a menacing expression, suddenly shouted: "Where are you going mademoiselle? And where have you come from?"

"That's no concern of yours, monsieur!"

"Oh yes it is, as a matter of fact, and more than you think." I was caught: he was from the Milice. Langourla was an excellent surveillance point on the way into the forest: I had been stupid. If only I had learned the message by heart! If I managed to get out of this I'd never make that mistake again.

He went on bombarding me with questions, trying to confuse me. "Where have you come from?"

"From Paris, there are too many bombs: I'm going home."

"Where did you spend the night? Quick, a name."

"With Madame Le Du, at a farm on the road."

"Which road? Tell me."

Don't say anything in the direction of La Moussaye, at all costs.

"I don't know anymore, I've taken so many roads! I didn't notice. Too tired."

Was he going to ask me which town I'd gone through? Was Fougères on the itinerary? I needed a route that would hold water. I blushed, began to stammer. Then pulled myself together. Come on, all was not lost. He went on:

"Who are you working for?"

"I'm not working for anyone, I'm a student."

"Oh yes you are, we know full well you're working for the Resistance."

His voice was downright malicious.

"I assure you I'm not; I'm just going to see my parents."

"Your name, your identity card."

I showed him my real one, and was deeply worried to see him writing down my name and all my particulars in a notebook. I was terrified of repercussions for my family. I called on all the saints in heaven to help me. With my identity card in its cellophane case were other papers, one of which was a Red Cross card, which he spotted.

"You're in the Red Cross?"

I had an inspiration.

"Yes, as you can see, and I'm a member of the emergency teams too. It's no joke clearing the rubble in Paris!"

With that, I launched into a long diatribe against the bombing.

He showed the card to the others.

"She's in the Red Cross."

Magic word! On a gentler note, he asked:

"Where are you going now?"

"To Pontivy."

"Where in Pontivy?"

I hesitated. Should I give the Bruhats' name?

"Tell the truth. We'll check everything you say immediately by telephone."

"With some people who have put me up sometimes, when I've been passing through Pontivy. They take paying guests but they probably won't remember me."

I was wary. If the police telephoned them the Bruhats might be terrified and deny it. I could only hope they would think to accept the story, which wouldn't compromise them in any way! It was all becoming very alarming; my head was thumping, and a cold sweat was trickling down my spine. But I could feel that I still appeared indifferent, calm and innocent, a little naive. I gave their name and address.

"OK, we're going to check to see if what you say is true. Anyway, you'll be stopped again between here and Pontivy."

He was still dubious, clearly, but didn't have a shred of proof. Finally he let me take my bicycle. Then he said, "Excuse me, you have a flat tyre, I'll pump it up for you." I wanted to refuse his help, but he insisted. That blasted message! With his manly grip he would force it out, or else the pump wouldn't work. My heart stopped until the operation was over – and he took his time! A miracle! The air went in, the tyre was pumped up, the unsavoury character unscrewed the connector with his long thin fingers and carefully replaced the pump. He smiled. He shook my hand. He almost apologised. I wanted to bite him.

Some distance from Langourla, I dismounted at the start of a track and with considerable difficulty extracted the piece of paper from the pump. It was black with grease. I read and reread it carefully, several times, and when it was engraved on my memory I tore it up into tiny pieces and shoved it into the mud under a large stone.

The sun was melting the surface of the road, but I pedalled faster and faster until I reached Pontivy, seventy kilometres away. All I could think of was one thing – my bed at the Bruhats' house. I pushed open the garden gate. The dog knew me and didn't bark. I was about to go round the corner of the house to the front steps, when I heard a whispered call from the road. Intrigued, I turned round:

"Mademoiselle, mademoiselle, where are you going?"

"To sleep at my friends' house." I carried on.

Then the woman opened the gate that I'd closed behind me and came running after me:

"Don't go there; the Gestapo have been there for six days!"

• • •

I thought I couldn't go another hundred metres, but I flew the twelve kilometres to Guern. M. Le Doze immediately took me to Deplante's new hideout, at a spot called "Le Château".

My arrival elicited the same exclamations as elsewhere: "You! Marie-Claire! We thought you'd been arrested, maybe shot!" Geo showed me the message they had received immediately after I'd left for the south: "Le Manchot reports Marienne and thirty men taken prisoner, stop, we cannot transmit your 387, stop, their code probably compromised." Message 387? The message in which Deplante asked Marienne to stop me!

So in England too they must have been wondering what I'd been up to. There was something amazing about this conversation through space.

"We were very frightened," said Geo.

Why did circumstances persist so stubbornly in bringing us back together?

Our attention was suddenly drawn by the shouts of a crowd of boys at the door of the manor house: tipsy young men from Guern, brought back by a parachutist who was no less the worse for wear.

Deplante fell into a furious rage: "So we're a curiosity to be shown off to the masses now!" he roared. "You want to get us all caught with your recklessness! OK then, since the entire village knows we're here, get your things, we're leaving."

As soon as our guide Le Pen arrived with his *pen-baz*, we followed him in single file. I'd hit the wall of my exhaustion and come out the other side, and now I kept up a good pace with the others. Geo took charge of my bicycle and my bag, naturally. We set up camp in a large apple orchard.

The patrols around Guern and our duel with the radio detection centre at Pontivy would continue right up to the Liberation.

CHAPTER 13

School Life

"Come along! Up you get lads! Time for your shift!" Deplante would stand first on Geo's side and then on Bailly's and repeat his refrain: "On your feet! Rise and shine!" They would groan, turn over under their blankets a few times, then sit up with their hair on end. Every night they would go to bed later than the others, working on messages or operating the Eureka beacon for parachute drops, and they never got enough sleep. Propped up on their elbows, they would slowly survey the field, glistening with dew, and the forms scattered around it. From the apple trees and the oaks on the banks there would be a merry warbling, and the crickets would soon be singing, for it was going to be a hot day. The dandelions, angelica and cow parsley would be standing erect, their stems stiffened by the cool of the night. The newly risen sun would shine through the woods like golden stars and cast long shadows across the meadow.

The wake-up call would rouse me too, like a school bell. Unlike Geo, I would have time to luxuriate in waking dreams in my bed, enjoying the purity of the air and the gentle warmth under the blanket, with a slight chill at my feet despite my woolly ankle socks. From time to time, Deplante's silhouette would cross my field of vision, and I would marvel at his energy so early in the morning. In my family lazing in bed was frowned on and we were constantly being reminded that the early bird catches the worm, but although I knew this was true I had never managed to conquer my loathing of getting out of bed. Soon the delightful aroma of hot coffee mingled with a wood fire would waft over to tickle my nostrils, and I would think, "Tony and René are just perfect!" The group now included a young assistant cook who worked wonders, a slight and frail young man whom Hitler would have rejected from his "master race" without mercy. Such stupidity and arrogance! So many of our great men had looked outwardly like the "failures" that he so despised!

A sudden call from the pit of my stomach would rouse me to action. I would undo the cord that I'd tied round the top of my yellow parachute to deter any unwelcome creatures, and there I would be, fully dressed beneath an apple tree that offered me its branches and leaves as a roof. Geo had had the charming idea of making it denser by interweaving it with ferns that we'd gathered together from hollows. I would put on the splendid new shoes that I'd managed to find in Pontivy, which I would turn upside down on two pieces of wood every night so that they wouldn't fill up with water if it rained. An adjustment of the skilful folds of my checked turban, a rummage in my bag for my mug, and I'd be off on my way to the enormous pot of coffee. Tony would give me a generous ladleful, saying: "Drink it while it's hot, it'll do you good, and then I'll give you some more with some milk, there's plenty here."

I would cut a slice of homemade bread, baked for us in Guern, and slather it with butter cut from the mound decorated with the traditional cow. Everyone would come and gather round the fire in a circle. Deplante would give out the jobs for the day: training to be continued in the neighbouring battalions, weapons to be cleaned in the morning, or operations to be carried out over several days. Antoinette and I wouldn't be forgotten either.

When we'd had our coffee, she and I would go off to have a wash. We would look for the clear springs, or *douëts*, with granite slabs where the women would come and do their laundry later on, or just a sandy stream with long water weeds undulating in the slow current. We would go far enough away from the camp to avoid any other enthusiasts. Our companions were perfect gentlemen, moreover, who behaved impeccably towards us in all circumstances, and who would do an about-turn if they happened to pick the same spot as us.

We always made a point of having a thorough wash, whatever the weather. Though not always fun, it was a discipline that would put us in a good mood for the rest of the day, and I never tired of soaping myself with that wonderful British soap and rinsing it off in the often freezing streams and springs. As we washed our underwear we would share confidences. We were very different but we accepted each other completely, and we both loved the Breton countryside with equal intensity. Together we would watch the sunrise and the clouds scudding across the sky. We would have liked to pick armfuls of buttercups and irises, foxgloves and cow parsley, but we no longer had a house to put them in. This life inspired Antoinette to compose more and more poems, which she diligently wrote down in fat exercise books; these were very important to her and followed her from one Maquis group to another. Bailly would tease her about it, poking fun at her attachment to her muse.

On the way back to the camp, we would see one or other of the lads shaving in front of a tiny mirror, or just a broken shard of mirror, stuck on a tree. When we got back, the cheerful strains of *Sur le Pont d'Avignon* would often be announcing the BBC messages: "*Allô Pierre 2, Allô Pierre 3*," immediately followed by the song and a varying number of Pierres. Then came the proper names, of which you needed just the initial to get the message, usually a prearranged phrase. The Pierres would talk to each other, as already mentioned, with London relaying the messages, and it was entertaining to listen in. I didn't know all these mysterious Pierres – far from it – but I pictured them all in my own way. Some of them disappeared, like Marienne, while others reappeared, like Pierre 1, Captain Puech-Samson, who had at last recuperated a radio group with Paulin and Hugonencq, and now that his leg was almost healed had taken the whole of the Josselin region in hand, as well as Michel de Camaret, Lesecq and others. This positive news helped to bolster our optimism, which on other fronts was sorely tried by the lack of any decisive developments in the war, day after day. The attempt on Hitler's life on 20 July showed the growing discontent in the enemy ranks, but in the end it had failed, and now the Führer believed he'd been sent by God. Radio Paris kindly presented us with his declaration of demented grandiosity: "I see in this state of affairs the confirmation of the mission with which Providence has entrusted me." His confidence in victory remained undiminished and was encouraged by the secret weapons he was using. For our part we were equally certain of final victory, but when?

All the same, despite all the impatience and anxiety, this was an exceptional time for me, and very valuable. It was a chance to put all that I had seen and experienced since I had been part of the Resistance into some kind of order, to build a philosophy on basic truths that I had time to think over at leisure, and to discuss all this with Antoinette and Geo. After such a nomadic lifestyle, I found this period of relative stability an absolute delight. Guern became my village. We would soon become the bourgeoisie of the Resistance, set in our ways. It wasn't without its charm. But there was one aspect in which we differed from the stability of the bourgeoisie: we were free of money, free of the desires and the needs that came with it. It was astonishing how much easier this made our relationships with each other. Differences in social background and wealth erect watertight barriers between people, so they no longer speak the same language. There it didn't matter to us whether anyone had more than anyone else. We had escaped the limits imposed by our social backgrounds: the walls had come tumbling down.

Thus men of very different backgrounds and types would come and show us their letters, the famous "Airgraphs"[56] that were parachuted in in canvas bags and brought news of their families or girlfriends left behind in Britain. They needed to pour out their feelings, to link their past to the present, to take stock, and it seemed to them that we could help them. For these letters forced them to relive the pain of separation and their worries for the future. They would have liked to forget them for a while, to inure themselves. Often the news was bad: Robineau learned of the great difficulties his wife was enduring in New Caledonia, and he was far from alone. The little paper envelopes scattered on the grass and sorted by the designated "mail officer" rekindled fears, particularly for those who knew nothing of those close to them, like our Captain and Antoinette.

Geo gave me his letters from his mother and father to read, letters that had come from so far away, that were full of tenderness and good advice, and I used to think that his parents were like mine. We were encoding and decoding together again. Lying flat on my stomach on the warm ground, the silk decoder nicely flattened out under the mica of the map holder, waving my legs in the air and occasionally nibbling a bilberry or blackberry, I would call out an endless stream of letters until my brains were scrambled and my cheeks burned. Nothing had apparently changed in our feelings towards each other, but running underneath our friendship was a far stronger emotion whose inevitable progress I occasionally noted without really knowing whether I felt happy about it or not.

Monsieur Le Doze or our friend Le Pen used to bring us visitors. I saw Michel again, very much thinner but happy: he was moving around a lot "doing" intelligence. I learned from him that Jacques

56. A system developed during the war by the British Post Office and Kodak, in which letters were photographed and the negatives sent to forces overseas by airmail or parachute drop.

Bruhat was with the Duboc family, over towards Kergrist, and that no one had heard anything of his parents since their arrest. Another visitor was Monsieur Taslé, a family friend from Pontivy, who reassured me that all was calm at Concarneau. I was massively relieved: I never stopped thinking about my father, and I was afraid for him.

• • •

We moved from one Maquis to another: to the first apple orchard after Coët-Niel, then the woods at Livouzec, then the mayor's field, then the second apple orchard, and finally the last Maquis. Our "guardian angels" from Guern, Monsieur Le Doze, our guide Le Pen, Jopé, Antoinette's cousins and the parish priest Abbé Bulot,[57] all had our complete trust. They would see which way the wind was blowing for us, and no sooner had we put our packs down somewhere than they would be looking for a fall-back position for us. So much so that if our Captain sensed that danger was near he would call for Le Pen and we would follow his lead. How many times did we escape the enemy in this way? And yet the Germans were ever closer on our heels. The radio detection van would tour the roads at a snail's pace and we knew that the exchange at Pontivy had sophisticated equipment. At our request the British had tried to destroy it, but with disappointing results, as our message noted. "From Pierre 5: Brittany exchange at Pontivy, stop, damage slight, now repaired, stop, your bombs useless, stop, note vulnerable areas, stop, amplifier in west part of blockhaus north of school and exchange itself at north-east point of school." And now the Germans had turned the bell tower of Notre Dame de Quelven into a look-out post, and from its slender spire they were able to survey a large part of inland Brittany.

---

57. Deplante would entrust Abbé Bulot with the completed message notebooks and he would hide them in the church at Guern.

Our guides did their best to keep us out of its sights, but it wasn't easy. Antoinette and I went to explore it when the Germans weren't there, but all I managed was to make a copy of a graduated dial; we didn't find any valuable instruments to take and there were no booby traps, the small camouflaged mines that the parachutists had warned us about. Deplante thought of having it bombed, but resigned himself to not doing so because the church was tightly surrounded by a small hamlet. "It's better if we move further away," he thought.

Often at night instead of going to bed we would be on the move again. During the last shift we would send a message: "Cancel special plane for tonight 900-520. Must get out quickly." We would have to pack our bags: I knew precisely how to pack my things: sandals, picnic kit, first aid manual, string, and a scrap of Geo's escape jumper, which had shrunk so much that he couldn't wear it anymore. I would roll up my blanket, wrap my yellow "sheet" in a scrap of rubber sheet, fold my raincoat on top if it was fine, and buckle the straps. Geo would pack "his bags" even faster than me, and I used to admire his strict orderliness.

We would wonder every time whether our guide was leading us to "the valley of Josaphat" a remote and wild spot that Deplante was attracted by. But Le Pen always had a better idea, so that for us the valley came to seem like a promised land, forever out of reach.

• • •

It was a very dark, overcast night when Le Pen led us into the "coppices", praising their charms. "We should all have flourescant palm torches," I said to Geo, "so we don't get lost." I had once held one of these in the hollow of my palm, as big as a good-sized egg and as bright as the light of the moon. Only officers had been issued with them, and most of them had been lost.

I was getting tangled up in some low branches when I heard our guide announcing: "Here we are; make yourselves at home." Here?

With my toe I dug into the layers of leaves, dry on top but rotting and damp underneath. I stumbled over a pile of stones, a perfect spot for adders. I went further on, spread my raincoat over a grassy patch away from the thicket and lay down. I was just drifting off into a lovely dream when an enormous raindrop plopped onto my forehead, followed by another, then another. I burrowed down under my blanket, determined to sleep however hard it rained. Which I did, but in the morning the results didn't make a pretty sight. The blanket was as heavy as lead, and my shoes and bag were completely saturated. And it was still raining. The only ones who were dry were men who had the regulation camouflage raincoat with a big pocket in the back for their haversack. They looked like huge beasts.

Tony and René had managed to light a fire and triumphantly handed out steaming mugs of coffee, but this state of affairs couldn't go on: we needed a roof over our heads, a farmhouse. Antoinette and I were dispatched to find one, which we did, and although the farmer was surly he had a room he said we could use. We burned a bundle of firewood in the hearth and, draping ourselves in our least wet items of clothing, frozen to the marrow and barefoot, in front of a motley assortment of garments hanging in front of the flames, we tried to warm up. This was the sight that greeted Jacques de Beaufort when he found us. The leader of an important FFI group near Hennebont, he wanted to establish contact with Deplante and wasn't remotely shocked by our strange appearance, which gave us all a good laugh.[58]

We had barely begun to dry off when Deplante took us back to the woods. No one was to stay in farmhouses: this was now the rule. We stretched a tarpaulin between some young trees and piled in underneath it. But the rain was now sheeting down, even more torrential than before. The tarpaulin was starting to develop worrying

---

58. Wounded by a grenade during an ambush on the night of 3-4 August 1944, not long after his visit to Guern, Jacques Grout de Beaufort was dragged behind a German gun carrier for some distance. His badly mutilated body was found in a ditch near Plouay on the morning of 4 August.

bulges. Here and there, the water was hosing down. "We have to get rid of this," said the Captain, "watch your backs!" With a huge effort, he heaved up the sagging pocket of water, only to be greeted by a loud yell. All the water was pouring through a gap and – as if by malicious design – straight down on to Geo, who happened to be bending down, before streaming out of his trouser legs above his puttees. I laughed and laughed until I could scarcely breathe: he shot me a furious look, then he burst out laughing too.

Whenever our mood grew sombre, Bailly would come to the rescue with his funny stories. But the radio shifts had to be respected, rain or no rain. The operators seemed to be having problems. We could see them moving their wires about and unplugging the quartz crystals and plugging them in again. "Something wrong?" yelled Deplante from our shelter to theirs.

"What do you think?" shot back Bailly, coming over to us with the wireless set. He turned the box upside down and it spewed out a good basinful of water. Deplante looked gloomy. What would he do without a wireless set?

"Have another go." He entreated the radio operators to try anything and everything – absolutely anything. They tinkered and fiddled with it for half an hour, tried again, and a shout of victory went up: "We've got them! They can hear us!"

When they saw the state of the wireless set after the campaign, the British couldn't believe their eyes.

• • •

As arranged, Commandant Bourgoin arrived with his radio operators, Hénin and Quittelier, and the section radio chief, Warrant Officer Hoffmann. To welcome him with due ceremony, a grand dinner was laid on. Left in sole charge by Tony, who had gone to put his SAS knowledge to better use elsewhere, René surpassed himself. We arranged ourselves comfortably on the grass for our picnic. Bourgoin presided over the feast; Antoinette had broken out a culotte-skirt for the occasion and I was wearing the blue skirt that her cousin had just made for me. The cider flowed freely, for a barrel full of it had followed us on one move after another, jolted and buffeted on a cart. Lightly sparkling, with the smoothness of a well-chosen draught, filling our mugs and glasses with its pale topaz tones, it magnified the joy of this reunion. It was to prove short-lived: after a few days, Tristan, an influential figure from Lorient, persuaded Le Manchot to leave with him, offering him a house in Saint-Hélène in the Ria Etel. But during this stay we saw visits from a succession of FFI and FTP chiefs of staff. Bourgoin even sent a message to London reading: "Meeting today with general commander FFI Paris."

After that we returned to our comparatively quiet way of life, despite all the exhausting errands for the war and chasing around for daily needs and sometimes quite simply for food supplies. Everyone did what they could. M. Le Doze would arrive with baskets full of dried sausage, steaks and bacon, or his daughter would come with her bicycle luggage rack engulfed by loaves of bread, or our guide would appear with a bag full of chickens.

But despite all René's efforts, mealtimes left a lot to be desired. "Lunch is served," was rarely heard before three in the afternoon at best, and sometimes it was nearer six. We'd forgotten how hungry we were, and everything tasted good to us: "everything" being for the most part a mishmash of potatoes and bacon, especially in the evening. In the morning, steak was very much in favour, and on days of plenty there would be second helpings ad lib. They were as big as dinner plates. But our rations were not often enough to satisfy our consuming hunger, and our constitutions, being creatures of habit, stubbornly persisted in demanding food at the customary times. I would fob off my annoying appetite by chewing on the green apples that filled the orchards.

We would settle down as best we could on the ground or on big stones close to the "kitchens". The parachutists looked very fine. The British uniform of combat jacket, narrow trousers caught in by canvas puttees and a wide belt laden with grenades gave the men a martial air, tall and lithe. "Put René in para uniform," I used to say to myself, "and he'd be a different man!" All the local recruits wanted nothing better, moreover. In many ways this Chouan[59] way of life suited them down to the ground.

Finally, when we'd finished eating, at around eleven o'clock or sometimes midnight, it was time to go and sleep. It was then that I would go back to Kerancalvez. If the sun had been beating down that day I would say to myself: "Papa will have watered the wilting flowers and the parched vegetables this evening. Did he eat a few cherries with Ginette and Arthur afterwards? They must be ripe now. Minette will have been prowling around them, suddenly springing in the air to play. She'll have had her kittens by now. Where will she have chosen to make her nest? In the bottom of a wardrobe, or a corner of the loft?" I liked to gaze up through the branches at the star-studded sky, and I had taught Geo our constellations. We would talk endlessly, and I was amazed at how we felt the same about absolutely everything. Some of the boys would linger around the glowing embers of the fire, softly singing *Adieu, clocher de mon village*,[60] but sleep would carry me off before they got to the end.

More and more, I was haunted by dark premonitions, and Deplante gave me permission to go to Le Faouët again. Surely there would be a letter waiting for me? I would leave one there. Why not go as far as Concarneau? The idea was almost irresisitible. But my brush with the Milice at Langourla was still vivid in my memory. They

---

59. "Chouans" (meaning "screech owl" in Breton) was the name adopted by supporters of a late-eighteenth-century anti-republican movement, chiefly among the Breton peasantry, protesting against government interference in traditional ways of life.

60. With its refrain *"Adieu je pars et je prends le maquis"*, this was billed on clandestine FFI sheet music as "the most popular song of the Maquis".

had copied my identity card, they might possibly have launched an investigation. And would I have the courage to leave again? No, it was better to send my news, and not go home.

The Fravals told me that my father had been there himself, in spite of the dangers, in the hope of seeing me. And Françoise had been there again two days earlier. She had entrusted our friends with a letter for me from Maman. I kept it for a few days, like a talisman, before destroying it.

With the letter Françoise had also brought a few cherries in a basket. Their beautiful pale red was blotched with brown, but I took no notice, and as I ate them one by one I closed my eyes and was transported away, over there. I was up in the tree with the magpies. The wind was rocking me and brought with it the smell of the sea. I picked a cherry, pulled off the stalk and bit into it, and it was so juicy that the juice ran down my fingers. Through the open window of the sitting room, I could hear Arthur playing. *Tristan and Isolde* or *Parsifal* cast their spell over me. Papa was arriving home from the boatyard for lunch, coming towards me with his long, determined strides. Maman was waiting for him on the path.

CHAPTER 14

Attrition and Hope Reborn

"When will it end?

"No one knows ..."

All around us nature was silent, as though overwhelmed. The storm had been circling for a while. We were stretched out on a slope, in the sparse shade of some broom bushes.

"The boys are getting more and more careless despite orders and instructions; guns are disappearing by themselves. The war is dormant and our luck is running out. You escaped the Germans by a whisker while I was at Le Faouët thanks to Deplante's instincts. I escaped the Milice at Langourla, the Gestapo at Pontivy, and the SS just a couple of days ago. They were in a tight knot at the top of a hill, and I couldn't avoid them. They'd seen me and were waiting for me. The curfew hadn't sounded, but it wasn't far off. The valley bottoms were full of midges, and I'd put my sunglasses on.

"They stopped me and took me to their officer, who had a Prussian's bull neck, thick and solid, and the jaw of a brute: 'You, terrorist,' he said. That old refrain that I was beginning to know so well.

'Of course!' I replied with a laugh. They'd formed an impenetrable circle around me, holding their black bicycles. 'You not laugh, because you can tell us where the terrorists are. Why you glasses and go so fast!' Oh Geo, try telling a man like that that I need sunglasses for the midges! You might as well be talking to a brick wall. He started to gibber away in German with the others. I was enjoying the fact that they were so frightened of the terrorists! Fear has eaten into every single one of them like a canker, and it's all our doing. I wish you could all have been there, along with my OCMJ friends, to see the furtive glances they kept shooting at the bushes, as if a devil was about to jump out of them. They drive their cars and lorries at a crazy speed on our roads to make them less vulnerable, with men lying on the mudguards, the running boards, anywhere they can hang on, machine guns and rifles cocked and ready to shoot. We've already defeated them, Geo."

"Not yet. There's a lot to do still. So how did you manage to escape their clutches this time?"

"By going on the attack. I said to the officer: 'Excuse me, monsieur, please could you tell me the time?' Disconcerted, he just looked at his watch: 'Half-past nine.'

'Oh heavens, the curfew! When I get to Pontivy they won't let me through! That's why I was going so fast. I didn't want to be late!' Hemmed in by that wall of grey-green topped by those expressionless faces, I felt as if I was suffocating. They closed in on me.

'You have time, mademoiselle, curfew is at ten o'clock. In any case, you will come with us.'

'Please don't go out of your way on my account.'

They hesitated, then at last the officer said, 'All right, but not too fast now, we will be watching you.'

I turned round several times. The patrol was standing there motionless, their faces white against the red sky. A lad was coming in the other direction with a blanket and a small bundle. I shouted: 'Watch out, Germans in a hundred metres!' He thanked me and leapt over the bank.

"Why did I say our luck was running out, Geo? We have to believe in it, and what do we know of God's plan for us? It's our bodies that are letting us down; I'm so tired. It wasn't really that far to Captain de Mauduit's camp and back. But yesterday I thought I'd never get to the end of that road to Mur-de-Bretagne."

I stopped talking, and for a long time we lay side by side in silence. I was reliving that exhausting journey back to Guern. The hills were so steep that I had to push the bike up them all, convinced every time that I'd never get to the top. When I couldn't go any further I stopped. The air above the road was shimmering in the heat, and the scorched vegetation crunched underfoot. A grey film of dust shrouded the thickets of brambles laden with big blackberries. I didn't even feel like eating them. I let my bicycle drop on the verge. My head was spinning. It was a waking nightmare.

I'd had to wait until I got my strength back, sitting in the ditch with my bicycle lying beside me.

We were all so tired of sleeping like cats, our senses on the alert, wide awake and clear-headed at the slightest strange noise: a twig cracking too loudly, a dog barking too close by, a rumbling on the road.

Tired, tired, tired. Tired of waiting for the landings, tired of waiting for battle and victory, tired of waiting to be captured, tired of living like savages, tired of being hunted down. Tired of being on the fringes of life. Renaud had told me that sometimes he felt an overwhelming temptation to take off his uniform, pick up a scythe and join in with the haymaking, cutting the ripe corn and gathering it into regular sheaves. Deplante had reached the point of wondering whether it wouldn't be better in the end to renounce the uniform. He had wanted to get a valid identity card, and Monsieur Le Doze had come in his role of photographer with his Kodak camera.

But just as he was developing the films a German patrol had rung at his door, and he'd thrown them down the lavatory.

His untimely visitors merely wanted to ask for directions. "You know, they've had enough too," he said. "They only went and looked in a barrel outside my door to check there weren't any terrorists hiding at the bottom of it. It doesn't make any sense!"

Suddenly Geo jumped: "Who's there?"

It was Morgane and Ginette, dishevelled and wild-eyed, running as if they had a mob baying at their heels. They raced up to Deplante, speaking in short bursts as they tried to catch their breath: "Captain, the camp's been taken, they've all been shot, all of them, and Martine, Christiane and two more; it's awful, awful." They were sobbing. Geo and I had rushed over. They were both friends of Nelly, a liaison agent who was part of our group, and we knew them well. Martine and Christiane used often to come to see us.

Deplante and Robineau tried to calm them down, letting them weep on their shoulders like children. Little by little, we heard the details of the tragedy. The FTP headquarters had been caught by surprise on a farm at Le Talhouët and the Germans had shot all the men on the spot, except for Armand, who could speak their language and whom they'd taken with them. The four liaison agents had managed to escape into the countryside at the back, running faster and faster, straight ahead, until the point when, gasping for breath, they had hidden on a hillside, clinging to one another. Some locals had seen them and described the scene to Ginette and Morgane, who had been away on a liaison mission. The Germans set out to hunt down the fugitives and spotted the pale patches made by their summer dresses against the grass. They caught them, tortured them (who will ever know what terrible things they did to them?) and finally machine-gunned them at point-blank range, there in the field. They hadn't betrayed a soul. A little while later, once the horde had gone, the locals went to collect the mutilated corpses: the Germans had sliced off their breasts.

With some wonderfully well-chosen words and the gentlest of gestures, the men soothed the terrified young girls, who had never come so close to death before. Morgane was shaking her head from side to side, her long golden hair brushing away her tears. Ginette was moaning: "My sister, my little sister Martine." Nelly was weeping with them. The horror of this violence intensified all the men's desire, harder to keep in check with every passing day, to finally go into battle for good and all and drive out the enemy. My outrage, which had subsided a little, was roused again, fresh as ever. Why such suffering? Why so many unjust deaths? I saw again Christiane's radiant face as she rode along beside me on our way back from Mellionnec.

Morgane had pulled herself together and was listening to Deplante now: they had to warn the other FTP battalions. "I'll go," she said, and when the message was written she put it inside her watch. For a long time I could see her hair shining like the sun under the apple trees in the orchard.

We were reaching the end of July. The days were getting shorter. The heather made purple splashes on the slopes, soon to be mingled with the blazing yellow of the second flowering on the heaths. Parachutists and patriots were being killed one after another, mown down like a harvest.

But there was movement in the war at last.

On 25 July, the Americans attacked in the south of Normandy. We learned of these final battles through a series of messages. We were still expecting landings at the full moon of 4 August, but whereabouts on the coast? Had the massive arrests in the southern Morbihan, including Marienne, compromised the landings on the Rhuys Peninsula for good? Whatever the case, the Allies were planning a large-scale operation, and we had been told to stand by to receive large numbers of airborne troops by glider. Could we please send details of usable landing zones? It was our deliverance at last, the culmination of all our efforts.

Where had our tiredness gone?

Pierre 5 replied: "Can receive three jeeps night 3 L or L on X 135 142, stop, terrain ideal for gliders on X 135642, stop, ground perfect and DCA anti-aircraft over 10 km away, stop, will send other drop zones." And they discussed these with other battalion leaders and company commanders.

During these days of intense preparation, Le Manchot came by car with Tristan to pay us another visit. Precise plans had to be drawn up for the moment of liberation, and we needed to decide how we would conduct ourselves vis-à-vis the Germans and the local authorities.

A small, slim distinguished man with a very firm handshake also came. He was strangely like my father. Lieutenant Désert and one of his friends brought us rigorous and detailed maps of the Lorient defences. It was an incredible feat and a concerted tour de force to have produced plans of such incalculable value. They would make it possible for us to capture the town and the port quickly and with minimal losses. Deplante and Désert had long discussions. The two men from Lorient went off full of hope, telling us that they would come back with more information in a few days. We sent messages of substance to London: "Have now in hand up-to-date plans of German defences in the Lorient region, stop, zone Bonhomme bridge to Port-Louis, stop, Le Pouldu zone, stop, wooden bridge at Keryado, stop, Bourgneuf manor, stop, plans of three gunpowder stores at Tréfaven, Mentac Sacqueven, stop, vital installations of port, do you want these and how?" And "Reporting battleship Rostock in Lorient Dock No.3."

• • •

This was the highly charged atmosphere we found ourselves in on Sunday 30 July when, on the eve of victory, the Germans came within a hair's breadth of finally snaring our group in their nets. Twenty-two lorry-loads of German troops arrived to torch and loot farms around our Maquis. They were on all the surrounding roads. I heard this in Guern, at the bakery where I'd gone after Mass to collect a gâteau Breton for Robineau's birthday. I sped off on my bike as fast as I could go. I had to warn them! I had to save them!

Deplante lost no time in packing up and getting out of the field where we'd made camp, and we spent an agonising day hiding out between a bank and a hillock of dry heathland. Henri kept watch, perched in a pollarded tree with his machine gun. We had the gâteau Breton for lunch, relishing it in spite of everything.

When night fell, we followed our guide on our last move. The moon rose, huge and yellow. The good weather seemed to be here to stay this time, which was a big advantage for the Allies. I was walking close to Geo. The balmy air enveloped us in a myriad of scents and the crickets were singing. At about two in the morning Le Pen left us in the hollow of a small valley. The rising sun revealed lush green meadows and a small beechwood on the slope.

The day after our arrival, the parachutists left en masse to receive a parachute drop that was intended specifically for us – with sleeping bags, shoes, uniforms and food supplies – and that we had been expecting for weeks. It took them a great deal of effort to bring back the containers, which turned out to be full of munitions, and only munitions! The parachutes were turned into tents. That was something at least. Geo used one to make a ridge tent. It was black. I was impressed.

In the message we sent back to the British we weren't so impressed. They apologised politely and promised to do better very soon.

• • •

Patton's army had broken through at Avranches on 31 July, this we now knew for certain, and he was pushing southwards. With them was Leclerc's army, and with Leclerc's army was my brother Pierre.

But still the message ordering the attack or announcing the arrival of the gliders didn't come. Yet they asked us again for the coordinates of the landing zones. What was going on? On 2 August, General Wood, leading the 20th Corps, was in Rennes and moving forwards, while General Troy Middleton was advancing towards the west.[61]

---

61. In September 1944, the airborne troops who had been intended for Brittany were sent to Arnhem as part of the ill-fated Operation "Market Garden".

Part Three

The End and the Beginning

CHAPTER 1

Engagement and Liberation

The increasing urgency of the radio work and the heightened danger of those last few days brought Geo and me much closer together. We had spent the whole day and evening of 2 August encoding and decoding, and when a storm got up we had taken shelter under Geo's black parachute. A terrible time, yet a privileged time too, was coming to an end, and we had no idea what the future held in store for us. But we were young and full of energy. From time to time I glanced at Geo and was astonished at how safe I felt when I was close to him. "It's because he's better than I am at getting to the heart of things," I thought.

"Marie-Claire," he said suddenly, "will you be my wife?" Then, pulling himself up immediately: "Why did I say anything? Forget it. Let's stay as we were, just friends. We're at war: I could be killed tomorrow."

I knew then that Geo loved me, and I thought: "This moment was always meant to be. This is how it should be."

"No, Geo I won't forget it," I replied. "Nothing will ever be the same as it used to be. I'll give you my answer tomorrow."

A night passed, the longest night of my life, lashed by howling, raging winds and more tormented even than that last night at Kerancalvez. I was buffeted by a thousand different thoughts. My head swam at the thought of ruling out forever all other possibilities for my future. The circumstances of our meeting were too unconventional for me not to feel troubled to the depths of my being, given how important it was to me to respect tradition – and necessary too, I knew – and I still made a habit of turning everything over in my mind. I searched back in my memory as far as I could, trying to remember what my mother had said to me about a woman's vocation and the conditions for its fulfilment. Were those conditions fulfilled?

That Geo loved me was a dazzling reality, and it was a rare blessing to encounter true love at twenty years old. He had been right to speak out. I had changed. The all-too tangible presence of death had made me realize that it wasn't the length of your life that mattered, but what you did with it. We shouldn't deny attachments that war rendered so fragile. We shouldn't be afraid of life, nor of death. Circumstances had always brought us back together, providentially. We shouldn't resist any longer.

On the morning of 3 August I said to Geo, "I will be your wife." We gazed at each other in wonder. The storm was over; the sun was shining.

• • •

Deplante was the first to know. He smiled, pleased in a fatherly way. Everyone found something nice to say. All of them were genuinely happy for us. They gave us ingenious little gifts. Tony fished some film spools out of his bag and Robineau found a square of green parachute silk, as he knew I'd been wanting some for ages. Antoinette gave me her blessing and advised me like a sister. The day was tranquil and beautiful.

Then the British started sending the same message over and over again, uncoded: "*Le chapeau de Napoléon est à Perros-Guirec*". "Napoleon's hat is at Perros-Guirec?" It was completely baffling. It had been agreed that on the day of the landings the operations to cut lines of communication would be launched by the message "*Le Manchot n'est pas mort!*" Everything pointed to our D-Day, but the right message wasn't there.

"Here we are, looking like idiots, trying to unravel some impenetrable enigma when we've gone to so much trouble!" said Deplante. "Oh well, it's just too bad, come on, *allons-y!*" But before we'd left to pass on the order to go on the attack, the British sent the famous message that we'd been waiting for.

Antoinette and I had to alert a few leaders; then we had multiple liaisons planned; young men and women were standing by and ready to go. The order flew from one place to the next. In the blink of an eye, roads were blocked by trees, the Germans were under attack from the front and the rear, and hamlets, villages and even towns were being liberated. Everywhere, on the roads and in the countryside, machine guns and automatic rifles were spitting bullets and grenades were exploding all around: railway lines were blown up and lorries and cars set on fire. Harried on all sides, the Germans didn't know which way to turn. The parachutists took up their positions in Guern, which was jubilant and festooned with flags, then went down to Pontivy, where Antoinette and I had been as couriers. The roads were deserted, the shutters were closed, as people waited in eerie silence. The Germans had gone. They were on the Sourn road, running away. Antoinette and I took another road just above it. It was steep and hard going, and we had dismounted and were walking parallel to the German column. Suddenly, we heard the drone of planes: British Spitfires.

They were flying quite high, and then, like birds of prey, they swooped vertically down onto the German column, machine-gunned them at ground level, then soared back up again as quickly as they had come down. We were so close that we were in danger of getting caught up in this hellish game. Flinging ourselves face down in the bottom of the ditch, blocking our ears and squeezing our eyes shut, we thought we had breathed our last. If the British saw us or our bicycles, how would they know the difference? Never had I seen the war so close up.

Part of the parachutists' group had stayed in the valley with the wireless set and radio operators. I went back there, still shocked by the British attack, for now every moment with Geo was precious. There were so many things we wanted to say to each other!

Lieutenant Désert had come back with more plans of Lorient. At the end of our frugal dinner, he proposed a toast in our honour. The quiet of our camp contrasted with the excitement in the newly liberated town. It would be hard for us to get used to town life again, I reflected. As the stars came out one by one, we wished each other goodnight and went off to bed. In the intoxication of the Liberation, we had forgotten about the British promise: our parachute drop! At about midnight we heard an aircraft. "It's ours, it's ours!" I cried. What were we to do? We knew the code letter, but we were too far away from the drop zone.

"Hang on a minute," said Hoffman, who had stayed with us after Bourgoin left, "I'll try; he might see us." The aircraft was flying round and round in circles. In the field next to our wood, Hoffman drew the letter with his torch, then "V" for victory. And the aircraft came, and it dropped its cargo in the field.

The farmers had heard it and ran to help us carry the baskets and containers under the trees. The moon was completely full and it was almost as light as day. We took out a few tins, unrolled a few sleeping bags. No doubt about it, this was "our" parachute drop. The next day, Deplante, Metz and Robineau distributed the treasures equally between us all.

"Not bad as a liberation gift, don't you think, Geo? How kind of the British!" I was delighted.

There would be no more parachute drops. There would be no gliders[62] and no landings. The Americans were arriving by road,[63] quite simply, and found before them a Brittany that had been largely liberated by her army within. For our part, our group was able to send the following message: "Results for Grog as of today: 86 aircraft and over 2000 containers received, stop, around 6000 men armed, stop, around 20 containers captured by the enemy."

But the Germans were falling back to the ports, to Brest, Lorient, Quiberon, Saint-Nazaire and Concarneau. They had to be stopped before they could entrench themselves in the fortifications. The Americans weren't going fast enough. General Ramcke and his German paratroopers, on their way to join the Normandy front, had been stopped by the FFI at Carhaix, but still had time to enter Brest. Lorient would not be taken by surprise, despite Lieutenant Désert's maps. And Captain Otto was determined to provide a "good ending" at Concarneau.

• • •

We spent a week at Pontivy. Deplante had been unanimously appointed garrison commander and tried his best to sort out the problems that cropped up between the different French factions and between the French and the Allies. The Allied Military Government for Occupied Territories (AMGOT), the administrative body set up by the British and the Americans for the liberated countries, deferred to his authority. "Restoring order to our country is essentially a French matter," he told the three delegates. "There will undoubtedly be difficult problems of a political nature to resolve in the days to

---

62. There were in fact twelve gliders, about sixty parachutists and some jeeps in the vicinity of Saint-Hélène, near Lorient.

63. Far fewer American troops were needed owing to the actions of the SAS and the FFI.

come. I must insist that you allow us to resolve them ourselves. For we are the only ones who are capable of fully understanding them. If we are proved wrong, there will still be time to ask you, to our great shame, to re-establish peace in our house." The parachutists thus ensured order where otherwise chaos would have reigned. Antoinette and I were in charge of the garrison's secretariat, and I was fascinated by this difficult transition between illegality and legality, which I had so often discussed with my friends in Paris and with my father in Concarneau.[64]

I had gone back to the restrictions and conveniences of town life, though not without some regrets for our green pastures: on the first night, unable to sleep in a house, I quietly slipped outside into the garden and laid out my nice new sleeping bag on the grass.

The Bruhats, released from prison after being dreadfully ill-treated, gave Geo and me a warm welcome, and brought out a bottle of cherries in eau-de-vie that had somehow escaped the looting. Jacques had joined an FFI company and Michel was fighting who knew where. We pooled what news we had about Paris, now a city effectively under siege. What had become of our friends? Sylvie was then on her way to Ravensbrück with Marie, and nearly everyone I knew had been sent to Buchenwald before being dispersed to other German camps. Frédéric, Claude, Nicole and Marie-Louise were preparing for the final battles, in which our group would take part with Cévennes[65] on the Boulevard Saint-Michel.

The news bulletins that we listened to were not wholly reassuring, for on 7 August, von Kluge had launched an offensive at Avranches. The war wasn't over yet!

There was plenty of news about Brittany, but it was constantly changing. One day you would hear a town had been taken, the next

---

64. The first measures were concerned primarily with the administration of justice, with a view to putting an end to private vendettas, kangaroo courts and summary justice.

65. Jean Pronteau, alias Lieutenant Colonel Cévennes, was a leader of the OCMJ and FUJP. He played an important role in the liberation of Paris.

day that it hadn't. But it was soon certain that on 4 August the FFI had begun the liberation of Quimper. "The French flag was flying from one of the cathedral's spires while German lorries were still driving around the streets," friends told us. On 8 August, Quimper was definitively "purged" of the enemy. I wondered what had become of my cousins during these uncertain days. Nantes and Angers would be captured on the 11th, Quimperlé and Châteaulin on the 13th.

What about Concarneau? I was haunted by the desire to go there, but everyone persuaded me not to: the roads were far from safe, groups of German soldiers were hiding out in the woods just as we had so recently, along with dubious gangs set on looting, and – most important of all – Captain Otto had not capitulated. "Why take the risk, when Concarneau will surrender any day now?" So I waited.

• • •

On 11 August, we went down to Vannes where the remainder of the battalion was regrouping. Some 60 per cent of the parachutists were missing and it would take some time to discover what had happened to them, or how they had died. Commandant Bourgoin and Commandant Morice had set up their HQ in Vannes in the first few days of the Liberation. The battalion was re-equipping before leaving again – this time in jeeps. Which combat zone were they headed for? Still a mystery. I hoped soon to join the regular army, as the British girls had done in their country. Many of the girls I knew shared my ambition.

Whatever happened, we were going to be separated, Geo and I. Gradually we had become convinced that our love was so rare and precious that we should seal it irrevocably, so that an indelible trace would remain if one of us should die.

As soon as I had arrived at Vannes, I had gone to see the Roret family. Lucienne, whom I had put in charge of the OCMJ's and Madame Lefaucheux's welfare departments when I was there at

Easter, introduced me to her parents and her sister Jacqueline, who was the same age as me and also engaged. The family offered us kindness and help, unreservedly and immediately; better still, they offered us affection. With Geo I often went to see them, and talked with them about how much we wanted to get married. They understood, gave us advice, and like us were on the lookout for any scrap of news about Concarneau. Alas! Concarneau was still "holding". But every day Bourgoin told us that it was about to fall.

We decided to start making plans for our wedding, which would be greatly simplified by the fact that we were "military personnel on operations". We would not have to produce our birth certificates, for example.

And so, one evening we stood at the presbytery door. Abbé Ezevan received us in a room that was as dark as a prison cell, with cold and austere Louis Philippe furniture, but he was pleasant and amenable. But the banns could only be read on a Sunday, and it had to be done three times. We were Monday 14 August, and we wanted to get married on Saturday 26th. The parachutists were leaving Vannes on the 28th.

The questionnaires were filled in, our details given from memory, since we had no papers apart from our identity cards, and after swearing on the Bible that we were telling the truth, we fixed the time for the marriage ceremony at half past nine. Naturally, it couldn't be decided definitely and the banns couldn't be read until after we had seen my parents. We hoped to get to Concarneau by the middle of the week. But I was strangely certain of their approval, and I didn't have any worries, not even the slightest apprehension, about their reaction: they could only agree with me. Geo felt the same way about his parents.

I could already picture myself walking up to the high altar in Vannes cathedral on my father's arm. Jacqueline had arranged for the cathedral choir to sing and had asked the scouts' chaplain if he would be kind enough to give the marriage sermon. It was all going to be marvellous, and everyone would share in our joy, as they were already. Especially our friend Devize, known as the "father" of the radio operators, whom I had at last got to know other than through his messages, and whom I often saw at the CP where Geo was staying and working. I had a room at the Hôtel du Commerce, which was run by veterans from Madagascar. They gave a dinner for the Madagascan parachutists, and I was amazed to see that there were so many of them. They talked to me about Geo's family. Renaud and Le Cudennec were missing, however: they were taking Paimpol with Captain de Mauduit. The town would surrender on 16 August, and Saint-Malo on the 17th, after a veritable siege by the Americans. The old city of the corsairs would go up in flames under murderous Allied bombardment. Only the ramparts would remain.

I was increasingly afraid that this would be the fate of Concarneau, despite what I was being told, and amid the succession of triumphant ceremonies, my anxiety took hold. Was it really such a triumph? The Allies didn't have the ports, not Brest, not Lorient, not Concarneau, not Quiberon and its bay. And their liberation was less urgent now, since Eisenhower's view had prevailed, and de Lattre's army had landed at Marseille on 15 August and was fighting its way up towards Lyon. The parachutists knew their next destination at last: they were to wait on the Loire for the Germans coming up from the south-west, blocking their route northwards.

• • •

On 17 August, Deplante sent Geo on a mission to Pontivy and I was given permission to go with him.

"Geo," I said, "we'll go on to Le Faouët afterwards. It's so close by car. There might be some letters for me there, or some news. I can't go on like this, not knowing anything."

"But where will we get any petrol?"

"Our friends in Pontivy will give us some, I'm sure." For every reasonable objection he put forward I had an answer. He gave in. What if I saw my father at the Fravals?

No. No one from my family was there: the Fravals gave me some letters that were already old. But they had heard some details about the siege of Concarneau.

CHAPTER 2

The Siege

In July, the Resistance groups on the coast, first Vengeance, then Libération, gradually pushed further inland, dividing between them the six tons of arms that the Coray Maquis had eventually received on 27 July, thanks to a Jedburgh team.[66] On 2 August, two hundred and fifty armed men thus descended on Concarneau.

The Germans had consolidated their defences. What was their military strength? A garrison of four or five hundred marines and about a hundred naval ratings; a Standortkommandantur commanded by Corvette Captain Otto and his second-in-command Lieutenant Niermann; and a flotilla under the command of Corvette Captain Neuthot based in the inner harbour, to which part of the Lorient Arsenal had retreated.

Fortified by the Romans, again during the Hundred Years' War and yet again by Vauban, for the Germans Concarneau had become a solid link in the Atlantic Wall, a genuine fortress.

The Todt organisation had done a good job, as a report on the siege makes clear: "All the access routes to the quays were blocked off,

---

66. The Jedburgh "Gilbert" team was made up of Captain Caron de la Carrière known as Pierre Charron (transmission code name Ardèche), Captain Christopher Blathwayt, and radio operator,Sergeant Neville Wood.

and the beaches filled with large numbers of chevaux-de-frise; small forts were erected all along the coast road; the villas of Les Sables-Blancs, some of which had been turned into blockhouses, bristled with defences of every description; a bunker at the Atlantic Hotel covered the Quai de l'Aiguillon and the Avenue de la Gare with its fire; posts near the Standortkommandantur, Rue Ernest-Renan and Rue Minez were armed with light cannon and heavy machine guns."

So much for Concarneau itself, but to the south there were numerous major military installations with massive firepower in Le Cabellou and, closer to the harbour entrance, Le Rouz, as well as at Kerviniou on the Quimperlé road, at the junction of the road to Le Cabellou. And to the north, finally, on the Quimper road, there was a heavily armed fortified line at Kernéac'h in the Beuzec-Conq district.

The Resistance planned to surround the town but did not have the necessary armaments to lay siege to such a powerful stronghold. Squadron Commandant Rincazaux and his ADC Captain Le Bourhis, who led the FTP groups, Vengeance and Libération, spread them out across the surrounding area: the FTP at Beuzec, Vengeance at Lanriec, and Libération at Trégunc. These groups were soon reinforced by others from Rosporden, La Forêt-Fouesnant, Pont-Aven and Quimper.

It had been hoped on 5 August that Concarneau could be liberated without too much suffering: the Americans were expected and dealings with Otto had been promising. Arrangements had been agreed whereby wounded patriots were given medical attention at the local hospital itself, in exchange for similar care for wounded Germans from the military hospital. Otto had conceded that "for the maintenance of order", it was necessary to arm an auxiliary gendarmerie, granting it ten rifles and two hundred and fifty-six cartridges, with the proviso, naturally, that they were not to be used against the Germans … All in all, if not a total surrender, there were at least some attempts at conciliation and hopes that everything would work out for the best when the Americans arrived, the only regular army deemed worthy of accepting the surrender of a German stronghold. There could be no question of parleying with franc tireurs and irregulars masquerading as an official, organised force!

Also on 5 August, a committee was set up of the three mayors of the Concarneau urban area, M. Aubert for the town of Concarneau, M. Rayer for Beuzec-Conq, and my father for Lanriec. Also on the committee was M. Jouannic, superintendent of police. My father was appointed as chair.

He was in constant communication with Otto, whether directly or through intermediaries. Otto agreed to inform him of all his decisions. My father asked him repeatedly: "What good would it be to you to destroy the town, when you have lost? Whatever you decide will be taken into account later on. Don't wait. To persist any further would be criminal." With each meeting, Otto's determination to carry on fighting and to follow his orders from Lorient to the letter was weakening. But some bloody skirmishes between the Germans and the FFI and an attempt by a trawler to block the channel strengthened his resolve once more, and my father would have to start undermining his defences all over again.

One evening, the police superintendent went to see Otto to ask him what he was going to do, once and for all. Incapable of making a decision, Otto replied: "I have entrusted the defence of Concarneau to Lieutenant Niermann. Address yourself to him."

And Lieutenant Niermann replied: "A veteran of the battle of Stalingrad does not surrender. I am from Munich, and Munich has been destroyed. I make war." With a dramatic gesture he pulled his shirt open to reveal a terrible scar on his chest, before adding inexplicably: "It is Captain Otto who commands. I obey."

• • •

As a historian, my mother was making notes that convey the atmosphere of the last days of the German occupation of Concarneau:

7 August: Machine-gun fire last night, but surprisingly quiet this morning. Shall I take Suche for a swim? Yes, I have made up my mind. It's such a beautiful day! Everything is so calm! Suche enjoyed her swim. However at about midday planes started flying overhead.

They say the Americans are at Château-Gontier, and that they are meeting with heavy resistance at Brest. They must be getting close to Lorient.

14.00: M. Pierre de Malherbe gallops past on his little horse. Sounds of heavy artillery from Trégunc, and lots of planes fly over just as I am due to take Suche for her lesson in Concarneau. A passer-by warns us that the town is full of troops and that the Russians are coming down from Trégunc.

15.00: They are coming down. Very odd with their vehicles coupled *à la russe* and decorated or rather camouflaged with greenery. A bit slack. Looking tired in the heat.

15.30: They're going up towards Trégunc. The same ones.

16.12: Concarneau very quiet. I buy three ties for my husband. Which one will he like?

A woman shopkeeper tells me: "The soldiers have advised us to keep our doors and windows shut. But everyone's outside. The children are playing."

17.00: M. de Malherbe goes past again.

17.45: A man in a horse-drawn carriage tells us the Americans are at Quimper.

My window is like a box at the theatre from which you see everything.

18.20: Rifle shots very close. We bring the children in from the garden.

19.00: Louis comes home and tells me about his day. All is well in Concarneau, all is quiet. He is approved by everyone and has been asked to preside over the three communes after the Liberation. He will be called "Administrator of the Concarneau urban area".

20.00: A few Germans go past looking weary. The heat and everything else. Although Ginette said one of them blew Sabine a kiss through the window. What are they thinking, under their warrior helmets? Probably that they've had enough, most of them. Yet a certain zeal still fires them into action against the Resistance, who harass them in any way they can.

Ginette is sewing (making Allied flags!), Françoise is helping, and Suche is drawing on some ribbon. Arthur is playing an anxious tune.

22.00: The safety of Concarneau is now in the hands of my husband. From now on he will spend the nights there, to be ready to intervene if necessary. He said to Arthur: "Now you are the head of the family."

• • •

The following day, he went back to Kerancalvez for lunch, saying that the Germans were definitely determined to resist and had given permission for children to be evacuated. So Maman left that afternoon to take Ginette, Suche and little Sabine to some friends at Pénanrun, eight kilometres the other side of Trégunc. The procession of babies had started on the roads, in prams or on bicycle luggage racks. When she came back, Maman helped Françoise to prepare a room in the house with a bed and materials to make dressings to treat any wounded. From then on, the pair of them (Anna had also left) would go every day, with our friends next door, to look after the inhabitants of Le Passage and Douric-ar-Zin. My sister Françoise, wearing her first-aid armband, could go everywhere. Caring for the sick, distributing milk, setting up a canteen in Le Passage: there was no shortage of work for these tireless and willing volunteers.

On 9 August, Otto announced that he had received imperative orders from Lorient to blow up the port and the fishing boats.

The mines were in place, the operation ready to be carried out, and Corvette Captain Otto was a soldier who "had" to obey orders. Immediately my father took a delegation to see him and made impassioned pleas on behalf of Concarneau. The German commander had a good deal of consideration for the men who stood before him and he liked their proud and dignified bearing – and he also liked Concarneau. "I shall not blow up the port," he concluded, "but only on condition that the Resistance do not attack." Commandant Rincazaux was informed immediately. But how difficult it would be to curb the impatience of the young FFI fighters!

On the morning of 10 August, however, shells whistled over the house. Two British destroyers had opened fire. They were off Le Cabellou. What did they want? To hit the Arsenal annexe in the heart of the harbour? Or just to frighten the Germans?

The Germans were extremely jumpy and part of the town's population was leaving. In the evening, we learned that the British ships had been pursuing two German ships from Bénodet that were coming to take shelter in the inner harbour.

On 11 August, my father came home, beaming. He had spent part of the day with the Resistance and had been given a wonderful welcome by them. "You see, we are united now," they told him. Commandant Rincazaux had given him a letter, his second, to give to Captain Otto. My father showed it to my mother before taking it down to Concarneau to deliver it personally.

But neither Otto nor Niermann would reply to Rincazaux, nor would they see him. They would only deal with the Americans, they said. And where were they, the Americans?

People said they didn't have enough infantry to attack such strong defences as those of the port, and their tanks would have to be scaled back. It would be another five days before they appeared over the hills to the north of the town, above the Kernéac'h line of defence at the Maison Blanche crossroads.

Meanwhile the Germans kept saying: "If the Resistance attacks, everything blows up." And my father wanted to save Concarneau. At last Otto had come round to the view of these stubborn Frenchmen: now he too, despite repeated orders from Lorient, wanted to save Concarneau.

He gazed at the port lying peacefully before him. The sun was setting. The heights of Le Moros were softening in the evening mists. Smoke was rising vertically from the crowded houses of Le Passage, at the far end of the harbour, behind our silent boatyard where half-built boats slumbered. The gold of the sky had spread over the smooth water and the still reflections of the resting trawlers and tuna boats. The quays were deserted, the fish market was empty, and the Ville Close was preparing for sleep behind the ancient walls that had protected it for so many centuries. "I love this town." he thought. "I cannot damage it." He went back inside and tore up his orders to destroy it.

• • •

On 16 August, at eight o'clock in the evening, my father found out that the Americans had really arrived at last. The police superintendent sent him a note to inform him, together with the ultimatum to the Germans. The messenger looked solemn. My father found the superintendent at the Maison Blanche with Colonel Brown and Captain Marina. His reception was somewhat cool. Young Captain Marina, in peacetime an engineer with a company in Virginia and the only one who could speak French, casually declared: "We've industrialised the war. You know nothing about it. We don't need your advice!" Matters are not always easy between different nations, even friendly ones, and a great deal of patience, a great deal of understanding and a great deal of tolerance were required. After all, without them we could do nothing.

A stentorian voice issued from the three loudspeakers mounted on a car at the top of the hill, carrying down towards the port where the Germans were listening: "Give yourselves up. No harm will come to you, your wounded will be well cared for."

The officers asked the two men to act as negotiators and immediately set off for the town. Otto arrived, discussed the situation and called for his ADC Niermann to agree the terms of the surrender with him. It was long drawn out, laborious, exhausting. Eventually the Americans said: "We want the surrender by 10.45pm at the latest." It was then ten o'clock. "If you do not surrender, the German garrison will be annihilated."

But Otto still insisted that he could only make a decision with all his officers, and summoned them to the Standortkommandantur. Discussions between the Nazis and anti-Nazis became so heated that they very nearly came to blows. Otto and his supporters prevailed, and he announced his surrender to Jouannic, superintendent of police. Still accompanied by Lieutenant Niermann, he headed back up to the Maison Blanche. Concarneau appeared to have been saved, with no bombardment and no bloodshed. And Concarneau would have been saved if Colonel Brown had listened to Jouannic, who begged him insistently not to accede to the demands of the German officers, who wanted a delay, just a brief delay, just a short one, so they wouldn't have to surrender at night. Brown granted an initial extension until the following day, the 17th, then until two o'clock in the morning, then until four o'clock, then until six o'clock.

While this was going on, my father, who had stayed at Concarneau town hall, was working on a notice, aided by Captain Dréau and another prominent local figure. To be posted the next day, it began:

"Our American allies have set us free. Let us show ourselves worthy of them by remaining very calm." They woke up a printer. The posters would be ready by seven o'clock. The police would stand guard on German military locations from five o'clock. The FFI would enter the town at ten o'clock. The Germans started to destroy some of their installations and scuttled two vessels that were under repair in the port.

But in the course of that night when everything was being tied up and untied again, Lieutenant Fuchs of the Gestapo had sent a wireless message to Lorient advising the German Admiralty that Otto and Lieutenant Niermann were surrendering Concarneau to the Americans. Blunt, peremptory orders to continue the fight arrived without delay.

"We should at least put up a fight to save our honour," said Captain Otto to Colonel Brown the next morning. "Make it limited," said Jouannic. And it was agreed that as soon as the first warning shots were fired by the tanks, the garrison would surrender.

At half past seven in the morning, when the shells started falling around them, about a hundred men came to give themselves up as prisoners, as had been arranged. But not the rest. At eight o'clock, the Americans issued another ultimatum to the diehards, and Captain Marina went down to the Standortkommandantur with a police officer carrying a white flag. The Germans would hear no more about it. At eleven o'clock, the tanks opened fire on the Atlantic Hotel and Le Cabellou, without retaliation. At around one in the afternoon, the FFI attacked.

It should have been the Americans who, acting with decisiveness and energy, put the final touches to the Germans' demoralisation and finally forced them to surrender. But they had left, weary of Concarneau.[67] My father was deeply disappointed: he had come so close to achieving his goal. In those last few days, Maman had seen

---

67. According to other reports the Americans were forced to withdraw for lack of infantry.

less and less of my father: he had pledged himself to the town. When he wanted to go back down that night, however, he found that a gun emplacement had been set up between Kerancalvez and Le Passage and the soldiers would not let him through. The bombardment was starting up again, this time by the Germans, and he said to Maman: "If it gets too dangerous, I would rather be with you."

Kerancalvez was surrounded, locked down, closed in by fighting. By the end of the day, the FFI had withdrawn from Concarneau, the Germans were unassailable in their bunkers, and Otto had asked to resume negotiations. Since the Americans had gone, the British Captain Price was asked to come from Quimper to meet with Otto at nine o'clock that night. But Otto was now a marked man, destined to be court-martialled and shot for treason. Professor Legendre[68] had heard that a launch was to take him to Lorient at midnight, and that it would bring his appointed successor, Corvette Captain Neuthot, who had recently left to see the Admiralty. "A madman," said someone who knew him.

But the former commander wanted to give himself up, to save his life. His wish was granted.

Hugging the walls, he reached the town hall at a quarter past eleven that night. Under cover of darkness, he was taken to Captain Mercier, one of the FFI chiefs, as the British officer had been slightly wounded. At that point the Americans, whose intentions everybody had stopped trying to work out by that time, reappeared and insisted that the unfortunate Otto be handed over to them. This time they ordered the complete evacuation of the town by half past twelve in the afternoon of 18 August. They were given six maps; they opened fire at four in the afternoon.

Niermann was extremely edgy and would hear nothing of any further negotiations (he would soon be arrested by his compatriots

---

68. Professor René Legendre, Director of the Marine Biology Laboratory of the Collège de France at Concarneau, was in constant contact with Louis Krebs.

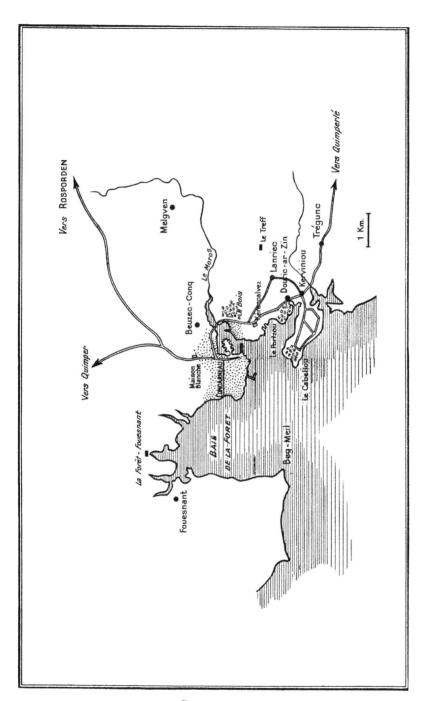

Concarneau

as Otto's accomplice); Neuthot was even more intransigent, and in a furious rage sprayed several neighbourhoods with shells and small torpedoes – in reprisal, he said. The Carnaud factory was in flames.

• • •

No one dared to speculate any more as to when the siege would end. Now that her work outside the house was limited, Maman was writing more than ever.

18 August: Arthur is playing the "Death of Isolde" and it changes the atmosphere in the house for me. It evokes all the beginnings of our old idyll …

Françoise spent the morning running round to all the farms to collect milk for the people who have stayed on in Le Passage, and she managed it.

19 August: The night was very quiet, but now it's come on to rain heavily and the wind has dropped. The Dervilles have suggested to my husband that we should stay with them at Le Manoir du Bois. We would perhaps be less exposed there than here. But if we go, what will happen to all the people living in Douric-ar-Zin, many of them old and sick? Le Passage, and Douric-ar-Zin are to be evacuated probably, but not completely. I should prefer to stay, and faced with my obstinacy Louis said: "We'll stay." Françoise can be useful as a nurse, but it would be better if Arthur went elsewhere. He doesn't seem keen and is playing the piano.

11.15: I am taking a table, my inkwell and my pen down to the cellar. I come from a long line of people who through events great and small have never forsaken pen and paper. And I shall remain of that lineage, if I can, to the end.

20 August: Françoise is allowed through and brings the news: the Cassegrain factory was completely burned down last night.

14.00: Two police officers have just brought Louis the evacuation order for the entire town. The Germans have taken their weapons and given them ten minutes to get back to the post, so they are in a hurry.

17.30: M. Jouannic comes to talk to Louis, warning him of the imminent bombardment of Le Cabellou. The truce obtained by Dr Carré and Commandant Perrier, head of Civil Defence, to enable civilians to leave is about to end. They wonder if there will be air raids and even naval bombardment.

21 August: The rain is torrential, which is both reassuring and dismal. The planes will certainly not come today, but the trenches are becoming a muddy morass.

The people of Douric-ar-Zin are more fearful of attacks from the sea than from the air. "If they send the fleet," they sigh, "we're done for." Despite this, there are still 175 people in the hamlet who don't want to evacuate, and 100 in Le Passage.

The 45 American tanks stationed near Rosporden left the day before yesterday, it appears.

19.00: Françoise has been to Concarneau, which is deserted. Only one doctor and one pharmacist are left.

• • •

Neuthot had calmed down a little, possibly because he now knew that in a few days he would be in Lorient. Indeed, preparations for the departure were underway: lorries were arriving on the quays, fully loaded; on 22 August, four German vessels, one of them a barge, entered the inner harbour. This refusal to surrender was assuming an epic scale, my parents reflected.

The rain was still torrential. Having managed to outwit the German surveillance, my father left for Quimper at ten o'clock, in response to an urgent summons. He had long discussions with M. Marchand and M. Arzel, the future mayor, and others. He was to play a major role in the future, more important than being Mayor of Concarneau. He was overjoyed to see his sister, my Aunt Guite, and they both hoped that the liberation of his town was only a matter of hours away.

It was late in the evening when he got back to Kerancalvez. For Maman it had been a long day. At around midday the sky had cleared, and she had gone out, venturing as far as Le Portzou. People were saying that the FFI had scattered leaflets in German and Russian urging the soldiers to surrender. But Maman had picked up a different bit of paper, one that in some strange manner had strayed into the house from a rally the previous summer, written by me. She read: "At the roundabout, look at the wall! *Courage!*"

CHAPTER 3

The Hour Draws Near

If we had not had to deal with one obstacle after another, we would have been in Quimper on 22 August with my father. For we had made our decision at Le Faouët: we would get as close as we could to Concarneau.

"I'll ask for two days' leave," Geo said.

"You'll need it," I replied, my eyes glued to the road, since he'd told me that German snipers were stretching very fine cables across the roads so as to make cars overturn. We were going through the forest of Pont-Calleck where the dense thickets concealed hidden dangers. Yet since Pontivy the threats had remained hidden and silent, and everything seemed quiet. "I don't think they'll let us go on our own," I added. "You should choose a few of your friends to come with us. Bourgoin is bound to give them leave as well."

"We'll have to get passes too. Impossible without them: just now I really thought the FFI sentry was going to make you get out of the car and stay there. We need to get hold of some weapons: a revolver isn't enough. And petrol. How many kilometres is it to Concarneau?"

I worked it out. "About a hundred and fifty if we have to make detours; and there are bound to be some, because the Lorient zone is in the hands of the Germans. Apparently Quimperlé has been liberated. I wonder if they destroyed La Villeneuve as they left."

Friday, Saturday and Sunday went by and still we couldn't set off. There was now very little chance that our wedding would take place on Saturday 26 August. I accepted this idea quite calmly, though with the feeling that the harm would be irreparable.

On the off-chance, and in case we managed to get back in time with my parents, we asked the lawyer to start preparing the documents; there was a "big one" to be done that was absolutely necessary for the town hall. Geo got our marriage licence from the public prosecutor and, naturally, obtained permission from Colonel Bourgoin. The banns had not been read out that Sunday at Mass, and they would not be read out at all if we were married on the Saturday. We were waiting until we'd been to Concarneau before we saw Abbé Ezevan again.

I had thought I would get married simply in a short dress, one that I would buy at the last minute, that I would bring from Kerancalvez, or that Jacqueline Roret would lend me. It was not without some sadness that I resigned myself to this, as I had always dreamed of the day when I would wear a wedding gown. I imagined a "princess" gown, tightly fitted at the waist and with metres of skirt billowing out below. There would be a long tulle veil attached to a little bonnet. Geo would have liked me to look like a queen.

It was then that Lieutenant Metz brought me back the Coët-Bigot parachute. He had been going round the farms where we had stayed to settle our outstanding accounts. As soon as he had seen Metz in the doorway, the little old man slipped out of the room and came back a moment later with the parachute in its bag. "Did I find a good hiding spot or what! The Hun didn't find nothing. That young girl will be well pleased!" I was indeed!

I took out the forty square metres of softest silk from the coarse khaki bag and draped it all around me.

"What a wonderful dress that would make for you," Geo said, "It would be so much better for the wedding!"

"Why not?" I replied. "The lawyer is prepared to get on with the 'big document', perhaps Jacqueline's dressmaker will be prepared to make the dress. I'll go and see her straight away."

Jacqueline was enthusiastic about the idea and took me to see her. The workshop was filled with fabrics of every type: every woman in Vannes wanted a revamp for those early days of the Liberation. But she thought my case was special and merited being given priority. "If you have a fitting on Wednesday, you'll have it for Friday." She had spread out the luminous white material and with a professional eye was examining the innumerable panels and tapes that gave the parachute its strength. "There will be a lot of seams, but the skirt will be so full that you won't see them," she said. Now she was holding it by the tip of the "funnel", where the panels shrank to almost nothing, and the parachute spread out like the calyx of a dried flower, but still fresh and dazzling. "I'm so pleased!" said Jacqueline. "No one will ever have had such an amazing wedding dress. I'll look for some tulle for the veil. It's off-ration, so I'll find some."

She looked at me almost tenderly with her big blue eyes, and her thick blonde hair shone in the half-light. "We're the same age and yet it's as though she were my mother," I thought. My mother. I felt an urgent, heart-wrenching need to have her with me.

Commandant Bourgoin was about to leave for England, but he would be back by Saturday and promised to come to the cathedral. Captain Deplante and our friend Devize agreed to be our witnesses at the town hall and the church.

Now we needed the rings. We had no gold to give in exchange, and the only rings we could afford at the jeweller's on the cathedral square were silver ones at twenty francs. These incidental details didn't matter to us in the least. The little shop sparkled and flashed with diamonds, rubies, sapphires and topazes, and the jeweller stared at us in astonishment. No engagement ring adorned my finger yet. We would think about that later.

$$\bullet \ \bullet \ \bullet$$

It was only on the Wednesday morning that Bourgoin relented and gave us permission to leave. Geo managed to get two days' leave, a Renault Viva Grand Sport and some petrol. "I'll come and pick you up straight after lunch," he said. I waited in my little hotel room, number 46. Big American lorries with pink streamers on their bonnets and white crosses, FFI cars and SAS jeeps were going past under my windows, making a tremendous din. But I was lost in thought. Besides, I'd had enough of wandering round the twisting streets of the medieval old town of Vannes, with its pot-bellied half-timbered houses, or along the ramparts, watching the river flow past and the long tresses of the weeping willows gently trailing in the current. I'd had enough of admiring the roofs covered with gold lichen above walls adorned with enormous clumps of wallflowers; enough of listening to the washerwomen chattering and banging their washboards beside the drawbridge; enough of enjoying the tranquillity of the port or the unruly comings and goings on the major roads flooded with FFI men coming to sign up with the parachutists and curious crowds free at last to wander at will. All this peace and joy weighed on me now, because Concarneau wasn't sharing in them.

Geo opened the door: "*Ma chérie*, I'm so sorry: the car's broken down. We can't repair it. I am going to try and find another one." And he went off again.

What dark forces were we up against?

All the same, I carried on packing my bag. I had put in some ration packs, chocolate, sweets, real wool socks and cigarettes, which would make them happy at home. In the pockets I added Geo's silk map and his evasion kit, as I wanted to tell them all about everything. I would probably spend the night there.

Geo was still on the hunt for a car when he bumped into Devès, a parachutist. "Listen," said Devès, "I'll happily take you to Concarneau in a Mercedes I've salvaged from the Germans. All you need to do is get Captain Deplante to give me permission and find some petrol." Devize volunteered for the trip, and they armed themselves with weapons and ammunition. Devize's belt was sagging under the weight of three grenades. We would have to be careful on the outskirts of Lorient. A radio operator lent me a big Colt pistol.

The car parked by the side of the road made an astonishing sight. It was camouflaged in every colour imaginable and all the windows were missing, including the windscreen; Devès had duly kitted himself out with a pair of motorcycle goggles. The bodywork was riddled with bullet holes. Truly an old warhorse, and a weary one! The tyres were in a lamentable state and went flat one after another. Between repairs we went at a good pace, as the engine was pulling well, and by a stroke of luck the weather was fine and dry. It was about four o'clock when we reached Le Faouët. As I went into the Fravals' shop I asked, "Has anything happened to my father?" They couldn't tell me, for Concarneau was still holding out.

More punctures held us up, and it wasn't until half past eight that we came to a stop outside the gendarmerie at Rosporden. I wanted to know where the nearest FFI post to Lanriec was. They directed us to Maison Blanche, on the road to Quimper.

In a house beside the road were some American and French officers. "Can I see my father," I asked, "the Mayor of Lanriec?"

"Oh, not here," a French officer replied. "He comes from the CP at Le Treff."

"Is he still living at Kerancalvez with his family?"

"Yes, and he very often comes to bring us intelligence. I'll ring Le Treff: he might be there."

He passed me the phone as soon as he got through. "Is the Mayor of Lanriec there? I'm his daughter."

I heard someone say: "He's not here now, but he will be tomorrow morning. We'll let him know. Come straight to the farm at Le Treff."

They convinced me that it was unthinkable to go as far as my house before the town was liberated, which was expected at any moment. It was true that I could wait until the next day, since I knew at last that my family was safe and I would see my father in the morning. I suggested to my companions that we should spend the night at Quimper, which was only twenty-five kilometres away. My aunt and cousins would put us up. They agreed.

The sea, glowing red in the setting sun, stretched to the horizon on both sides of us. We could just make out the dark outline of Les Glénans and the Ile aux Moutons. We were at the summit of the heights overlooking the bay to the north and I could imagine the port glittering down below, amid the dark mass of the houses of Concarneau, the Ville Close and Le Passage. Kerancalvez was just there, a little to the left, behind the dense trees of the Bois. I was overwhelmed with emotion. Geo stood beside me, in silence.

A tyre let us down halfway to Quimper. While the men busied themselves around the car with torches, I walked a little way along the road; sitting still on the journey had made me drowsy. The sky was aflame, brilliant scarlet, blood red. Suddenly I was bitterly sorry not have found my father that night. And all because of breakdowns!

I was afraid, afraid of what might happen. My joy gave way to anguish. But I tried to reason with myself. This dark feeling of dread was probably due to nothing more than the pervasive silence of the night, the heaviness of the atmosphere, and the blood-red reflections on the concrete of the road. Of course everything would be all right!

"*Don't worry, tomorrow is always a day away,*" Geo would often say to me in English.

• • •

It had been a quiet day, almost like a holiday. In the morning my father had been able to go down to Concarneau again, although had it not been for the intervention of Charly the interpreter the Germans would have kept him prisoner. Near the Kommandantur, an armed soldier had said to him "The war is long. When will it end?" "Soon, my boy," he replied. Françoise had also got through the barrier with her milk cans. The soldiers at the checkpoint had seen her coming and going so often that in the end they'd got to know her. The Germans had nonetheless decided to impose draconian measures in the town and the surrounding area under their control, so that the civilians who remained would not be able to observe their departure. The lorries were constantly shuttling to and fro between the port and Le Cabellou. The military hospital at the Hôtel de Cornouailles had already been evacuated to Lorient.

After lunch, my father wanted to go back down to the Kommandantur to collect the passes that had been promised that morning for the Red Cross women. "But you know," he said to Françoise as she arrived from Le Portzou, "there's no way of getting through. There's a soldier posted at the corner. He's so apologetic it's almost touching. He told me that no civilians are allowed to move about, then in a low voice he said: 'Tomorrow, *nicht Kommandant*, for now Gestapo in charge.' Your mother tried to negotiate in German. No use. Stay here. The women won't get through any more than I can. At least I shall have a day off." He went off to Douric-ar-Zin to check that a partial evacuation, if not a complete one, had gone ahead as planned, and then came back into the garden and busied himself with a few jobs.

"It's a bit much when the mayor is reduced to sorting onions!" said Maman.

He sent Françoise to Lanriec by the Le Pontic path to warn the Resistance that the Germans were on the point of leaving.

It was nearly time for tea, which my father liked to take with us on his days off. My mother would have wanted to prepare the tray, setting it beside the white roses that my father had arranged the day before in the Salins vase he had given her during their engagement. She would not have put tea in the teapot because there hadn't been any for a long time now, but would have used mint from the garden instead, and she would have enjoyed a private moment on her own with her husband. But it wasn't to be, because jobs and chores were forever intruding on every waking moment. Someone had just arrived and was saying: "You can go and pick the tomatoes in the Pezennec garden." There they stood on the other side of our garden hedge, scarlet and tempting, some that were already overripe lying on the ground beneath the plants. My father encouraged her to go: "Yes, you can go because you're a woman; but for a man, it's probably too close to the pinewood." And he waited for her in the garden. He picked and ate a pear that he had been watching as it slowly ripened over the previous few days. It had swelled beautifully in the generous August sun and its melting flesh was sweet and juicy. "Is any fruit more delicious than a good pear?" he said to Maman over the hedge. At that moment, our friends Geneviève and Marie-Cécile were going past with a wheelbarrow full of vegetables meant for the canteen at Le Passage; but they had been turned back at the checkpoint and were on their way back to Le Portzou, crestfallen. My father went over to them with Maman and Françoise. Smiling, he said: "Tomorrow it will all be over."

Later, when she had given the rabbits their grass rations, Maman lingered a moment in the garden, listening to the guttural voices of the Germans in the pinewood and the sound of lorries on the road. They were carrying troops. Françoise was back up at her observation post. She called out: "Papa, come and look at this boat anchored offshore."

He went up with his binoculars and tried to look through the windowpane. Irritated at not being able to see clearly, he half-opened the window to look: "It's a tugboat towing a barge. They're waiting for it to get dark before they leave." He closed the window and went back downstairs.

He found Maman in their bedroom, looking out at the view that always held us spellbound. A sliver of a crescent moon shone delicately in a cloudless pink sky, framed by two narrow bands of grey cloud. "Look how wonderful this view is!" said Maman. "And the moon – it seems to be mocking the quarrels of men!"

In a voice filled with warmth and tenderness, he replied: "Ah yes, what pleasure this view has given me!" Then he added: "There are so many beautiful landscapes in the world, so many beautiful things … and mankind doesn't know how to love them! The sea will be soon free. I should like to go sailing with you again." He pointed towards the beechwood: "If we build there we'll have to do some cutting back, for we should always have sky, lots of sky."

At that very moment I was at Maison Blanche with Geo.

CHAPTER 4

The Hour Comes

The following day, as usual, Françoise got up at about seven o'clock and my father half an hour later. He opened the bedroom shutters, looked out towards the pinewood and said: "I can't see anything; they must have gone. I'll go upstairs to check there aren't a few of them still about." He was also thinking: "I'll see if the sea is really free."

He knocked discreetly on Françoise's door: "May I come in? I want to check that the Germans have gone."

"Yes, come in," said Françoise. He kissed her, and together they gazed at the view. It was very calm and the rising sun was dispelling the mists of the night. "There doesn't seem to be anything moving around the mill," said Françoise. "Wait a minute! I can see a man walking down beside the pine trees. He's stopping."

"Where?" asked my father, "I can't see him." He picked up the binoculars from the table, good German binoculars, and not being able to see very well through the glass, just like the day before, he opened the window slightly and looked out: "The door of the mill isn't shut properly; there's a pile of things outside that looks like a hasty departure..." He stopped. Françoise was very close to him. Suddenly she saw something pass through the window. He turned his head, hoping to avoid it, but it entered his ear, the binoculars dropped, and he fell backwards.

Françoise shouted from the landing: "Maman, come up here! Come quickly!"

"Where are you? Upstairs or downstairs?"

"Upstairs. They've killed Papa!"

Maman thought: "This is it. In another moment my happiness will end. When I have climbed these stairs, when I have seen, it will all be over."

She went up all the same and saw the body stretched out at the other side of the room, face down in a pool of blood.

"Where?" she asked Françoise.

"In his ear."

"All is lost," thought Maman.

At that moment a second burst of gunfire came through the window, which had swung shut again. The bullets passed over them and buried themselves in the ceiling. The shattered windowpane fell with a loud crash. Maman rushed over to him, saying: "Let's get him away from here, they'll finish him off, if they haven't already," and with her daughter, she dragged the inert body onto the landing. Then Françoise went to find a doctor.

My father was now lying on his back and she put her head to his chest but could hear nothing. She felt for his pulse, but there was none. It was as though all life and all suffering had stopped within her. The beloved blood was still flowing. Maman kept thinking: "Always alone and never again." From the very depths of her heart there rose the dying Isolde's lament for her beloved:

> *How sweetly he opens his eyes,*
>
> *Do you see, my friends,*
>
> *Can you not see?*
>
> *How he glows ever brighter,*

Shining like a star on high.

Can you not see?

Do I alone hear this melody?

So wondrous

And so sublime.

In bliss lamenting, all-expressing,

Gently soothing from within him,

It quivers within me,

Echoes softly within me

And the sounds that float around me

Are they the rippling of the breeze?

Are they clouds of heavenly fragrance

That swell and surge around me?

Shall I breathe them,

Shall I hear them,

Shall I drink of them, Drown in them?

Must I lose myself in these sweet scents?

In the heaving swell,

In the ringing echoes,

In the vast stream of the world's breath [...]

Tristan was dead, Louis was dead. There was no more day or night, no more life or death. Everything was intertwined. But yes, there was death: it rose like a great impregnable wall, and Isolde's lament rose again, as haunting as the waves of the sea.

Now Arthur stood behind her, too overcome to weep.

"Why?" she thought. "Why has God taken him?" Then she was tortured with regrets. Why had she not gone to the Manoir du Bois, to Lanriec, to Pénanrun, anywhere! No, she had stayed there – and so he had too – thinking that it was the right thing to do for Douric-ar-Zin. Regrets were useless, yet she could not help herself.

• • •

I knew the crossroads at Le Treff well: we had often gone that way, my father and I, on our way to collect the milk from Pen-ar-Hoat on Sundays. He would look at the fields and explain the crops to me. He would say: "This year the wheat will be splendid," or, "the rapeseed hasn't flowered well," and the walk never seemed long. The country people of Lanriec would greet their mayor, who understood them, as he understood the fishermen of Le Passage, of Douric-ar-Zin and of Concarneau.

It was midday when we got to the farm.

Getting out of the car first, I went through the gate, across a courtyard, and into a dark, narrow passageway. I was still dazzled by the sun, and at first I could only see the fire on my right: it was burning in a huge fireplace and a little girl was stirring a pot of buckwheat porridge.

"Excuse me, can you tell me if the Mayor of Lanriec is here?"

She looked at me and replied placidly, "*Monsieur le maire*? He was killed at his window at about seven o'clock this morning."

A cry erupted from me, instantly and instinctively, and hung before me like a shield: "That can't be true!" My heart stopped; I thought I was going to die. "He's my father," I whispered. The girl leapt to her feet, her eyes wide with shock and terror.

I turned towards Geo, whose outline was silhouetted against the light in the doorway. "Geo, they've killed Papa." He put his arms around me:

"My little one, my own little one, it may not be true."

He hugged me very tight. I thought: "They've killed Papa. What about the others? Have they killed them too? Geo is all I have left now." He was alive, and I felt dead. The blood was running warm in his veins. His heart was beating against my cheek. His skin was quivering to my touch. He spoke, and his eyes were full of tenderness. But he was dead, my father, he was cold and white, stiff already. Geo could be like him tomorrow. What we had to do was to make another life that would have more chance of lasting, one in which we could live on. Marry Geo and have a child. Then death would be easier to accept. All that had been felt, loved, done and created by my father and by us would be passed on and would live again.

The sun was blinding: it shouldn't have been shining; the birds shouldn't have been singing, the green grass shouldn't have been swaying so gently in the breeze.

Devize and Devès arrived and said the same thing: "It may not be true." But I knew they were wrong.

Lieutenant Martin and some other officers appeared before me in a fog. They said that there were indeed some rumours about my father, but none of them seemed to have any real foundation. An ambulance with a doctor on board had gone to the German outposts on the road to Lanriec to try to find out more.

"We've got to go there" I said, and we went. The ambulance had returned to Lanriec and I saw the doctor. "An officer confirmed to us that your father had indeed been wounded this morning, but only lightly, nothing serious. A head wound may be either fatal or benign, as it seems to be in this case." He spoke calmly, with confidence. I could see the others were reassured. But although I felt the faint stirrings of hope, I could hear the little girl's words ringing in my ears: *Monsieur le maire? He was killed at his window this morning.* But he was more or less certain that the Germans hadn't hurt the rest of my family.

I asked if it might be possible for me to go to Kerancalvez by the country paths: I was so close, a mere eight hundred metres or so! In the end, they convinced me that it would be pure folly. The Germans were ready to kill anyone on the road. And anyway, if they stopped me might I not be compromising my family even more? Ever since the Milice had copied my identity card, had I not been on their list of "terrorists"?

So we set off back to Le Treff. Commandant Le Bourhis greeted me solemnly. I could see that there too I wouldn't be able to persuade anyone to let me go home.

"We're attacking Kerviniou at about two or half-past two; we can't delay the attack and we don't know how the operation will turn out; you mustn't get in the way. Wait until tomorrow. Then we think that Concarneau will be liberated." What could I say? What should I do? The parachutists had to go back to Vannes that night, it was imperative. Where should I go? To Quimper. To Aunt Guite. To tell her what I knew. To decide with her what was best to do. We had to go back to Quimper; I would come back the next day. I would leave a letter for Maman in case someone could get to Kerancalvez before I did.

The large farm was filled with a loud confusion of comings and goings. The farmyard too. An ambulance was being got ready, and lorries full of soldiers were setting off in clouds of dust. In a field a little way off, with Geo's help, I wrote a long letter. Folding it in four, I gave it to Commandant Le Bourhis.

Aunt Guite was sitting on a bench at the bottom of the garden, knitting; she was amazed to see us again so soon and very distressed by what I told her. Our triumphant arrival at her house the day before seemed very far away. Devize and Devès left Geo and me alone with her. My cousin Anneck had left two days earlier with my father's brother to open up La Villeneuve again. We talked for a long time. Postponing the wedding and waiting for my father to get better was the sensible solution. Geo would go back to Vannes without me that evening and he would come back the next day or the day after. We fetched the things we had brought from the car.

Claudine Mélo, an old family friend, came to join us. She lived in Concarneau but had taken refuge at my aunt's house, leaving her husband behind in Concarneau. Louise, the cook, called her. Claudine turned pale and went in, then immediately reappeared at the stop of the steps and beckoned to Aunt Guite. I understood that it concerned me, and a few minutes later Claudine called me in too. In the living room, Aunt Guite was weeping:

"It's true, my little Mie, this morning they shot your father." I knew it, with all my body and all my soul, and I said nothing. I saw a pale boy who was watching us sadly; he had crossed enemy lines, risking his life to reach us.

"What will you do?" asked my aunt.

"I can't leave Geo now," I said. "I think we should try to get married tomorrow, then come straight back. I'd like someone from the family to come with us."

"I think you're right," she said. "You're bound to meet Anneck and Uncle Arthur on their way back from La Villeneuve, which the Germans have left at last. Take them to Vannes." We were both filled with a great faith in the future.

· · ·

Since we didn't see either my cousin or my uncle on the way, Geo and I looked round the garden at La Villeneuve. There was no one there. We stopped beside the veranda outside the drawing room. White cyclamens were flowering in drifts along the side of the path, among the long grass that the gardener wasn't cutting anymore. Geraniums made splashes of red where neat ornamental flowerbeds used to sit in the lawn. I could feel a throng of family presences around me. This was where my parents had met and fallen in love.

"Mie," said Geo, "It would be better if we waited to get married."

At first I said nothing, then all at once: "If we don't get married tomorrow, we'll never get married."

He hugged me: "In that case we'll do as you wish."

I didn't care in the slightest what other people might think. The only opinion that mattered was Maman's, and I knew that already. In any case, girls who had been bold enough to share the adventurous life of the Maquis, even with the regular army, as I had, would be viewed askance. The only thing that really mattered to me was that my conscience should be at peace. I had to marry Geo because his heritage had to go on, the heritage of men who had risked everything and who had done so freely, and who must not be allowed to disappear. The heritage of my father.

CHAPTER 5

Survival

There was no respite from my despair, but by the time we reached Vannes I was more resolved than ever. The first thing was to go to the town hall, to save half a day. The staff threw their hands in the air: they wouldn't have time to draw up the marriage certificate! Then they promised the marriage could take place at eleven o'clock the following morning if we could bring the papers at ten o'clock sharp, the ones from the lawyer, whose office was shut. But after we'd knocked for ages the door finally opened. The senior clerk and his subordinates conferred: they would have to work late into the evening to finish the "big one". "Come back at ten tomorrow morning and it will all be ready," they assured us.

Finally, and most importantly, we still had to see Abbé Ezevan. By a stroke of luck, he was at the presbytery. Our request threw him into a panic.

"Listen, I can't decide anything about this, you'll have to see the canon. I'll take you." He led us through the dark streets. The maid made me wait with Geo in a parlour. I sat down, then stood up again: I couldn't stay still.

Through the curtains we could see the priest talking to the canon, who was digging his garden. It took forever. We couldn't make out what they were saying, we could just hear a murmur of words. In the end, however, the canon said in a louder voice: "Well, marry them tomorrow then!"

"That's settled," Abbé Ezevan confirmed as he came back to collect us, "I shall bless your marriage tomorrow morning in the Chapel of the Virgin in the cathedral, at noon. You won't have a Mass, just the blessing."

There was no need for the dressmaker to rush with my wedding dress, since I wouldn't be wearing it. I went round to see her. "Try it on anyway," she said, "we've worked most of the night, me and the others; we're going to finish it, my poor young lady!"

I twirled in front of the mirror and twirled again. No dress had ever suited me so well, making me look slimmer and taller. The "V" of the décolleté was cut a little low: "I'd have caught it together higher up with the cross of Lorraine from Saint-Marcel," I thought. The skirt, which measured five metres round at the hem, had a few yellow stains from the damp straw in its hiding place. What did it matter? The dressmaker made alterations here and adjustments there, and evened out the fall of the innumerable folds. "How beautiful it is! How beautiful it is!" she kept saying. Was there something unseemly about having this fitting? No: my father would have loved to see me in that dress.

Deeply distressed and full of comfort and affection, Jacqueline Roret promised to be at the cathedral at midday. Geo never left my side. He spoke very little, just saying what was needed. His tenderness and decisiveness restored some of my composure. He made sure that Deplante was warned to be at the town hall at eleven o'clock. Bourgoin would not be with us: he wasn't due back from London until Friday evening.

I didn't sleep: I thought about my father, and meditated on my union with Geo.

• • •

When night fell on that Thursday, 24 August, Maman relived every tiny detail of that long day, which she would have wished could be longer while she still had her husband's body beside her. It was only a semblance of him, but it was something of him, all the same.

Immediately after the terrible event, Françoise, after telling our neighbours and the rector of church in Le Passage, had gone to the Manoir du Bois, hoping to find a decent bicycle to go down to Concarneau, but it was all shut up. Going back to Kerancalvez, she endeavoured to pump up her flat tyres, then set off for the town as fast as she could go; she got through the Moulin guard post, but when she reached the inner harbour post a soldier held his rifle across the road to stop her. Without slowing down, she raised her hand and shouted, "Military hospital!" and he immediately drew his rifle back. She only stopped when she reached the quay.

Dr Carré dressed very quickly, put on a white helmet and came out:

"Is your father wounded?"

"Yes, a bullet in his ear."

He pulled a face. "How long ago?"

"Seven thirty, and now it's eight o'clock: you have to go up to the house straight away.

"Where exactly do you live?"

Françoise explained, lent him her bicycle, and he left with a white flag, saying:

"Stay here and find a car."

She went to the town hall square where there was a group of gendarmes. The ambulance was busy, Françoise couldn't have it. Then she saw Mélo, Claudine's husband, crossing the square.

He looked at her, astonished:

"Is something wrong, Mademoiselle Françoise?" he asked.

"Papa has been shot in the head." His face fell. He drew away a little, and with an expression of terrible pain he groaned: "Oh Louis, my little Louis!" For he had known my father since he was tiny. Then he drew closer:

"Mademoiselle Françoise, would you like my car? I've got petrol, we can drive him to Quimper."

"Cars can't get through," said the crowd who had gathered.

"With you we'll get through. Tell the pharmacist Diraison, I'm going to get my car." The pharmacist fetched a flag from his house and Mélo arrived: "Get in the back, mademoiselle, Monsieur Diraison will hold the flag in front."

But at the guard post on the harbour they were stopped. "Get out, mademoiselle," said Mélo, which she did, tense with energy. She marched straight up to the sentry post: an officer was emerging in his shirtsleeves, disturbed in his lie-in. "We are going to fetch a gravely wounded man at Le Passage, you must let us through," Françoise snapped, her voice harsh. He acquiesced.

Meanwhile, the rector from Le Passage had come to kneel beside Maman, who was holding her husband's head on her lap. Then our neighbours came: they carried my father into Anna's room, helped Dr Carré to bandage him and dress him in the suit he wore every day, so that above all he wouldn't look like an invalid, he who had a horror of illness, then laid him out on my parents' bed. With the helmet-like bandages and the large red cross on his armband he looked like a crusader.

The parish priest of Concarneau, Superintendent Jouannic and other dignitaries wanted to go up to Kerancalvez, but the Germans were ferocious in stopping everyone, and were killing people. The only people to sit with my father that day were Françoise, Arthur, the neighbours and people from Le Passage and Douric-ar-Zin.

In the morning, three Germans came into the house, looking nervously to right and left as though it was a terrorists' lair, and went up to Françoise's room where Maman joined them. "*Warum?*" she asked.

"Because of the binoculars," answered the second lieutenant, but he had only just spotted them. They were still on the table; he took them and added: "The commanding officer will come in half an hour." (What was the point of saying that? All the officers had already left for Lorient.) They stopped in front of my father, who seemed to be resting with a slight smile on his lips, as if he were thinking: "How petty the quarrels of men seem when viewed from on high!" They saluted solemnly and left. More came a little later; not the commanding officer, who they said was away until the evening. Maman received them coldly and calmly in the sitting room. She was determined to live by my father's words, repeated so often in those last few days when he was expected to make decisions on everything: "I must stay calm." They told her that no one could go to Lanriec that day, and that she should not go beyond the Bois, or Kerviniou, but the following day everyone would be able to go to Lanriec. They left a guard in the garden.

Someone told Maman about some poor man in Douric-ar-Zin who had been gunned down on his doorstep when the Russians who were evacuating Le Cabellou went past. His wife was in hospital, and he had hardly any family. They wanted to bury him that Saturday afternoon, after my father.

"No," said Maman, "he shall have the same ceremony as my husband, with the same hymns and the same honours." It was what he would have done, she thought. Henceforth, everything she did would be decided by the answer to the little phrase that haunted her: "What would he have done?"

The rector of Le Passage, followed in the afternoon by our friends Geneviève and Marie-Cécile, slipped into Lanriec by the path to Le

Pontic to tell the Resistance what had happened. The younger ones wanted to come and collect the body and lay it in a chapel of rest that they were getting ready. The older ones persuaded them not to. They gave my letter to our friends. We had only just left. Maman read it and thought "That's good. But how can I get to Vannes?" She gazed for a long time at our photographs, which I had slipped into the letter. I was alive, when for so many days she had been expecting news of my death, and God had given me a protector! She knew me well enough to know that I had not chosen lightly. Then she wished fervently that we could see my father again, so handsome by her side. Our neighbours, concerned at the Germans' attitude, burned any papers that they thought might have been compromising in any way in the stove, which they had lit to make some food. As the light faded, all of them had to go, leaving Maman, Françoise and Arthur to keep vigil over the body. They had been warned not to worry if they heard any noise as there were plans to attack the post at Kerviniou. Soon there were bursts of machine-gun fire, followed by a lull. Lieutenant Martin's men had taken the position.

• • •

The night began, filled with rumblings and gunfire. There was no electricity, but people had brought candles and Maman had put one in an antique candlestick with royal blue decoration that she had given my father for the feast of Saint-Louis the year before. She had laughed then, saying: "It's for the last candle on the last night of bombardment." That night, the slender yellow flame lit up my father's face, still and very white like the recumbent stone effigies in cathedrals.

The two women prayed, but for my mother there was no peace yet.

"What can I do for Maman?" thought Arthur. He lit a candle, sat down at the piano, and started to play. Suddenly the lament of

Amfortas from *Parsifal* filled the grief-stricken house. The richness and grandeur of the music – which no one could have played more beautifully than Arthur at that moment – soothed the devastation of my mother's soul. Her husband loved *Parsifal* so much that he had given the name to his boat. My parents had first sailed together in that boat, and Maman relived that first trip that night; then Arthur played the "Good Friday Spell", which brought acceptance to her heart. Fridays were holy days; and that one especially so, because the new day that dawned on 25 August was the feast day of St Louis, King of France, the saint of duty, courage and love.

Fearing the candles would burn down too quickly, Françoise blew them out from time to time, and they kept watch in the darkness.

Around two o'clock in the morning, the extraordinary glow of flares and searchlights lit up the room, and an aircraft circled interminably over the house, LeCabellou and Concarneau. Bursts of machine-gun fire rattled across the countryside and bombs exploded. On the road, German soldiers were running towards the bridge, panic-stricken and in chaos. Maman extinguished the lights, this time because of the danger. At four o'clock, the danger appeared so great that she told Françoise and Arthur that they should go down to the cellar. But every now and then she would go back up to be with her husband. At five o'clock, a terrifying explosion shook the house, as two mines went up on the quays. A trivial matter, in the end, compared with the destruction that had been planned.

Finally, at half past six, several shells coming from the sea skimmed the house. It was the parting salvo from the Germans in a boat passing off Porz-Guir. It was meant for Kerancalvez.

At a quarter past seven, Leclerc's division was entering Paris. The "Dio" group, under Colonel Dio, was heading for the Porte d'Orléans. After relieving the Gare Montparnasse and Les Invalides and capturing the Latour-Maubourg barracks, General Rouvillois was attacking the Senate. My brother Pierre was under his command.

Under cover of fire from his tank, he took the Luxembourg defence post at the entrance to Rue Vavin, reducing it to silence, and advanced towards the Palais, through the gardens where we had played as children. He thought of his father, whose saint's day it was, and who would be so happy to see him again.

At that same moment, I was getting ready for eight o'clock Mass in Vannes cathedral, where we were to be married.

The best I could find to wear for this Mass was a white long-sleeved blouse that didn't suit me, a jacket someone had given me, the well-worn cotton skirt made for me at Guern, and a beret from the last parachute drop. Geo was wearing his customary uniform with a white shirt ironed with great care.

It was a normal Mass, but I read the office of Saint-Louis, making the prayers my own, applying them to my father and my friends who had died: "In death thou art triumphant: death takes thee and ensures victory to thee."

While Geo went to the lawyer to fetch the papers and then take them to the town hall, Jacqueline came to see me in my room, bringing me a pair of sheer stockings, my sole shred of elegance that day.

Just a quarter of an hour late, the civil wedding took place in front of Deplante, Metz, Devize and Antoinette. Geo and I led them down the steps of the town hall. It promised to be a beautiful day, with wonderful weather from the west and a few white cumulus clouds beginning to form. As we walked the twists and turns of the road to the cathedral, I kept telling myself, still astonished, that I was Geo's wife in the eyes of the law: but the main thing, the only thing that really mattered to us, was the religious ceremony.

A verger in purple led us into the Lady Chapel. The Virgin leaned forward, gracious and tender, showing us her Son. I prayed for her help.

The verger lit two large candles on either side of us. Geo glanced at me now and then: before we went in I'd asked him if he'd remembered the rings, and he had. The chaplain had not been able to get away, so Abbé Ezevan spoke to us as a priest and a friend, then he pronounced the words of the ritual and we said "yes", loudly and without hesitation. At last we were joined together, never to be put asunder. The war couldn't get us now. Only death could sever the ties that bound us, and I didn't even believe that anymore: can death separate those who love each other?

Behind us, our friends who had been at the town hall, and Jacqueline Roret too, were listening. There was no one from my family, no one from Geo's family. We were alone.

On our way back from the cathedral, Jacqueline and Devize gave us some white carnations, whose fragrance filled the air. What kindness there was in their friendship!

We left very early in the afternoon, hoping to reach Concarneau before evening. Deplante gave Geo an extra two days' leave, an SAS car with the parachutists' insignia on the doors, and a driver, Amiel, a charming boy, who at only twenty-three had served with the SAS since Libya. Several more breakdowns meant we had to spend the night at Pontivy.

• • •

Maman was waiting for us. With every hour that passed she kept saying, "Why haven't they arrived yet?"

At about half past ten, Ginette had managed to reach the house, in black already. Then, just before eleven, two FFI men approached with great caution, one to the right of the road and the other to the left, to let those behind them know it was safe. And in the first hour of Concarneau's liberation, Captain Mercier came to salute my father in the name of the whole of the Resistance; for he, my father, had been the principal architect of the town's liberation, and through his persistence and determination, which he had transmitted to others, in the end he had saved it from destruction.

The day was one of triumph and glory. Maman could see this for her husband; and she could see that she had to share in this glory for his sake. The bells of Lanriec began to ring.

Also for this moment of glory, Françoise spread over her father the large flag they had bought together for the day of victory. Then the crucifixes were brought from the churches of Lanriec and Le Passage, and one was put at the head of the bed and the other beside it. Finally, Françoise picked some blue hydrangeas from the front of the house – the bed was in full bloom – and arranged them on the white sheet.

The local people who had stayed and those who had managed to come from the surrounding area filed past in a steady stream, after the military and officials. The hostility that some people had shown when my father first arrived in the region was completely forgotten: whether from the right or the left, they wept for him as for one of their own. The parish priest of Lanriec said, "He was reborn at Lanriec." The wake went on, with many men and many women. Speaking in low voices, they reminded each other of all the things he had done for them. This continuous chant was like a balm to Maman.

By about half past nine on the morning of the 26th, she had become resigned to the fact that I would not see my father again. Françoise covered him with the large flag and placed a single hydrangea in the coffin. Four of his workmen carried him down into the garden.

• • •

Not knowing whether the Germans had left Concarneau and if we could go there, we made a detour via Quimper, where Louise urged us: "Hurry! The funeral is at ten o'clock." There was no one now at the barriers on the road out of town, after Maison Blanche. Boats were sailing out of the harbour, the sea was free.

At the top of the hill at Le Passage, I saw a crowd walking towards us in silence; I could see a coffin draped with a flag, and

then a second one. Amiel stopped the car; I got out, walked on with
Geo, and joined the procession as it turned in front of the granite
cross at the Quimperlé and Lanriec crossroads. The people parted
to let us through. I went up to Maman and kissed her beneath her
long black veils. Geo waited a little behind with Amiel. Françoise,
Ginette, Arthur and Suche surrounded me and very quietly told
me that Maman had had my letter the day before, and that it had
comforted her. Anneck brought Geo over to be with the family, and
he walked beside Maman. I was glad I'd married him. Every now
and then I glanced down at my wedding ring. It was a bit too big and
twisted around on my finger. When would I tell Maman that we were
married? There was no possible happiness for her today or for a long
time yet, or for any of us, but perhaps it would help her to know?
Perhaps she would love Geo straight away. And so my thoughts ran
on. Was the weather fine? For me there was no colour in the sky, nor
in the earth. My eyes were dry and burning. I hadn't wept. It was
impossible. The bugle sounded the Last Post, I saw the flags draped
over the coffins, the wheels squeaked a little, and the dull thud of the
crowd's footsteps lulled me imperceptibly. Maman was offered a lift
in a car. She refused, thinking: "I shall follow my husband on foot,
on foot to the very end, on this road that he has walked so often and
that he loved."

Outside the church at Lanriec, under the lime trees that my father
had had pollarded in the spring, the FFI men, with Commandant
Rincazaux, Captain Le Bourhis and Lieutenant Martin, gave him
full military honours.

Shafts of sunshine cut across the nave like flaming swords and
a throng of farming and fishing folk crowded between the granite
pillars. The women's tall mourning headdresses trembled with their
sobbing.

I was in the front row, beside Maman and within touching distance
of the coffin. Geo was on the other side with Arthur. Standing with

my arms crossed, I wept at last. My grief was so unbearable that I wanted to stretch out on the coffin and howl, like women in earlier times. But for centuries we had been taught to control ourselves, to hold ourselves in check, ever since Christ brought us the Promise. Through my tears, which I let stream down my cheeks, not wiping them away, familiar images of my father unfolded; more and more they came, rising before my eyes like hallucinations. And I wept not only for him but for all those who had died for the same ideal, in Paris, in Brittany, in the whole of France and further afield.

They carried my father's body out through the main portal and laid it outside a chapel where he would lie until he could be laid to rest in the old graveyard at Lanriec. Then I took Geo by the hand and went up to my mother.

"Maman," I said, "this is your son." She embraced him and asked him to stand beside her. We shook countless hands. Yet most of the local people had not come back yet. When the last friend had gone past, known or unknown, a workman from the boatyard folded up the flag from the coffin.

"Isn't that a flag from a boat?" Françoise asked our manager. "Yes, mademoiselle."

"Take it. Give it to the owner of the next boat to leave the boatyard, and it will bear my father's name."

• • •

Back at Kerancalvez, while Maman and Geo were talking in the garden, I went up to Françoise's room, to the spot where he had been killed. During the whole of that war I had never seen a man die, nor witnessed any bloodshed; here the house was soaked with my father's blood.

Like him on that last day, I gazed out to sea. A feeling that rose from my innermost being surged up within me, and I learned then what real hatred was, a wild, uncontrollable hatred of war. But at the same time there grew within me an implacable determination to carry on the fight, until Nazism and all the poisonous ideologies like it were crushed.

My father's death was the beginning of my own death, and I would continue to die a little more throughout my life with those I loved. Life was nothing but death and creation, and there was a great deal that remained to be created. My father had passed down a message to me that I would pass down to our children, the children that Geo and I would have. I understood it now: what mattered to him in the end was not himself anymore but those around him, his family, his parish, his town, other people. In that the whole truth lay.

Appendices

The Organisation Civile et Militaire des Jeunes

The OCMJ was entrusted to Charles Verny in November 1942 by Captain O'Neil, a former naval officer responsible for the Ile-de-France section of the Organisation Civile et Militaire (OCM), one of the most important Resistance movements in the Occupied Zone, then under the leadership of Colonel Touny.

Captain O'Neil (alias Marc) initially instructed Charles to set up clandestine military training sessions. He began this among the student population, and soon fifty teams of four young men were working under the orders of officers and NCOs. Once they had completed the preparatory courses, the young people naturally wanted to take things further, so they were steered towards existing OCM operations: intelligence, organising the Maquis, escape routes to Spain and parachute drops of weapons. They set up departments for forging papers and carrying out direct actions (*coups de main*), among others.

Until February 1943, recruitment was very largely limited to within Paris; but seeing the results obtained by these young teams, Colonel Touny and Maxime Blocq-Mascart decided to extend the youth movement to all areas where the OCM was then established, in other words throughout a large part of the Occupied Zone (with some 100,000 members). Charles Verny would be its leader. He had enough contacts among student and Catholic circles, among the young people in the Mouvements Unis de Résistance (MUR) in the southern zone, and through his family with Pierre-Henri Teitgen and many others to be able to attract followers from all quarters. The new laws made it a matter of urgency to fight against the Service du Travail Obligatoire, and Maquis were immediately set up in the Ardennes, the Loiret, Normandy and elsewhere, where young men were sent after being provided with immaculate false papers supplied by the OCMJ. The OCMJ department for forging papers was soon one of the best organised in the Resistance. They produced over 16,000 false identity cards and supplied them to organisations including the Comité anti-déportation. Eventually they secured some 40 different official forms and, by dint of a series of raids, some 200 official stamps, including the most important German stamps.

In September 1943, the organisation was put on a definitive footing, with Charles Verny as secretary general, Roger Perret as his deputy, and a national headquarters.

Charles was responsible for liaison with the leadership of the OCM and soon that of the FFI, which – on the impetus of London and the Comité National de la Résistance – was taking shape with the aim of imposing unity. Charles was in control of the distribution of funds and the general running of the organisation.

His deputy was responsible for coordinating the operations of the different bureaux within the national headquarters (see structure below) and for running the Premier Bureau (manpower and officers).

Premier Bureau: manpower and officers.
Deuxième Bureau: intelligence and security.
Troisième Bureau: direct action, arms, military preparations and the Maquis.
Quatrième Bureau: False papers and fighting deportation.

Roger Perret was also responsible for liaison operations, escape routes to Spain (through Mme Vassias, who had replaced Mme Jullien, and Père Riquet), press and propaganda and political matters.

The northern zone was divided into six regions which needed to be organised as rapidly as possible:

P: Seine and Ile-de-France
A: The North
B: Bordeaux
D: Dijon
C: Reims
M: Normandy and Brittany

In Normandy, we had a large number of Maquis groups, including one under the admirable leadership of Commandant Hamel. Claude Desjardins was still in charge of the region when he took me to Caen and Vire in October and November 1943.

In Brittany, the OCM worked with, and was more or less answerable to, Libération, which had about six thousand members in each department.

In the southern zone, the Lyon group was extremely active.

I looked after secretarial work and liaisons for Richard, while Nicole took care of secretarial work for Charles as well as liaisons with external individuals and bodies (OCM, the secret army, national military delegates, regional military delegates, etc., including Blocq-Mascart, Pierre Pène [alias Péricot] ADC to colonel Touny, General Delestraint [alias Vidal], also Colonel Dejussieu-Pontcarral, Bourgès-Manoury, André Rondenay [alias Jarry], Chaban-Delmas, André Boulloche.) We also arranged liaisons with agents from other movements, such as the Jeunes Chrétiens and Jeunesse Communiste.

• • •

Operation Ouessant: Francis-Boeuf

One day, Professor Legendre, Director of the Laboratoire Maritime of the Collège de France in Concarneau, received a message from the College de France in Paris: "We accept your request for an assistant. He will arrive very shortly." Professor Legendre had made no such request. He suspected something but said nothing. After several more letters on the subject of the mysterious assistant, the latter finally appeared.

"*Monsieur le Professor*, I should like to speak with you."

The professor closed his office door: "I'm listening."

"I'll be very frank and I don't want you to incur any risks without agreeing to do so. I'm here because I need a good cover for moving about in the forbidden zone along the coast. No cover could be no better than being your assistant. I'm in the Resistance and I have important missions to carry out. One in particular, for which, if you agree, you could be of great assistance to me: to make preparations for the destruction of the radar installation on Ouessant."

"I understand, I will help you," said Professor Legendre.

The most astounding operation was then put in place. They went to find the German services responsible for the U-boats that were then inflicting terrible losses on Allied convoys in the Atlantic, and that were being directed to these convoys by the notorious radar installation on Ouessant (Ushant). They managed to convince the Kriegsmarine that its precious U-boats were running great risks in the vicinity of Ouessant because of the inaccuracies of submarine navigation charts. These, they said, had been drawn up before the war, without the aid of a truly remarkable instrument that they had just perfected, which would enable them to measure the currents with the greatest precision. Consequently, they strongly advised the Germans to authorise a hydrographic operation by the relevant branch of the French Navy (which set the whole business up with

Francis-Boeuf and Professor Legendre) to re-measure the currents and draw up accurate charts.

The Germans affixed a flurry of official stamps to the required papers, and Francis-Boeuf set off with his instrument. He was able to examine the coastline and defences of Ouessant at his leisure, not hesitating when necessary to get into a dinghy and paddle as close as he could to the cliffs to get a better view. Every now and then he would dip his current-measuring instrument into the sea – where it would measure precisely nothing at all.

At this point it was virtually impossible for anyone to land on the island of Ouessant, where the tiny population was meticulously checked by the Germans every time there was any contact with the mainland. Yet Francis-Boeuf could land wherever he wanted, and made contact there with a handful of staunch islanders, preparing them for the task that lay ahead: meeting and helping the British commando unit who were going to land one night to destroy the radar installation.

Everything was now in place: the coast had been scrutinised, cove by cove; the defences on the cliffs and inland had been recorded; the garrison had been inventoried. Mission accomplished. Francis-Boeuf went back to Paris and sent Professor Legendre a postcard: "The measurement of the currents went well."

One moonless night three or four weeks later, a British commando unit landed on Ouessant, at the spot chosen by Francis-Boeuf, and with the help of the few islanders who had been forewarned reduced the radar station to rubble. Then the commando unit slipped away again in the darkness, just as they had come.

Beside themselves with fury, the Germans began to go through the registers of journeys to and from the island with a fine-tooth comb. Then the operation occurred to them, and this brought them straight to the laboratory at Concarneau. They took Professor Legendre away to Quimper, where for three days they endeavoured to make him admit that his assistant was responsible for the outrage. But with great dignity the professor stood his ground, sticking to the story of the urgency of drawing up new sea charts for the safety of the Reich's U-boats. With no clues and no proof, the shattered Germans gave up trying to find the guilty party.

Soon afterwards, Claude Francis-Boeuf was arrested with his young wife, aged twenty. They both survived the deportation camps. In 1952, Francis-Boeuf was killed on a mission, in an air crash near Addis Ababa, just before he was due to make the first descent in Professor Piccard's bathyscaphe in the Gulf of Guinea.

• • •

Making hiding places on the trawlers Papillon des Vagues and Général Charette in our boatyard at Concarneau for liaisons with England

As early as 1941, my father was in contact with the intelligence network set up by Rémy, the Confrérie Notre-Dame (CND, later CND-Castille). In 1943, Francis-Boeuf came to ask him to prepare and fit out two trawlers, the *Papillon des Vagues* and the *Général Charette*, Narval 1 and 2 for the network, which had been damaged during the bombing at Lorient. Specifically, they wanted hiding places to be created in the ice storage areas.

The hiding places were installed in the boats by a workman who had volunteered to run the risks of doing this job on his own, and who did it after the other workmen had gone home and on Sundays.

In the forward compartment, he made two hatches opening into the ice storage space. The hatches were concealed in the bunks and were very difficult to detect. In the first forward compartment, the ice storage space was divided and a shelf about 30cm high was installed against the bulkhead to the crew room and above the hiding place. This left a space 1.5m high and 3.5m long with a gap of 80cm between the bulkheads.

This 30cm shelf would be completely covered with ice when the boat left port. At customs control, the Germans would see that the refrigeration space was filled with ice, as was normal for any fishing trip. Never would they have suspected that four or five people were hidden underneath that ice, though not perhaps in the most comfortable of positions. As soon as the trawler left harbour the crew would lose no time in letting them out and into the relative comfort of their own accommodation.

• • •

The Clinique des Augustines at Malestroit

The hospital run by the Augustinian nuns in Malestroit would take in anyone who was severely wounded and could reach them. Dr Queinnec operated on the wounded and stitched them up, Germans, patriots and parachutists alike, for after the battle of Saint-Marcel they admitted everyone, and the enemy even thanked them for the unstinting care they received. This made it all the easier for them to treat those who were outside the law. On 23 June, however, the clinic was surrounded by the Germans and put under siege. That same morning, a car had brought four exhausted men with five-day-old wounds that they had only been able to treat with alcohol from their flasks. On the third floor, four other parachutists had already passed themselves off as victims of the Ploërmel bombings, thanking their lucky stars that they had not suffered the tragic fate of many of the wounded, who had been killed the day after the battle in the slate mines and quarries around Sérent, or in hollows in the woods, or even in the beds where brave farming people were caring for them.

Only Dr Queinnec, Mother Superior Yvonne-Aimée and the doctor's assistants, Mother Marie de la Trinité and Mother Marie de l'Eucharistie, knew who the clinic was sheltering. But everyone knew the dangers that a search meant, so when the Germans arrived at twelve thirty in the afternoon Sister Marie-Gabrielle rang the bell furiously to alert Mother Marie de la Trinité. She instantly warned the Mother Superior, who told her to go quickly and fetch the two parachutists, Roger Berthelot and Philippe Reinhart, who had just been operated on. Mother Marie bundled them out of bed without ceremony. Weaving an unsteady course, the poor men followed her as fast as they could down the corridors and stairways. On the first floor, a soldier was keeping watch on the lift, standing with his back to them. In an instant they turned on their heels and tore through the glass aviary, where panicked parakeets and canaries flew off in all directions. They crouched down so as not to be spotted by the Germans who were now swarming all over the gardens. They were about to reach the door in the wall where the Mother Superior was waiting for them when it suddenly occurred to Mother Marie that she could transform these smooth-cheeked young men into two blameless nuns. No sooner said than done. A few seconds later, two pale Augustinian sisters were stretched out on chaises longues in the gallery of the chapel where other nuns were praying. There the parachutists spent two hours in silent meditation.

Meanwhile, Mother Marie de la Eucharistie rushed upstairs to check that nothing compromising had been left behind in the rooms. She grabbed their bloodstained pyjamas from the bottom of the cupboards, stuffed them in her apron and went back downstairs, wondering where she could get rid of them. On the landing below, a German soldier was standing on the bottom step, watching her. She stopped dead, slapped her hand to her forehead as though she had suddenly remembered something, and went back upstairs again, at an unhurried pace. Encountering a young nun, she told her to put the pyjamas in the bins in the operating theatre, along with the parachutist's belt that Mother Econome had just slipped her when they passed each other in the corridor.

The nuns had managed to drag the Germans' visit out, so that by the time they reached the rooms a lady visitor and a small girl were occupying the beds, which were still warm from their previous occupants. Nothing suspicious to be seen! Yet the Germans had it on good authority that four parachutists had come into the hospital that morning. Suspecting that the wool was being pulled over their eyes, they said in German that they would go and check the identities of the supposed victims of the bombings. One of the nuns understood what they were saying, and in the twinkling of an eye the Mother Superior had despatched a young boy to the town hall in Ploërmel to add the names of the four suspicious parachutists to the list of the dead. Two anguished hours had passed, two hours of countering every threat with a plausible defence, but in the end victory was theirs. The following day, Berthelot and Reinhart were taken to a remote wooded area where some local people took care of them.

On 25 June, the Feldgendarmerie sealed off Malestroit and there was no chance of using motor transport. The most able-bodied of the patients left on foot, one by one, while Maurice Trouvé, a parachutist with a severe leg wound, was put in a cart filled with manure and fitted with a double bottom pierced with holes so that he could breathe.

• • •

François d'Humières
11 April 1922–31 January 1945
An OCMJ fighter killed in action in Alsace
by Jean Pronteau (Cévennes)[69]

"Second lieutenant François d'Humières, 'Frédéric' in the Résistance, has fallen. He was killed at Dürrennentzen, east of Colmar, during the offensive to liberate the town and bring French forces to the Rhine. He died a glorious death, faithful to all the promise of his life. He was not yet twenty-three.

"In September 1944, François d'Humières was one of the survivors of that unequal struggle that was nevertheless decisive in the liberation of the country. He used to say, and we would cheerfully agree with him, that he led a charmed life. In 1942, he had 'organised' a group of students into a military training group, a training that too often was punished by deportation or death: assembling and disassembling machine guns, recuperating and transporting arms and the like. In May 1943, he was one of those who regrouped to launch the OCMJ. From the founding of the Union des Étudiants Patriotes, which united all the young patriots at the University, communists and Christians alike, he brought to this work his tireless zeal, his energy and his faith.

"Last spring, by a 'miracle', he escaped the brutal repression that rained down on the national officers of the OCMJ. With every day that passed, the cheerful Frédéric we knew became more ardent and more 'wound up'. The young leader who fell at the head of his commando unit in Alsace grew into a man during those months of underground struggle. We had to fight every inch of the way and rebuild the tottering organisation thread by thread, as we used to say. Then, through direct actions and 'recuperations', to restore its means of action and prepare it for the uprising. The Gestapo was tightening

---

69. Jean Pronteau, alias Lieutenant Colonel Cévennes, was a leader of the OCMJ and FUJP who played a prominent part in the Liberation of Paris.

its net. Every day, tried and tested leaders, 'veteran' activists of twenty or twenty-three were falling and had to be replaced. In this exhausting running battle between us and the enemy during those final weeks, Frédéric gave of himself as only he knew how. Heedless of the consequences, he led from the front with the reckless courage and the determination to succeed that had become the twin pillars of his life.

"By 19 August, Frédéric was already 'liberated': the day to bring the fight out into the open had come! Amid the many heroic exploits that were seen in Paris during those days, he was beyond compare. Suffice to say that few others could fight as well as he did. Those who fought with him around Boulevard Saint-Michel remember it well. As second-in-command in this sector from 19 to 25 August, he demonstrated the full measure of his outstanding qualities, and like so many of our comrades proved that their clandestine training was the toughest training of all for military leadership, and that the 'officers' who emerged from the Maquis were officers through and through.

"Two years of living outside the law were not enough for him! He still had things to prove, French soil to liberate, the dead to avenge and the future of his country to shape. That phrase on the OCMJ posters – 'To make the new France in the image of our youth and our struggle' – was by him.

"He left our organisation, along with many of our comrades, for a while, or so we thought. He helped to train the commando unit that, on 31 January, broke the defences at Dürrennentzen. He fought as we knew he would.

"They have entrusted us – he and all those young French men and women who have fallen over the past five years in this war of volunteers – with the task of building this future, a future that will now have to be built without them. For the accomplishment of this task, they have bequeathed us the glory of their memory and the example of their sacrifice. This is their final and supreme presence. Tomorrow as yesterday, they will always be at our side in our struggles for the greatness of France."

Voyage to England

Written by Marie Chamming's following her voyage to England from the 13 to 18 November 1944.[70] Translated by Catherine Cary-Elwes, and edited by Marie's son, Louis Chamming's.

The sheer coastline was illuminated by the setting sun, spreading pink, with mauve hills in the background. We left Dieppe in the direction of Guernsey on a Royal Navy ship that had transported commandos for the D-Day landings. Earlier, we had been hit by a terrible squall, complete with hailstones, but the sea was calm now.

I was anxious to be at last "a guest" of the British, because our departure from France had been somewhat shambolic. First of all, we had to wait for a long time in the cold and rain on the esplanade of Les Invalides.

Francois d'Humières (known as Frédéric) had told me to go to Rue de Grenelle where I would meet the parachutists, who would be wearing their new red berets, conferred on them at last by the British SAS in recognition of their exploits. I saw Deplante sheltering in the doorway of a house (because it was already raining). He had drawn

70. Contemporary Newsreel footage of the FFI visit to London is available on these websites:
http://www.aparchive.com/metadata/youtube/68b55617a5944246806e07ea1f827b7b
https://www.youtube.com/watch?v=Pg11UUWOqiU

up a document that would authorise me to obtain the army pay that was due to Geo, if possible. Deplante was particularly keen that I should contact Colonel Collins, who wanted to see me and Madame Piriou, because he, Deplante, had sent him citations relating to our activities. I needed to locate the SAS Brigade in London. They told us that we would march past General de Gaulle or maybe even Churchill. In the event we had only Duff Cooper; which wasn't bad at all.

The British boarded us onto the *La Combattante*, the boat that had brought de Gaulle to France! Once on board I found my way to the hold, where a number of couchettes had been installed. It was very stuffy, so during the night I went up on deck to cool down and breathe a bit of sea air. At Newhaven we had to wait until the tide was favourable for us to disembark, at around eight o'clock in the evening. The sky was clear and scintillating with stars. But goodness, it was cold. Brigitte, Gabrielle and I sat leaning against one of the big chimneys. It was deliciously warm, but I worried that it might melt my black oilskin. A group of sailors soon joined us. One of them sang the whole repertoire of Navy songs. And I was quite a hit with my rendition of "Around the Block". Later, we searched the skies together to find the pole star and other constellations.

At last, we disembarked on a darkened quay, dark because of the blackout, which was very strict here. Those unfortunates in our group who had been seasick and had spent the crossing collapsed on deck, and who were still rather green, gradually came back to life. The train station was very close and we had a reserved carriage. For short journeys, for instance between London and Newhaven, there were no corridors in the trains, like on those trains we used to take when I was a child and we travelled to Brittany.

I was horribly tired. I hoped I would not become ill on this journey. I had hesitated to say "yes" to François (Frédéric) because I was a month into my first pregnancy. We arrived in London at around half-past ten. An enthusiastic crowd greeted us at Victoria Station. I was surprised to discover that one stepped out of the train at the same level as the platform. It was clear that many things were different when one crossed the Channel.

Suddenly, we heard an enormous "boom!" "A V2 bomb", people said casually. Although not much reassured, we remained impassive, of course. We formed ranks "in columns..." The manoeuvre was lengthy and I thought I was going to faint. But then a pretty and kind English girl, who worked for the French FFL (*Forces Françaises Libres*) and spoke our language perfectly, came to fetch me and took me to a coach, where the others soon joined me. This is where we were first assailed by reporters and photographers. They didn't give us any peace for the whole journey, neither in London, nor in Liverpool, where my own group was to go, while others went to Scotland and other cities in England. In London itself, the coaches took us to different places. We were two hundred, not very many to represent the French Resistance, but too numerous for the ATS barracks where we ended up.[71]

The ATS barracks in Gower Street were housed in an enormous building with a maze of corridors in which, admitted the ATS, they themselves sometimes got lost. It was very modern, clean and spartan. As I was feeling a bit dizzy, an ATS took me aside and asked if I wanted something to drink. I answered, "something strong..." She looked at me in astonishment. I was hoping for some rum, or sherry, something like that. She was a little shocked, I think, and offered me some coffee. It was the real thing but served in a large white cup, thick with lots of concentrated milk. It was perfectly nauseating.

They took me to the infirmary. The poor nurse had to be woken up. She appeared in her dressing gown, a flamboyant red affair decorated with a leafy pattern. She made me sit down and took my temperature with a very small thermometer that she put in my

71. Auxiliary Territorial Service, the women's branch of the regular army.

mouth.[72] It was normal, therefore I was not ill. Same logic as was applied in my family! Luckily a young girl made up my bed for me. I wouldn't have had the strength to do it myself. I was trembling with exhaustion.

The English have mattresses made up of three sections. They are as flat as pancakes and as hard as a plank of wood. My unfortunate friends had to climb six floors carrying sheets and blankets – we were sleeping directly under the roof. Dominique collapsed on the other bed in the room. We were freezing. I slept, or rather I didn't sleep. In spite of the rabbit-skin jerkin I had been given when we left France, a lining to go with the oilskin jacket, I was shivering with cold.

There were two air raid alerts. The siren went off when the V1 bombers were overhead and had been seen and heard.[73] Most of them were shot down by the Anti-Aircraft Brigade or by fighter planes. They rumbled for a long time, giving us plenty of time to say to ourselves, "it will go over, it won't go over". The final "boom" was deafening, but it meant that all was well; they hadn't fallen on top of us. We could hear Air Defence firing repeatedly At the FAFL[74] they told me that these were rockets being fired against the V2 bombs. The people were blessed with an imperturbable calm. Around six-thirty, everything stopped, but we had hardly slept and no one had been down into the shelter. The ATS did not move when the alert sounded, so we dared not move either, not wanting them to think we were afraid!

Next morning, we had a fantastically copious breakfast in an enormous hall on the ground floor. Again, coffee, inevitably; porridge, jam, margarine, toast, bacon, etc ... I was suffering from morning sickness. It was heartbreaking to feel so unwell when offered all this good food, most of which couldn't be found in France. We

---

72. In France, they took a patient's temperature at the rear end.
73. Known as "buzz bombs" because of the buzzing or rattling sound made by their engines.
74. Forces Aériennes Francaises Libres.

then climbed back into our coaches and were taken to where we were to parade through London. The newspapers published our route. I was too tired to make this journey on foot and I followed the last group that was marching, in a coach with the wounded who were no less acclaimed for that. The British people gave us a wild welcome, shouting *"Vive la France!"* in their English accents. The elderly women waved and cheered; it couldn't have been more moving. When we marched from the equestrian statue of Ferdinand Foch to the Cenotaph, I got down from the coach. The traffic was stopped, the band of the Scots Guards played the *Marseillaise* and everyone stood to attention.

Then we reached Mansion House, Horse Guards pushed back the crowds in front of the building. We lined up in a square formation. The Lord Mayor appeared, bedecked in his red robes and enormous chain of office. Other officials followed wearing frizzy wigs in the style of Louis XV. Two of them were wearing sable coats and hats as well as their red robes. They processed slowly past us while the Guards continued to play. We were, once again, standing to attention.

Finally, we went inside Mansion House and were guided through a series of immense formal rooms. One by one, each man and woman was announced by name and came forward to shake the Lord Mayor's hand. We also shook hands with his wife who was wearing a garnet-coloured velvet dress and her blonde hair was tied back into a tight bun. She carried a diamond-encrusted sword. We were formed into a semi-circle in the main reception room and a band played mournful tunes, rather formal in nature, and then they surprised us by playing an extract from the song, *"La Petite Tonkinoise"*.[75]

There followed another procession of notables: two magnificent figures in goodness knows what uniform, or more precisely in costumes from the Middle Ages. One was carrying a golden sceptre with a large crown on top, and the other the glittering sword that the

---

75. A song made famous by Josephine Baker.

wife of the Lord Mayor had brought in. They placed their burdens on a table. The Lord Mayor, with his Lady seated beside him, stood up and delivered a moving and eulogistic speech, somewhat shorter than the speech made by the President of the Two Houses of Parliament, who was pleased to use the few words of French *argot* that he knew. During his speech, the Lord Mayor halted mid-sentence and a total silence fell on the room. From the sky came the rumbling sound of a V1 bomb. Once the reassuring "boom" sounded elsewhere, the Lord Mayor continued his speech picking up from the exact place where he had broken off. We were then ushered into a large adjoining hall. All along the walls, tables were laid out with cakes, mainly fruitcakes, arranged on silver platters. Tea and coffee were served. I ate well because I was hungry and I thought this was lunch. The Lord Mayor's deputy couldn't believe that I was 21 and already married.

We formed a line once again (this time, I was part of it, for I felt greatly restored by my hearty breakfast). A visit was organised to the Guildhall, which had been practically demolished by a bomb. Only the section chiefs were to go there, including, I believe, Frédéric. The various groups then went off separately to inspect those London boroughs that had been badly hit by the V1 and V2 bombs. The Londoners wanted absolutely to demonstrate to us that they had also suffered. I was in group 5 and we went to Hackney. Once again, the bigwigs were waiting for us ... and it was again lunch time. We were led to a large metal table in the shape of a horseshoe, its surface covered in exquisite fried dishes. And, thankfully, with the fish, and all the rest, we were served a good light ale.

The Lord Mayor was a small, thin man, and that day he was wearing a comfortable beige suit made of good quality wool. Around his neck he wore the heavy chain of office, made of gold. Another link was added with each new Mayor appointed, and the chain was already very long! Embroidered on his jacket was a rich array of coats of arms, the same ones that decorated the sceptre placed before him on the table. We raised our glasses to toast the health of the King, as we did at every meal we took in the kingdom of His Majesty George VI. From that moment, smoking was permitted, but not before. The Mayor made another short speech (how many had we heard already?). He spoke in English and Pivetot, our interpreter, translated. That day we were joined by members of the Civil Defence, who, every day and every night, continued to protect the population, often showing great heroism. Daniel replied to the Mayor's speech with some difficulty and then Brigitte spoke rather more fluently. She was careful to mention those of our comrades who had been taken to Germany and confined in appalling deportation camps, and whose fate was unknown. It was too easy to forget about them. For my part, every day I thought about Charles, Sylvie, Richard and the others.

We were in an area that had been badly hit by the V1 bombs, and I was not very at ease. After lunch, a reporter wouldn't leave me alone. The girls were surrounded by photographers who took their pictures, two at a time. We were a huge success with the Londoners. Everyone wanted us to sign their visitors' books; they asked for our addresses so that they could send us copies of the photographs they were taking. An English Captain asked me every five minutes if I was feeling all right. Someone must have told him that I was tired. He made a great fuss of me.

Then we were off again in our coaches to visit Hackney, a borough of some 200,000 inhabitants. Whole districts had been reduced to rubble. And a great expanse of ruins was the work of a single V1 bomb! And that is not counting the houses with their doors blown off, their shop fronts crumpled and front steps cracked and pitted. Luckily, there were few victims relative to the physical damage. This is because the Londoners constructed excellent air raid shelters that were generally long, low buildings. The blast could do little against these defences, and the impact of the blast was the principal danger of the VI bombs.[76] We visited another type of shelter, one that was built vertically, with recessed windows. Every night, the women and children of the district slept in these ultra-modern shelters. It was very cold inside and there were rows of bunk beds made of wood. There was also a recreation room for the children, and a library.

During the morning march past, I had got down from the coach and caught up with some members of the 4th Battalion. They had given me the address of the centre for the French parachutists. On our way back to Gower Street, I asked my knight protector if Bryanston Square was far away. It wasn't and he took me there in spite of the fact that I wasn't on official free time. At the centre, I was very warmly received. I brought them a little of the air of France. I showed them the document Deplante had given me and timidly asked whether it was possible to be remitted my husband's salary. I said that I was Marie-Claire and a delighted Sergeant Taxis said that they knew me well via the Intelligence Service. I couldn't get over it. He immediately gave me ten pounds, which did me no harm – we had no English currency. He told me to come back on Friday and I would be handed Geo's supplies allocation: cigarettes, a big woollen pullover, some warm khaki socks, and his pay. I then had to navigate a labyrinth of stairways and corridors in order to visit various offices where I could settle my business. My captain waited for me very patiently for three-quarters of an hour, without flinching. He took me by taxi to the Ministry of Information, located in Senate House, formerly part of the University of London, a vast building in the style of 1930s New York architecture.[77] He showed me the room where news items from all over the world were received. He introduced me to the editor of the most important English daily newspaper – *The Times*, I think. Finally, he took me back to Gower Street.

---

76. These community shelters were later abandoned because, although they were built of brick and concrete, they collapsed on the occupants if a bomb dropped too close. Increasingly, Londoners took refuge in the Underground system.

77. Senate House reverted to the University after the war.

The day had not ended for me because we were taken to the biggest dance hall in Piccadilly to have dinner and dance. The food was excellent. Everything was excellent, but I really wasn't hungry anymore. Most of the waitresses spoke French. Those who had been chosen to go to Scotland, to Edinburgh, had to leave by nine o'clock and were sorry to go because there was to be dancing. I didn't regret the dancing, but I envied the trip to Scotland. Geo had told me so much about it. A group of young people from the BBC dragged me off with another girl from my group. We struggled to push our way through the cosmopolitan crowd of dancers in the big hall on the first floor and we reached the green room for the artists. There, I was photographed by numerous reporters with Françoise Rosay, the great French actress. I was completely blinded by the flashes. One of the reporters told us that we would be on the front page of a Canadian journal. I was obliged to speak in English into the BBC microphone. I hoped that Geo would hear me. I told the story of the parachutists in Brittany.

Then we went and danced. There were many Americans, as many if not more than English people. Chantal, who I was with, and who knew nothing about uniforms, made a terrible faux pas. She was dancing with an officer, and he asked her, "Do you like Americans?" "Not at all", she replied, "they are so thoughtless and rude", and she continued in this vein. Her dancing partner's face clouded. He was an American.

After we watched a few numbers onstage, we left to catch our train at Euston Station. We were very late and we had to run and run. Luckily we were travelling in first class carriages, which was a good thing, and we reached Liverpool at half-past four in the morning. A number of brave notables of the city were waiting for us at the station. I remember in particular a very tall and imposing gentleman from the Ministry of Information. He was a born orator, who showered us with compliments and called us the nobility of France!

A cheerfully decorated coach drove us a long way out of the city, many kilometres' distance. Were we ever going to arrive? I was longing for a bed. Suddenly, we came to a stop in front of some metal fencing that could have surrounded a prison camp, but, no, it was a camp for women who worked in an armaments factory. We were offered a "coffee" in the canteen after which we were directed to a single-storey building, half-timbered, half brick. It was well heated and comfortable. We were given small rooms with blue checked curtains with flounces, very "cosy" as they said. The beds were reasonably comfortable and we were supplied with little bars of soap that I had only known in my dreams. I was too honest and left them behind when it was time to depart.

Rising at nine o'clock in the morning was something of a trial. We were served a superabundant breakfast of fish fingers, porridge, raspberry jam, margarine, fried bread and American bread, like bagels, in thin slices.

Arrival in Liverpool! I wanted to see the massive port where Geo disembarked in 1943, but we were taken to a grand monument and cenotaph in the city. Photographers and reporters swarmed around us and stuck with us for the duration. We were given a rapid tour of the city. Each one of us gasped at the shop windows stuffed with tins of food, breads, meat, fruit and I don't know what else. But there wasn't a moment to go shopping. Had we been so deprived that this material aspect of England became of intense interest to us? This was presumably the case.

We admired Liverpool Cathedral, which was indeed splendid although building had only begun forty-five years before to plans drawn up by Giles Gilbert Scott, a young architect, only 21 years old at the time: such brilliance! A clergyman walked us around this imposing edifice, pointing out that it had the greatest Gothic arch in the world, without the support of side aisles. The stained-glass windows looked very old, but they were not. The clergyman was in civilian dress but wore a small, stiff white collar around his neck. He was delighted to receive French people because he had spent many years in our country. The Catholics, not to be outdone, were in the process of building in Liverpool the largest cathedral in the world, but had only got as far as laying the foundations, and I don't know if it was ever completed.[78]

Near the statue of Queen Victoria, the great pride of Liverpool, an entire district of the city had disappeared. There were 24,000 victims and thousands of houses were destroyed in eight days of bombing. However, the citizens gave thanks that this monument, one that we considered to be of little artistic merit, remained intact. It was valued as a symbol, I daresay. Further off, we could see a building that reminded us of Les Invalides, but the dome had caved in. There was still no suggestion of a visit to the port, maybe because it was a "top-secret" zone. Instead we departed to visit a large factory in Halifax, some distance to the north of Liverpool. People stared at us from buses and on double-decker trams. Once they realised that we were the renowned FFI delegation that they were expecting, they cheered us on. As we drove through the suburbs we were astonished to see rows of individual houses, more or less all the same, built in red brick and blackened with age. They all had large bay windows as well as big guillotine-style windows (sash windows). They must have been comfortable homes. There was no indication of deprivation. Everything was clean and tidy. And this was no false impression; taken as a whole, these suburbs were in better condition than certain areas of Paris.

We arrived at an airfield where planes were continuously landing and taking off. There were camouflaged hangars. The design of camouflage seems to be the same in every country. In one of the hangars, young women were folding parachutes. The directors of the factory greeted us warmly, and, of course, offered us coffee as well

---

78. Liverpool Metropolitan Cathedral was completed in 1967.

as absolutely delicious biscuits. And then they led us to a stage, like that of a theatre. The curtain was still down. We were organised into a semi-circle in front of a black banner onto which had been sewn large white letters spelling out "*Vive la France, Vive les FFI; ÉGALITÉ, LIBERTÉ*". The curtain was raised. An invisible orchestra struck up with the *Marseillaise*. We now faced an immense hall where workers and service personnel – there were 10,000 of them – were sitting down to a meal.

A very imposing gentleman made a rousing speech that I had no difficulty understanding. The audience stamped its feet and called out "Bravo!" Daniel said a few words with the help of an interpreter and then I was pushed in front of the microphone. In spite of crippling stage fright, I spoke out loudly. One lady said how astonished she was at the "purity" of my English accent. I was just as astonished as she was! There followed wild applause. The dream went on.

We sat down to a grand luncheon with wonderful-looking dishes, but for me the spread was pretty nauseating. The table was arranged in the shape of the Cross of Lorraine,[79] and enlivened by vases of white chrysanthemums. I spoke at length, in English, with my very charming neighbour at the table. Over dessert there were more speeches, of course. (The dessert was a fantastic pyramid-shaped confection divided into yellow, green and red sections). We were invited to sign the big visitors' book and we were asked for our autographs. When we were about to leave, it was discovered that the Director's fine pen had disappeared. Daniel gave him his own, saying, "It is a gift, not a compensation." The Director was so delighted that he repeated these words at least three or four times.

After this we were given a tour of the factory, which built airplanes. They said that the rear gunner, out on a limb at the back of the aircraft and separated from the rest of the crew, is more or less sacrificed. If he survives four sorties, that is an achievement. The

---

79. The Cross of Lorraine was the insignia of the Free French Forces and the Resistance.

women workers were dressed in green overalls and were very friendly to us. They were off for their midday meal, carrying their big white mugs. In England, all the women were working, rich and poor alike.

When we got back to the coach, we found that they had decorated the front of it with a large Cross of Lorraine flanked by two French *Tricolore* flags. The women workers still chased after us with bits of paper for us to autograph. One of them gave me her brooch; it was made of blue enamel with three little birds sitting on the branch of a tree. Another girl gave me a penny. Chantal was offered some crocheted shoes; they gave us all kinds of things. It was time now to leave and head back to Liverpool where we were to be received by the Lord Mayor, the Earl of Sefton.

I was really exhausted. Back in Liverpool, we waited in an imposing room with the Lord Mayor's portrait hanging on the wall. A good fire was burning in the grate, under a chimney that pulled magnificently. What a fine man that Lord Mayor turned out to be! His wife was a slight figure next to him, but she had a charming smile. She was wearing a blue dress with flounces, not in the latest fashion, at least not by the standards of French fashion. It is true that fashion continued to evolve during the war as if nothing extraordinary was happening. Women used alternative materials or old curtains to make astonishing dresses and skirts.

The Lord Mayor, in his official robes, was at least 1.90 meters tall and proportioned accordingly. He stood up very straight and had a large, majestic forehead. He made a speech and, as usual, Daniel responded. We had been told to address the Mayor as "My Lord..." but Daniel began *"Monsieur le Lord Maire"* We looked at each other and had to stifle our giggles. We thought he hadn't understood anything, but Daniel insisted "I have understood perfectly well ..."

We visited all the reception rooms at the Town Hall, a rare privilege, so we were told. In one of them, the Lord Mayor invited us to admire some chandeliers that, he said, each weighed a ton.

As there were mirrors on all sides, the chandeliers were reflected to infinity. In the council meeting room, which looked like a courtroom, we sat down to another lavish buffet. And once again, the reporters were in attendance. The Lord Mayor and his wife, both decked out in their heavy gold chains of office, were extremely kind and modest in their manner.

At last we returned to our camp where we were able to beautify ourselves for dinner. On the way back there, we stopped at a bookshop-stationers to buy a few souvenirs, but there wasn't much on the shelves. However, I found a dark green leather frame, which I intended to use for the photograph of Geo taken at Apers' – it was a photo I was very fond of. Once again, the people in the shop wanted to give us their merchandise as gifts and they jostled to get our autographs.

We had dinner that night at the Allied Centre in Liverpool. Apparently Geo was received there when he first arrived from Madagascar in 1943. There was great rivalry among our hosts to cater to all our needs. We were very impressed by the purity of the French spoken by an Englishwoman who made a little speech. I sat next to a very respectable and important Englishman and I told him many stories of our exploits in France. The beer was excellent, which may have accounted for our heightened understanding of the English language. Opposite me sat a charming French parachutist who had just come back from Arnhem. I had heard about this operation, but I was unaware of its scale. This young man had waited a long time in England before being sent in to support operatives in Brittany. Indeed, at the end of July and beginning of August, we had indicated by radio message suitable drop zones and landing strips for parachutists and gliders. The Allies were being slowed up in Normandy and Allied command was considering launching a diversionary operation to free up the offensive on the Normandy front. But General Patton broke through at Avranches and the French parachutists waiting in

England were once again disappointed. However, on 17 September, they were sent to Holland with the British 1st Airborne Division under Major General Urquhart, the "Red Devils". They took part in the extraordinary combined operation known as "Market Garden", a plan conceived by Field Marshal Montgomery and intended to speedily circumvent Germany from the west, thus enabling the crushing of the Nazis before winter set in. Unfortunately, a series of unforeseen circumstances prevented the advance of ground troops coming from the south. They were unable to join up with the parachutists within the expected timeframe. The hapless parachutists found themselves in a desperate situation; having held out for around eight days, they were either killed or taken prisoner, except for about 2000 men who managed to escape by crossing the Rhine, as did my dinner companion. They had survived by taking Benzedrine tablets. (I had taken them myself when I had to walk the length of the Nantes to Brest canal at night, with Major Smith. The effect was immediate and I found myself in terrific form once again.) Practically all the food stocks parachuted in by the British and the Americans fell into the hands of the Germans. And to relieve the wounded they only had injections of sedative. In short, my French parachutist was plagued by nightmare memories of this hopeless battle and still suffered from its impact. However, the operation ended between 26 and 27 September and we were now in November. The most unexpected coincidence was that, a little while later, I met the parachutist's fiancée in London, when I went to buy some shoes. She was standing in line next to me.

After we had eaten in the great hall, we were surrounded by people including French nationals who were delighted to see us. I found myself with arms full of gifts of chocolate and sweets. A French woman married to an Englishman and some French sailors took me up to the bar for a smoke and some beer. When we got back to camp, we were completely exhausted but we went to the canteen for yet another "coffee". The lads making conquests among the English girls, who asked for nothing better, seemed to have more stamina. We could hear the factory girls singing in the corridors. I thought of a kind lady I met at their club, who said to me that if she had known that there were shortages of everything in France, she would have supplied us, from head to foot, so to speak. But there was no time; we were leaving the next morning, heading back to London. That day, a dreadful storm broke, complete with diluvian rain.

We struggled to get up at six-thirty in the morning and we made our way along narrow tarmacked lanes, heads down, braving the storm. Luckily, as always, we had been served a copious breakfast. When we left, the friendly atmosphere was such that the factory girls cut off strands of their hair and gave them to the boys!

It was still dark when we reached the railway station. The night before, some French sailors had promised to bring us some chocolates. And true to their word, they were there, in spite of the storm. As well as chocolates, they brought us packets of sweets with soft centres, cigarettes and, in a big bag, some oranges. These were what pleased me most. One of the sailors came from Canada. He brought with him enough clothes to outfit us all, but he hadn't had time to tie them into parcels. So, he gave me a little dog from Montreal made from reconstituted marble dust. Our coach driver was a sweet man, who couldn't think of a way of expressing his joy at having driven us to our various meetings. Finally, he pulled all the buttons off his uniform and gave one to each of us, with a beaming smile. I wonder what his wife said when he got home! The two representatives from the Ministry of Information couldn't bear to part from us. One of them attempted to compliment Brigitte on her shoes with wooden soles by saying: *"Comme vous avez de jolies petites boîtes à vos pieds..."* / "What pretty little boxes you have on your feet."

As we travelled, I watched the English countryside unfold. It was saturated from the rain. I liked the big green fields surrounded by hedgerows and pretty wooden gates. The Canadian sailor travelled with us to London and related the terrible odyssey of transport ships attacked by torpedoes. He was so happy to meet French people coming from France that he chatted the whole time we were together.

Once we got to London he took me and Chantal to a French restaurant. I was dreaming of roast beef but there wasn't any to be had. And none to be had anywhere else. But we went shopping for coffee, Van Houten cocoa, mustard and many other marvellous things. We felt as if we were in a land flowing with milk and honey. In a pharmacy, I met a parachutist from Madagascar who knew Geo. If only he had been with me! When we got to Piccadilly, the French sailor gave us some coupons to buy ourselves some shoes. They were so solidly made and elegant that I wore mine for fifteen years! It was in this shop that I met the fiancée of the parachutist from Arnhem. We were in a terrible hurry, but people were eager to continue serving us because they wanted to hear the news from France.

We had some trouble finding a taxi, but eventually we arrived at 7 Bryanston Square where I was to pick up Geo's belongings ... and the money. That meant another big bundle to take back with me. From there we went back to Gower Street and then on to the French Embassy. There was a great crowd of people there including many AVF.[80] Ambassador René Massigli welcomed us all. Photographs were taken; reporters made notes. I remember talking to a very charming American woman and I told her all about the parachutists, Papa and Marie-Hélène Lefaucheux. There was cake, cake and more cake ... and it was terribly hot.

We went back to our ATS barracks. Some of the girls were missing. I trembled at the thought that we would not be able to leave on time. I had had enough. Just then, the alarm sounded. We listened to a V1 bomb passing overhead. I was dismayed at the sight of my two canvas bags, my handbag (the leather bag from the Maquis), my back pack and Geo's bundle. How would I carry all that? A young ATS

---

80. All Volunteer Force.

girl tore off her badges and her buttons and gave them to me. The joy these people expressed in meeting us was incredible. We were astonished and very moved.

At last, we arrived at Victoria Station. A great crowd thronged the platform shouting *"Vive la France!"* I was sorry that it hadn't been possible for us to visit Buckingham Palace and meet the King himself. The royal family was in mourning for the death of Princess Beatrice. The British government requested that we remain an extra two days, but the French government refused.

We arrived at Newhaven in the dead of night and the storm raged around us. We embarked immediately. Two kind souls from my group carried my two big bags for me. The boat was another troop carrier. We settled into the hold where bunks were stacked one above the other. I wondered how many men had lain here thinking about the pitiless war that awaited them, and how many of them did not return. I climbed into an upper bunk but the aroma of coffee drove me up on deck. My heavy baggage was heaped up in a corner and I counted the ninety pounds, in five-pound notes, of Geo's pay; it would be difficult to change them into francs back home. I stuffed the money into my bra; it was forbidden to take money across to France and we would probably be searched on arrival.

The sea was rough and we didn't leave until six o'clock in the morning. I thought about the danger of mines, fixed or adrift in the Channel. This time we were to sail towards Calais because the Germans might well know of our departure and they still had U-boats patrolling the sector. God willing, we would get home safely.

We were all issued with a small waterproof bag for ... I didn't feel well, but I wasn't seasick. That big boat heaved a lot less than *Le Marsouin*.[81] I slept for a while and then went up on deck at around nine o'clock. There is no more splendid a sight than the sea in a raging storm. Foam flew over my head and big waves broke over the

---

81. *Le Marsouin* was the name of the yacht belonging to my father, Louis Krebs.

ship's railings. In the ship's wake the swell was emerald green, and was skimmed by gulls that circled and glided on the wind. Suddenly Dieppe came into view, and not Calais.

We had zigzagged a good deal before the blunt coast of France appeared on the horizon. The waves were breaking on the jetties of the port, now half destroyed by the war. The sailors showed us where the Canadians had landed, many of them only to be killed and others to be taken prisoner. You could say that it was a terrible adventure, but it provided the Allies with invaluable information for the main D-Day landings. I could see that many houses, most of those around the port, had been pulverised and burned. Some German prisoners were working on clearing up the rubble.

Our buses were awaiting us and we set off immediately. But before we reached Paris, we had our fair share of breakdowns. We passed the launch ramps of the V1 bombs and the fields round about were completely ploughed up by bombing. I was so tired that Frédéric looked at me with concern; he had promised Geo to bring me back in good condition! He accompanied me to the apartment in Rue Madame, right up to the front door. I rang but there was nobody home. I went upstairs to our neighbour's flat. Madame Harambure told me that Geo was ill and at the Val-de-Grâce hospital and I wondered whether it was malaria or something else. I was very worried as was Frédéric, and he was unwilling to leave me alone in this state of anxiety. I rang the bell again in the hope that my brother Albert had returned. Thankfully he was there and reassured me about Geo's health. He had indeed suffered an attack of malaria. Frédéric prepared to leave me. We said how we would never forget this extraordinary journey to visit our allies. I was never to see Frédéric again. He rejoined the army in Alsace and death was awaiting him near Colmar at the end of January. What a tragic loss for us all![82] How many of us would still be alive on the day of victory, I wondered.

---

82. He died on 31 January 1945.

The next day I was finally reunited with Geo. We embraced passionately. Geo had been so afraid that a V1 or V2 would land on my head! We undid all the parcels, those from London and all the treats: cakes, cookies, cigarettes, etc. that the sailors on board had given me. It was like Christmas Day. We felt so privileged, oh, painfully so, when our friends from the Resistance were dying of hunger and cold in the concentration camps. If the Arnhem operation had been a success, they would not have been living through another terrible winter, which many would be unable to survive.

Marie-Claire Chamming's, Paris, 1945.

THE MINISTRY OF WAR

FFI DIRECTORATE

JOURNEY TO ENGLAND

By invitation of the British Government of a contingent of FFI (FUJP) under the command of Lt Colonel Cévennes

Travel document N° 124

Issued to Mme CHAMMING'S

• • •

"...ardent youth who answered the call of their country, banded together to fight in our French Forces of the Interior, and brought to the National Army the richness of its zeal and its valour."

Charles de Gaulle

"In France itself, the French Forces of the Interior astonished their allies - not to mention their enemies - by the skill, audacity and scope of their operations."

Antony Eden

(Extract from a speech made 14 July 1944)

A FEW WORDS BEFORE LEAVING

As you have had the honour of being chosen from among thousands of your comrades to be part of this trip, the first to be organised in an allied, friendly country since the Liberation, you MUST appreciate the importance of a mission whose repercussions abroad will make each and every one of you an ambassador for our young French combatants. You are not undertaking a tourist trip. Understand that this journey operates at a much higher level, and that, by its very nature, it carries unavoidable responsibilities.

Never forget that, while you are in England, you will be representing the FFI. It is on your comments, your attitude and your behaviour that many British people, unaware of the exact conditions of our struggle, will judge this surge of national determination, which, from the maquis to the barricades, has made France equal to her own destiny, and tomorrow, will claim her rightful place in the world.

Neither must you forget, in your exchanges with our friends across the Channel, the heroism the English people showed in 1940, when, alone, they stood up against the common enemy and endured devastating bombing. Express your lasting gratitude to our allies for the glorious role the British army played in the liberation of France.

Tell them too that the united will of France is, each day, to take an increasingly active part in the war, and that, once again, we need them to equip our troops, to arm them and ensure their supplies. Think of the thousands of our men who died and those comrades who were deported, who knew neither the glory of the Liberation, nor the pleasure of this journey, and be worthy of your mission.

In this way, you can contribute to making known, in an allied country, the valiant unity of the French youth and further enhance the reputation of the FFI, and so of France, in the eyes of the world.

Lt Colonel CEVENNES (Jean Pronteau)

VOYAGE PROGRAMME

Mon. 13 November
09.00 sharp: meeting of the group outside les INVALIDES metro station.
09.30: inspection of the party on the platform at les Invalides.
10.15: departure by bus for the port of embarkation - cold lunch on route - arrival at the port for dinner and accommodation.

Tues. 14 November
All-day journey to London - dinner and accommodation in London hotel.

Wed. 15 November
Official receptions all day - inspection of the devastation caused by the 1940 bombing and the V-1 flying bombs.

Thurs. 16 November
Official reception for the 8 sections by the town councils of 8 large provincial towns.

Fri. 17 November
In the morning - free time in London
In the afternoon - depart London for return journey.
Dinner and accommodation at the French disembarkation port.

Sat. 18 November
Transfer by bus from the disembarkation port to Paris.
Cold lunch en route - arrival in Paris at about 16.00.

Don't forget to have your bread ration cards and MG for the meals that will be taken in France both for the outgoing and return trip.

During the journey you will join up with Section No. 5. This is obligatory.

GENERAL KOENIG

Paris, 25 March 1965
51bis, Bd de Latour-Maubourg

Madame,

Please excuse my lateness in thanking you for the book that you have so kindly dedicated to me and put in my hands. I wanted to at least glance through it before acknowledging its receipt.

I may tell you that, though initially flattered that you should have thought of me, I was also a little concerned. The vein of feminine literature is not abundant in France and the Resistance has so often been betrayed – and by the pens of its own! But I am happy to tell you in all sincerity that I very soon realised that my fears were unfounded: your book, Madame, is excellent.

Excellent first of all because the style flows beautifully and is full of life, devoid of all sentimentality. Excellent above all because in counterpoint we feel the presence of a beating heart, a heart that knew and dared to choose. I love those who have Faith and who know how to make choices. While our daily lives are woven from minor weaknesses and little white lies – if only to avoid upsetting those around us! – by contrast I love, and I will say it again, those who have Faith, and who are able to confess it. You are one of those.

Please accept, Madame, my gratitude and congratulations once again for this fine book, together with my deepest respects.

General Koenig

GÉNÉRAL DE GAULLE

Paris, 30 April 1965

Madame,

You chose to serve France at a time when it was particularly difficult and commendable to do so. You have given us a lively and vivid account of what led you to make that choice, which is at once a testimony and a lesson in courage.

Allow me to offer you my congratulations and my sincere thanks for it. Please know too that while reading your book, my thoughts turned to the memory of Monsieur Louis Krebs, your father, whose courageous actions and whose sacrifice you evoke so movingly.

Veuillez agréer, Madame, mes respectueux hommages.

C de Gaulle

Général de Gaulle

The Earl of Sefton
Lord Mayor

The Town Hall
Liverpool

16 November 1944

To the members of the Free French Forces of the Interior

Welcome to Liverpool. We are delighted that you are able to visit our city: words cannot express our profound admiration for the heroic part you have played in the liberation of your country and for the common cause of freedom. We hope that you will have happy memories of your short stay in our city. For our part, we will always remember your visit, and this memory will strengthen the unbreakable bonds of friendship that henceforth will unite our two countries.

Sefton

LORD MAYOR

Principal members of the OCMJ with whom Marie Chamming's worked

CHARLES (deported to a concentration camp) — Charles Verny

RICHARD (deported to a concentration camp) — Roger Perret

SYLVIE (deported to a concentration camp) — Maryton Girard

NICOLE — Nicole de Boisguilbert

CLAUDE — Claude Desjardins

DELEUZE (deported) — Georges d'Argenlieu

FREDERIC (killed in action in Alsace in 1945) — François d'Humières

JEAN-MARIE (died in a concentration camp) — Jean-Marie West

FRANCIS (shot by the Germans in 1944) — Francis Belmas

DANIEL (deported to a concentration camp) — Daniel Piquée-Audrain

MICHEL — Marcel Quilliou

List of Abbreviations

AMGOT		Allied Military Government Occupied Territories
BCRA	Bureau Central de Renseignements et d'Action	Central Bureau of Intelligence and Operation (Free French intelligence service based in London)
BOA	Bureau des Opérations Aériennes	Office of Aerial Operations (created in 1943 on the initiative of BCRA)
CAD	Comité d'Action contre la Déportation	Anti-deportation committee (set up in 1943 to resist STO)
CFAD	Comité Féminin Anti-Déportation	Women's anti-deportation committee
CND	Confrérie Notre-Dame	Catholic Resistance network founded by Colonel Rémy in 1940
CNR	Conseil National de la Résistance	National Council for the Resistance: central coordinating body set up in 1943
DCA	Défense Contre l'Aviation	Anti-aircraft defence
DZ		Drop zone
FAT(354)	Front Aufklärungstruppen	Collaborationist group (reconnaissance division)
FFI	Forces Françaises de l'Intérieur	French Forces of the Interior

FFL	Forces Françaises Libres	Free French Forces
FTP	Francs-Tireurs et Partisans	Armed Resistance group founded by leaders of the French Communist Party
FUJP	Forces Unies de la Jeunesse Patriotique	Umbrella movement for numerous Resistance youth groups, set up in 1943
LVF	Légion Volontaire Française	Unit of the German army made up of French volunteers, founded in 1941
MUR	Mouvements Unis de Résistance (Zone sud)	Movement uniting the three main Resistance groups in the southern zone (Combat, Libération-Sud and Francs-Tireurs), created in January 1943)
OCM	Organisation Civile et Militaire	One of the major Resistance organisations in the Occupied zone
OCMJ	Organisation Civile et Militaire des Jeunes	Youth organisation of the OCM
PPF	Partie Populaire Française	Fascist, antisemitic and extreme collaborationist party led by Jacques Doriot
SAS		Special Air Service
STO	Service du Travail Obligatoire	Set up in 1942 to provide French forced labour for Germany

Looking back to the French S.A.S. in Brittany, 1944

This true narrative of the exploits of the S.A.S. was written by Lt.Col. O.A.J. Cary-Elwes who took part in Operation 'LOST'.

Introduction

The Allied Invasion Plan of 1944 included the dropping of S.A.S. parties to cut the lines of communication joining Brittany to the rest of France on the night of D minus I.

This task, allotted to the 2nd [sic] French S.A.S. Bn. was successfully carried out with the assistance of the local Maquis. On its completion the Bn. Commander, Colonel Blanc [Bourgoin], was ordered to organise the speedy arming and training of the Breton Maquis with a view to their playing their part in subsequent operations by the Allied Army in Brittany.

In the South the Bn. Commander met with such enthusiasm from the local inhabitants that he proceeded to call up the Maquis, and by the 13th June had formed a camp of 6,000 men at St. Marcel (Morbihan) to whom no less than thirty aeroplanes had dropped arms in one night. This camp of untrained men was subsequently attacked by the Germans on the 18th June. A battle raged all day, and during the night the S.A.S. and Maquis disappeared into thin air, having killed some 400–500 Germans and only losing a combined total of approximately 30.

The last signal received in England from the Colonel was to the effect that his camp was surrounded and that he could not continue to keep the wireless open in case the Germans pin-pointed his exact location with their detector apparatus.

Meanwhile smaller and equally premature concentrations of the Maquis and S.A.S. in other parts of Brittany had been attacked and dispersed, with the result that the Bde. Commander [Brigadier McLeod] at his Headquarters in London had some 300–400 men launched in Brittany and was out of contact with them all. No signals were received from anyone for three days – on the third day the Brigadier decided to send me to the South to re-establish contact. I took with me a fresh radio team of three Frenchmen [with Sergeant Mati in charge], my own English batman [Corporal Eric Mills], another French Officer [Lieutenant Fleuriot] and two French parachutists. We went the same night – there was no moon nor was there anyone on the ground to signal the location of a reconnoitred dropping zone to the pilot. The pilot and I selected a likely spot off the map, and he did his best, with the aid of "George" to put us out over it. In actual fact we arrived about seven miles wide of the mark, but we all landed safely in the right general area at about 3 a.m.

• • •

Gaining contact

The fact that we were being dropped on that particular night had been broadcast in code over the B.B.C. and we had been allotted a code sentence to be broadcast on the European Services at special times for the next two days to help us establish our authenticity with any well-disposed locals. Apart from hiding our parachutes and kitbags, we did nothing until dawn except move a few kilometres away from where we actually landed. Being combatant troops we were, of course, all in ordinary parachutist uniform.

Our efforts the next day to make contact with the local farmers were not very successful – although they were not hostile they disclaimed all knowledge of the Maquis or any battle or of the one-armed Colonel Blanc [Bourgoin]. This was hardly surprising as the Germans had captured many of our uniforms, and, dressed in them, were doing exactly as I was in order to trace down the S.A.S. who were lying up in the area.

During the day the party split in two and moved off by different routes to a rendezvous in the woods where I had decided we should stay the night. We missed each other that night and did not meet again until the following morning, the other half having also failed to make useful contacts. We moved on again, and, at about midday, having chosen a safe lying-up place for the rest of the party, I moved off with one Frenchman to tackle various farmers. After talking to one or two who were unresponsive I came across one who, while denying all knowledge of everything connected with the Maquis, gave me the impression that he would have helped had he been confident of our authenticity. He explained that if, after he had given us information about the Maquis, we turned out to be Germans, his wife and five children would probably be shot and his farm burnt. It was unfortunate at this stage that the Frenchman accompanying me was an Alsacien who spoke French with a German accent!

We left the farmer saying we would come back at 6 p.m. with our wireless and he could listen to our phrase which I told him would be broadcast at 6. (This, incidentally, was the last broadcast.) We duly came back, tuned in to the Service, but by the time it was all set we were too late for the broadcast. However, the farmer was a good chap and was sufficiently impressed with our English equipment and our wireless set to have some confidence in us. He agreed to take my identity card and that of the French Officer accompanying me which he would show to some of his friends whom he thought knew the whereabouts of some of the S.A.S. These latter, if they recognized us from photographs, might be able to put us in touch with the Colonel. As a result of this, two days later a guide collected me in the morning and took me to a cottage where the Colonel had his Headquarters. At this time the whole area was full of Germans hunting for him and they had put a large price on his head, but in spite of this, he had re-opened his wireless communications with Bde. Headquarters. We, therefore decided, in order to avoid having two wirelesses operating in the same place and also to avoid swelling the numbers of his Headquarters, that I should go with my party to join Captain Maurice [Marienne] near Trédion. This Officer was one of the S.A.S. Company Commanders who was controlling the Maquis in that particular area. This part of Brittany consists of very small fields surrounded by high banks and hedges and has few main roads but hundreds of winding lanes. For this reason we were able to dodge the Germans and go from one place to another, even by day, provided we had a good guide.

· · ·

Arming the Maquis

Our task now was to arm and train as many Maquis as possible but not to concentrate them in large numbers until ordered to do so from London. We were told that, in all probability, a subsidiary landing would take place somewhere in Brittany during the coming full-moon period.

The general system which was adopted by all Commanders in the area for arming and training the Maquis was now roughly the same. This was to farm out their trained soldiers to each group of Maquis, and then the Commander, through his wireless link with

London, would arrange for each group to be supplied with arms and equipment in turn in their own area. This system worked well as no large concentration of Maquisards was necessary for a drop of arms to any one place, and also the local Commander kept control of each group as it depended on him for its arms, ammunition and also money.

Captain Maurice's [Marienne] headquarters was between 16 and 20 strong and was situated around the edges of a field with sentries posted at each corner. In spite of the incessant rain they did not go into the farm even at night and all their food was provided by the neighbouring farmers. I stayed with Maurice for a few days and assisted in the re-organization of the various Maquis Bns. in this area. For our communications to London and to the other H.Q. groups in Brittany we used wireless. As each group was on a different net to London, direct communication between groups was not possible, but London could relay messages as requested. Our communication on the ground was by means of runners called locally "agents de liaison". The majority of these were young girls between the ages of sixteen and twenty-five who at this stage were not suspected by the Germans and who were allowed to circulate freely. Even if stopped they were seldom searched. Later on some were captured and tortured by the Germans for information, but none gave anything away.

After I had been with Maurice [Marienne] about a week I was ordered by Brigade Headquarters to go northwards and join Captain David [Deplante] and his group near Guern, a distance of about 40 kilometres as the crow flies and considerably more by the devious route we were forced to take. The area was still full of German detachments who actually were Russians with German officers, a proportion of them being mounted and known locally as Cossacks. We, therefore, made most of the journey at night or in the middle of the day (when the Germans were eating) on foot through the lanes. I took with me my wireless team and my batman. The French officer and two men were left with Captain Maurice.

Within 48 hours of my leaving Maurice's Headquarters it was surprised at night and all in it, with the exception of two, were taken prisoner and subsequently shot or, as in the case of Maurice [Marienne] himself, tortured to death. The reason for this disaster was that French *miliciens* working for the Gestapo had infiltrated into the camp at night dressed as parachutists. In my opinion Maurice [Marienne] stayed too long in the same place and his presence there was much too widely known in the area. At the best of times the French are not security-minded – when one is dealing with enthusiastic peasants with a liking for strong cider, it is impossible to keep anything secret.

Our trip to Guern was uneventful except for one rather tricky period when we crossed the river Blavet at about midday. We were paddling over in a very unseaworthy little rowing boat, and one of the oars which were rotten broke in two and we were left in the middle of the river with the boat going rapidly downstream in circles. However, eventually we got across without being noticed. We also visited on the way up about four small Maquis and arranged for arms to be dropped to them.

It was my experience that the best way to go from one place to another, even if one knew the exact location of one's destination, was to be handed on from guide to guide, and never to take any one guide for any great distance. The inhabitants of this part of Brittany were very primitive and, although knowing their immediate surroundings like the back of their hands, had no idea of the lanes outside a radius of about five miles from their own farms.

Captain David [Deplante] had his Headquarters organized differently from Maurice's. It consisted only of himself, his wireless team of three, one parachutist, and his "agent de liaison". He only stayed in one place for about forty-eight hours, and only a few people of whom he was 100 per cent sure knew his exact location. During the day he kept well away from buildings but at night he went into the lofts of farms. He successfully arranged almost nightly parachutings of arms and equipment to all the various Maquis in his sector over which he had an extraordinarily high measure of control.

Meanwhile, the weather continued to be so bad that the moon period came and went without any subsidiary landing being possible. This meant that the parachutists and the Maquis would have to wait either for the next full-moon or until the breakthrough in Normandy took place before being relieved. Every day more and more of the Maquis leaders and the S.A.S. were being rounded up, and this fact, not unnaturally, was beginning to affect the morale of those who were left.

After I had been with David [Deplante] about a week and the battle at Caen was in full swing, I received a signal ordering me to return to England as soon as possible and to contact a man named Robert at a certain spot in the north of Brittany referred to in the signal simply by a map reference – actually in the vicinity of Guingamp. This Robert was to put me into the M.I.9 escape channel. As Guingamp was some 70 kilometres away, I decided to make the journey in a car at night. Before leaving David [Deplante] I had been given maps showing some details of the defence plans of the ports of Morlaix in the north and Vannes and Lorient in the south. These I was to take with me to England. I left my wireless team with David [Deplante] and set off with only my batman and the two Maquisard owners of the car. The driver left us on the road near to where Robert was supposed to be and went home. At first light we approached the farm and the farmer denied all knowledge of anyone of the name of Robert. We then went to the outskirts of the nearest village and asked another man if he had heard of Robert. No such man existed and nor was there anyone in the village except one very old yokel who even had the Christian name of Robert.

So there I was with all contacts broken and in a hell of a hurry to get to London with my maps and other information!

I regretted very much having broken my principle of always being handed on from contact to contact. It was obvious that I had received a corrupted map reference from Brigade Headquarters but as I had left my wireless sending set behind at Guern I had no way of getting a connection. I was obviously going to waste all the time I had saved by my car journey before I could get in touch with Robert.

• • •

Regaining contact

After going up to several people we eventually found one youngish man who seemed helpful. I put our position to him and did my best to convince him of our bona fides. I arranged with him that we should go and lie up in a small wood well away from the lanes and that he should come back to us at midday with some food, and that in the meantime he should report our presence to the head of the local Maquis. From his point of view, this was a sound arrangement, but from ours it was not quite so good because, had he gone to the Germans instead of to the Maquis, we should not have known until it was too late. He came back as arranged, not only with food, but also with an active Maquisard called "Tristan" who said that he had heard of Robert, would tell him that we were in the area, and that if Robert had information about us from London he would send guides to fetch us the following day.

I explained to "Tristan" ["Frederick"] that we were in a hurry and that Robert was going to arrange for our swift return to England. He then told us that he knew of an R.A.F. Sergeant-Pilot [Fargher] who had been shot down and was hiding in the area, but who had not been able to find anybody to help him to get home. I decided that he should join us the following day and go with us to Robert. We spent that night in the farm we had visited that morning where the old man, now reassured that we were British, was only too pleased to have us.

• • •

Robert's Maquis

The next morning the Sergeant-Pilot joined us, and in the afternoon the three of us set off with Robert's guides to join his Maquis some miles away. This Maquis was by far the most efficient I had seen. Although Robert was only a young Serjeant in the French S.A.S. Battalion, it was he that commanded this Maquis consisting of some two hundred men – all the officers (mostly French Army Reserve officers) willingly accepted him as their Commanding Officer. The camp itself was in a large wood near a big lake, and the inmates really conducted themselves as trained soldiers. Guards were mounted properly, organized parades held, and the Tricolour was hoisted with due ceremony at dawn and similarly lowered at dusk. Strong pickets guarded every approach to the wood and Robert had even put anti-personnel mines round what he considered the most dangerous approaches. These mines stood him in good stead when his camp was attacked by the Germans shortly after I had left him.

While at Robert's camp, where we stayed two days, we were joined by another British S.A.S. liaison officer, Sqn-Ldr. Pat Smith, and also by an American Army Air Force Major [Jones], who, like the Sergeant-Pilot, had been shot down some weeks before. Our party for the homeward journey was, therefore, five.

We had to stay at Robert's camp for two days (a) to turn ourselves into civilians, and (b) so as to give time for the M.I.9 contacts to arrange for us to be collected by the Royal Navy from the coast. We all had passport photographs taken, and false identity cards were prepared for us by the local Mayor. My batman was a yokel, and I was a shipping agent. We were dressed in plain clothes accordingly, but contrary to the normal practice on these occasions, we all kept arms and grenades. It seemed strange to us not to be in uniform and theoretically to be able to go where we liked.

• • •

M.I.9 channels

In the early morning of the third day of our stay with Robert we left in a farm cart driven by one of the Maquis for our first staging post on our route to the coast. We had about thirty kilometres to go, and as usual our destination was a small unobtrusive little farm. On the way, feeling somewhat overconfident of our disguise, I suggested to our driver that we should stop at a bistro and have a drink. To this he agree with alacrity, and we went into a small cafe. I ordered a Calvados to which, unfortunately, my companions were unused, and, not realising how strong it was, swallowed a good gulp each. The splutterings which followed not unnaturally attracted the attention of the other people in the cafe, so as soon as my companions had recovered sufficiently we left in haste!

The rest of our trip was uneventful. At the farm we met the head of the M.I.9 organization for that particular part of the world – a Canadian called Lt. "Labrosse" who had been doing this job for just under a year. He told us that his orders were to get me home as soon as possible, but so far as he had not been able to make the final arrangements for a boat. He did not stay long with us but said that he would be back in the evening.

That evening he came to our farm and took me off to his hide-out. There he explained to me that normally we should have waited for two days at the farm, but as it was so urgent he had managed to arrange for our getaway the following night. This meant that later on in the early part of the night we should have to move on foot to our last "staging" farm. He also told me that I was the first person he had ever actually shown where he lived – it was in a loft! Normally, he always arranges to meet all his agents and contacts at cafes or anywhere other than where he had his wireless link to England. His radio operator was also a Canadian, and one of the toughest men I have ever seen.

I rejoined the others, and we waited for nightfall to be guided to the last farm.

Apart from having to cross roads on which the Germans had motorized patrols – we were very near the coast by this time – the journey was quite simple.

• • •

The last halt

We arrived at the farm and all was in darkness. "Labrosse" said that in our case he had not had time to warn the farmer that we were coming. However, he was soon woken up and lit a lamp, and we went in. Then, thirsty and hungry after the long walk, we had some cider and chocolate and biscuits before being dispersed to the various lofts to sleep.

Our Canadian friend left us, and we had been chatting for about a quarter of an hour when suddenly there were shouts outside and a few rounds from a rifle were fired through the door. Obviously a patrol had come on the farm and, as we found out later, the farmer, who had not been expecting us, had not put up his black-out. Pat Smith had the presence of mind to dash out the light and the farmer just had time to push us up some stairs into the loft before unlocking his door.

Luckily one of us had a torch and at once we saw that the loft was divided into two by a wall with a doorway in it. We stumbled into the far compartment while downstairs the farmer's wife wailed and screamed to try to drown the noise of our steps. She had a baby of two months old who helped to swell the racket!

The patrol, all Russians, had seen through the window that there were obviously more people in the house than just the farmer and his wife, and finding some of our English sweets and biscuits on the table downstairs, shouted up the stairs demanding that we should come down.

Upstairs we were in a tricky position; in plain clothes, all armed and I with the ports defence plans on me. Furthermore, I knew the location of the Canadian's hideout. If we came down, we were obviously going to have a very bad time – we all knew the fate of so many of our friends. There was no way out of the loft except by the stairs. (Usually in these lofts there was a sort of window by which the corn could be loaded, and by which people like ourselves could escape). If we tried to blast our way out by throwing a couple of grenades down the stairs we would have blown the farmer and his wife to bits as well as the patrol.

The only hope seemed to be to stay where we were behind the wall dividing the loft, and if they came up after us to lob the grenades into the other half and hope that the thin wall between us would protect us. Of course, it was far more likely that they would sit tight, send for reinforcements, surround the building, and then burn it down – quite a normal practice.

We waited and meanwhile downstairs the shouts for us or even two of us to go down increased, and the screams of the woman got more and more voluble. Suddenly another shot was fired, there was a shout of pain and piercing screams from the woman. Our visions of what might be going on downstairs were appalling but we made no move and the demands for us to go down ceased. Instead, thick voices demanded "cognac", and, to our relief, we heard the farmer answer that he had some, and he produced.

Shortly afterwards someone went out and again a little later on we heard a cart arrive. Naturally, in our frame of mind, we imagined reinforcements, but we stayed still and listened. To our amazement we heard a lot of shuffling downstairs, some comparatively subdued talk, everyone going outside, the cart moving off, and then, for a few moments – silence. A minute later we heard running feet in the parlour and on the stairs and the farmer was with us. He said that the Russians had gone and it was the one chance for us to get to hell out of it. He did not have to tell us twice. In a moment we had gone, but a second before we dashed off, I managed to arrange with him roughly where we would be – lying under a hedge about three fields away in the direction he pointed.

• • •

The last lap

Just at first light, we heard footsteps coming in our direction. We peered through the top of the corn in the half light of the morning, and to our relief, we saw Labrosse and our farmer. We were at once taken off on foot to a safer hiding place in a thicket some five or six miles away. On the way we sometimes redoubled on our tracks to confuse any German police dogs which might be tracking us. We thought of dogs for the whole of the rest of that day!

Apparently, what had happened in the farm was that the farmer had been standing on the first of the stairs that led up to our loft with two Russians below covering him from either side of the entrance to the staircase. Luckily they were slightly drunk, and when he made a move to pass them and go down into the parlour, one of them loosed off his trigger, but, instead of getting the farmer, he hit his fellow-countryman opposite. From that moment the whole patrol temporarily lost interest in us and concentrated on the badly-wounded man. The farmer at once suggested that his friend from next door had a horse and cart in which the Russian could be taken back to the camp, and so it was that they all left and we were able to slip away. They did not forget about us or the farm for long because at dawn they came and burned it to the ground. By that time the farmer had hidden his wife and child in a friend's farm nearby and arrangements were made for him to join our party for England.

All the next day we lay up in the thicket and that night we were guided down to the beach. A young girl led us through the minefield – she put white handkerchiefs or rags on each mine along the path, and we followed in single file after her, being very careful not to step on the white patches.

We were picked up according to plan, the Navy arriving within literally a few seconds of the time arranged. By midday we were at Brigade Headquarters, and that night, having made my report and arranged the conferences for the morrow, I went in a party to the Dorchester, and I don't think Bollinger '28 has ever tasted so good!

Bibliography

There are hundreds of websites and books devoted to the Resistance. These are just a few of the main sites and books that were helpful in the translation of this book.

https://fflsas.org/fr/menucontent/200
Dedicated to the FFL and SAS. In French and English.

http://maitron-fusilles-40-44.univ-paris1.fr
Biographical dictionary of executed *résistants* and SAS. In French.

www.ordredelaliberation.fr/fr
List of Compagnons de la Libération and decorations awarded. In French.

www.francaislibres.net
Livre d'Or of the Free French. In French.

https://kristianhamon.blogspot.com/2016/09/
Extremely detailed blog with reliable sources. In French.

www.museedelaresistanceenligne.org

http://41emeri3945.eklablog.com/05-le-

maquis-de-st-marcel-c25651658
1939–1945 – events in the Morbihan with an account of the Saint-Marcel battle. In French.

www.memoresist.org
Amis de la Fondation de la Résistance. In French.

http://memoiredeguerre.free.fr/ph-doc/vie-quotidienne/vie-quotidienne.htm
Ration cards and daily life under the Occupation. In French.

https://french-genealogy.typepad.com/genealogie/2012/07/a-french-familys-ration-cards-and-what-they-reveal-about-names.html
Ration cards. In English.

www.cia.gov/library/center-for-the-study-of-intelligence/csi-publications/csi-studies/studies/winter98_99/art03.html
An account of Jedburgh team Frederick. In English.

https://fr.wikipedia.org/wiki/Louis_Krebs
Louis Krebs, Marie Chamming's father. In French.

https://www.reseau-canope.fr/cnrd/glossaire/
Resistance glossary. In French.

http://www.39-45.org/portailv2/news/news.php
Second World War forum. In French.

Calmette, A. "Les Équipes Jedburgh dans la Bataille de France." *Revue D'histoire De La Deuxième Guerre Mondiale* 16, no. 61 (1966): 35-48. www.jstor.org/ stable/25730024.

Cobb, Matthew, *The Resistance: The French Fight against the Nazis*, Simon & Schuster, 2009.

——, *Elevan Days in August: The Liberation of Paris in 1944*, Simon & Schuster 2013.

De Montergon, Camille, *Histoire de Concarneau*, Concarneau: Librairie E. Le Tendre, 1953.

Eisenhower, Dwight, *Crusade in Europe*, London, William Heinemann Ltd, 1948.

Guil, Jean-Claude and Pierre Cherel, *Saint-Marcel dans la Tourmente*: *18 juin, 1944*, Témoignages, 2012.

Huc, André and Ewen Southby-Tailyour, *The Next Moon*, London, Penguin Books Ltd, 2005.

Le Guénic, René, *Morbihan Mémorial de la Résistance*, Quéven, Imprimerie Basse Bretagne, 2013.

Thomas, Georges-Michel and Alain Le Grand, *Le Finistère dans la Guerre – La Libération*, Brest, Éditions de la Cité, 1981.

Maps